SIMPLE
MONEY
SOLUTIONS

SIMPLE
MONEY
SOLUTIONS

*10 Ways You Can Stop Feeling
Overwhelmed by Money and
Start Making It Work for You*

NANCY LLOYD

TIMES BUSINESS

RANDOM HOUSE

Library of Congress Cataloging-in-Publication data is available.

ISBN: 0-8129-3175-0

Random House Website address: www.randomhouse.com

Manufactured in the United States of America on acid-free paper

9 8 7 6 5 4 3 2

First Edition

SPECIAL SALES: Times Books are available at special discounts for bulk purchases for sales promotions or premiums. Special editions, including personalized covers, excerpts of existing books, and corporate imprints, can be created in large quantities for special needs. For more information, write to Special Markets, Times Books, 201 East 50th Street, New York, New York 10022, or call 800-800-3246.

For my parents who taught me many things,
including the value of a dollar,
the simplest way to balance a checkbook, and
the joy of giving one's time, in addition to money, to charity.

Preface

As a financial print and broadcast journalist and a former Federal Reserve Board economist I often give personal finance talks. During the talks my audiences open up about the major financial issues they are confronting: teaching their kids about money, finding the money to pay for their kids' college education, saving for what they hope will be their own comfortable retirement, finding the money to pay for their first or second home, cutting their taxes, taking charge of their credit, and cutting their bank fees.

I wrote this book in response to their questions about those issues and many others. I chose its title carefully so that readers would know exactly what they're getting: "SIMPLE MONEY SOLUTIONS: 10 Ways You Can Stop Feeling Overwhelmed By Money and Start Making It Work For You." In this book I will show you how to:

- Free-up cash each month but not have to live within a budget.
- Slash ATM fees and other bank costs.
- Take charge of your credit.
- Maximize your pay and perks at work including 401(k) and other retirement savings plans.
- Use a personal computer and the Internet to manage your financial life faster and better.
- Shave thousands off the cost of a home, mortgage, and car.
- Ensure your safety net is not riddled with holes.
- Understand what makes stocks, bonds, and mutual funds work.
- Start and manage an investment portfolio—for retirement or your kids' college education—with just a few dollars a month.
- Improve your tax situation the rest of the year.
- Easily boost your money IQ—and understand why "free" financial seminars could end up costing you a bundle.

Why did I call it "Simple Money Solutions?" Because the ways to accumulate wealth and the solutions to most money concerns are simple, practical and easy to follow—it's just that no one may have ever let you in on them.

I kept the information user-friendly and very focused, in response to the many people who have said to me, "I don't have a lot of time to deal with my money, so *just tell me what to do and tell me how to do it.*"

Over the years, my audiences have generously shared their stories of financial struggles—their very personal financial and consumer lives—with me. Their stories revealed new financial and consumer minefields that could devastate the financial plans of any of us.

Often they would ask me for specific advice. Here are a few examples:

- "I pay my credit card bill on time and in full each month, but instead of thanking me, my credit card company canceled my card with no notice. Several of my friends tell me that the same thing happened to them and we are all having trouble finding a new card that won't charge us exorbitant fees. Why aren't credit card companies jumping at the chance to have customers like us?"
- "After paying one credit card bill a couple of days late, my five other credit cards jacked up my interest rate (two of them doubled the rate I had been paying!). How do the other card issuers know that I paid one bill late? And, since I followed all of *their* cards' rules, what right do they have to punish me for paying another card issuer late?"
- "My company just went public and is offering its stock as part of their retirement savings plan. The company's share prices shot up the first few days of trading, so did I miss the boat? When, if ever, is owning shares of my employer's stock a good idea? This is the first place I've ever been offered stock options, so how can I maximize them?"
- "I invested most of my life's savings in what a financial adviser swore to me was a 'totally safe investment.' But instead of going up, the investment is now worth less than half of what I paid for it, so now I won't have enough money to send my 15- and 16-year-old children to college. Should I take what's left of my money and put it in something that could pay off big, even though I know that this particular investment is very risky? I want my kids to get a good education, so is there any other way to pay for their education if I can't make up for the shortfall?"
- "My company was bought out by its main competitor and several departments, including mine, will soon be abolished. I haven't been in the job market for 13 years, so how can I quickly find a new job and what do I say to a potential employer about why I'm leaving my current company? Also, what should I do with the lump-sum payment—part severance pay and part retirement

savings money—that my current employer will be handing me when I leave the company?"

I wish to thank everyone who took the time to share a personal story with me. In this book I recount some of their stories (although most names and identifying details have been changed to protect their privacy). The simple solutions that follow their stories can help keep you from being snagged by the same "gotchas."

Throughout the book I provide time-tested, straightforward, practical financial and consumer advice that you can start using today. There are a variety of resources (Web sites and toll-free numbers) so you can also get up-to-the-minute information before making a financial decision. You can use this book in several ways:

1. You can read it straight through over a few days.
2. You can turn to a specific chapter when you want some immediate help. Maybe you are considering buying or selling a house, leasing or buying a car, buying or selling mutual funds, looking for a better paying job, weighing a buyout offer from your employer, or weighing the pros and cons of various college savings plans. In this book you'll get lots of easy-to-follow advice that will make your decision-making process easier.
3. You can read it at your leisure, in any order you choose, to boost your overall money IQ.

I hope you find these solutions helpful. Let me know what you think. You can e-mail me at my Web site: www.nancylloyd.com.

It's time to end the nagging feeling that you *should* be taking charge of your money if you only knew how, so what are you waiting for?

NANCY LLOYD

January 2000

Acknowledgment

My sincere thanks go to Chip Gibson, Steve Ross, and Tina Constable for their enthusiastic support of this book.

I also wish to thank Bob Edwards, who as host of NPR's *Morning Edition,* is graciously sharing his extensive broadcast insights and patiently teaching me the fine art of doing a radio interview that is both informative and entertaining. Special thanks to NPR's Jeffrey Dvorkin, Ellen McDonnell, and Greg Allen who regularly let me share my financial advice with their millions and millions of *Morning Edition* listeners and who, while I was writing this book, were flexible with my schedule.

My deep gratitude goes to *Family Circle's* Susan Ungaro, Nancy Clark, and Ann Matturro, who since 1991 have given me a great hands-on education on writing magazine articles.

My sincere appreciation goes to ABC Radio's Chris Berry, Merrilee Cox, Steve Jones, Hank Weinbloom, and Dick Rosenbaum, for giving me the opportunity to tell money stories in nontraditional and sometimes musical ways.

I wish to say thank you to Dr. Joyce Brothers for kindly taking the time to teach me the many ways that money affects personal relationships.

My profound gratitude goes to Sue Vogelsinger for her invaluable wisdom, common sense, and always helpful suggestions.

I want to thank Carie Freimuth, who believed in this project from day one, and who kept me focused on the big picture, and to acknowledge the tireless efforts of Sabrina Hicks and Annsley Rosner.

Thanks to *The Washington Post's* Peggy Hackman who, in 1990, took a chance on an unknown writer and who still gives me wide latitude in writing stories the way I want to write them. I also wish to thank Sylvia Barsotti who gave me my first magazine assignment and encouraged me to expand the types of articles I write. My appreciation goes to Robert Hunter, who over the years has taken the time to share his vast knowledge of insurance matters with me. My boundless gratitude to superagent, Mel Berger.

Last, but certainly not least, I wish to thank Maria Shriver, Forrest Sawyer, Jim Farley, Bill Tucker, Susan Zirinsky, and Letitia Baldrige for their words of wisdom, advice, and encouragement at various stages of my journalism career.

Contents

Solution 2

Improve Your Credit and Slash Bank Fees

Solution 4

Stop the Squabbling (or Break the Family Silence) About Money

Chapter 12

Look Out for Loved Ones with Trusts and More   136

Solution 5

Strengthen Your Safety Net

Chapter 13

Shop Smart for Life Insurance   151

Chapter 14

Protect Your Earnings with Good Disability Insurance   158

Solution 7

Shave Thousands Off the Cost of a
Home and a Mortgage

Solution 8

Start and Manage an Investment Portfolio with Only a Few Dollars a Month

- Choosing the Right Mutual Funds for Your Situation—Separating the Market Hype from the Facts About Fees and Performance
- Understanding How Index Funds Could Work for You
- Determining if You Are Ready—and Willing—to Do Your Homework to Invest in Individual Stocks
- How to Diversify with Just a Handful of Stocks Plus Using Dividend Reinvestment Plans (DRIPS) to Keep Costs to a Minimum
- Understanding How Buying Bonds Can Cut Your Risk
- Keeping Your Wits When the Market Tumbles

Chapter 28

- Deciding How Much Advice You Need—Full-Service versus Discount Brokers
- Selecting the Terms and Conditions of Your Brokerage Account with Care
- Knowing What You're Getting and Giving Up with an Online Broker versus a Live Broker, Plus How to Comparison Shop for an Online Broker

Solution 9

Make the Most of the New Retirement Realities

Chapter 29

- Setting Goals That Are Important to You So You Know What You're Saving for and Can Stay Motivated
- Taking a Stab at What Retirement Will Cost
- Taking a Stab at What You Will Earn (Fill-in-the-Blank Form)
- Creating Ways to Improve the Quality of Your Postretirement Life

Chapter 30

Maximize Your 401(k), IRA, Keogh, and Other Retirement Savings Plans

- Understanding the Differences Between Traditional Pensions and Newer Retirement Savings Plans

- What You Need to Know About Your 401(k) Retirement Savings Plan

- Exploring Other Retirement Savings Options if You Work for a Nonprofit Organization or the Government

- Choosing Between a Roth IRA and a Traditional IRA

- What a Variable Annuity Is and Deciding When (or If) It Would Benefit You

- Special Retirement Savings Plans for the Self-Employed—Keogh, SEP, and Simple IRAs

Solution 10

Put Your Kids Through College Even if You Can't Save Enough Money

Chapter 31

Bankroll Your Kids' College Years Creatively

- Learning and Following the New Rules of Financial Aid

- Understanding the Pros and Cons of Popular Tuition Savings Plans—Prepaid State Tuition Plans, Education IRAs, 529 Plans— and Choosing the Best One for Your Situation

- Letting Hope and Other Tax Credits Help

- Choosing Between an IRA and an Education Tax Credit

- Looking High and Low for Loans

- Understanding the Hidden Costs and Risks of "Easy" Money

- Positioning Yourself for More Financial Aid

- Sizing Up Last-Minute Tuition Stretchers if You Couldn't Save Enough

- Surfing for Dollars

I Know I Should Be Saving for My Future, But Life Keeps Getting in My Way

You know you should be saving for your future. You don't need to hear it from me. And in a perfect world, you would be able to pay your bills *and* put away enough money to buy your dream house, pay for your children's college education, start a business, travel around the world, save for a comfortable retirement, or even decide to quit your job. But if you're like millions of people, your financial goals are eluding you. Why?

> **It's *not* because you lack motivation or good intentions or follow-through.**

The real reason you've fallen short of your goals may simply be because: You have no money left over at the end of the month. Or, you have so little left that you say to yourself, "It's not enough to start investing."

For many people, the culprit is their crushing credit card debt. Couple that with outstanding student loans and day-to-day living expenses and it's easy to get discouraged.

The sad fact is: *Debt Diets have failure rates that exceed those of food diets.* That's why so many people—regardless of income or education— are perpetually hungry for financial advice that will work for them. It's why many fall for fixes that ultimately make their situation worse.

Despite their good intentions, most people cannot pay off their debts without some outside advice. For instance, they don't know the secrets of getting the amount of their debt reduced. They just take their creditors' word that they must pay off every cent that appears on their bill.

This book will show you simple, proven ways to negotiate a lower balance. I will also show you where you can get free help if you just don't want to negotiate with your creditors yourself.

When debt diets fail, you know what happens. You grow frustrated and you stop trying. Small problems mushroom into big ones. And it doesn't stop there. You may be passing on to your children your financial fears, frustrations, and feelings of failure.

Does any of this strike a chord with you? If so, then this book is for you. Is paying off your credit card balance your number one goal? If so, which card should you pay off first—the one with the highest balance or the one with the highest interest rate? I will answer that question and show you other ways to pay off your debts more quickly.

Even if you don't carry a credit card balance from month to month, you may have other financial goals, such as buying a house, paying for children's college education, retiring comfortably, but other things in life get in the way. Wouldn't your financial goals be easier to reach if only you could:

1. Choose some good investments that can go the distance—and find the money to start making those investments.
2. Convince your boss to pay you what you're really worth—what you truly deserve.
3. Stop the squabbling (or break the family silence) about money.

Here's the good news: you *can* free up cash each month and learn to make good investments that can get you to your financial goals. You *can* ask for and get better pay and perks at work. You *can* begin having productive talks with your parents, in-laws, and kids about money and debt, so you don't have to repeat your financial past or pass your financial fears or frustrations on to your kids.

Over the years I've worked with many people who were facing similar money struggles. I understand your questions and frustrations. That's why I wrote this book and filled it with time-tested, straightforward, practical money and consumer advice that you can start using today.

In "SIMPLE MONEY SOLUTIONS: 10 Ways You Can Stop Feeling Overwhelmed By Money and Start Making It Work For You," I show you

LLOYD'S LAW

There are no secrets to money. But there are some simple rules that no one—until now—may have told you. I will tell you the simple rules and will show you step-by-step how you can start using them today.

Don't give up.

You can get yourself out of self-defeating money habits.

You can take charge of your finances.

You can start saving money and planning for a financially secure future.

how to get yourself out of self-defeating money habits. And show that everyday choices you make can spell the difference between wealth and a life-long struggle for financial security.

In this book, I give you time-tested, proven strategies, so that you can take control of your finances—and realize your dreams.

Throughout the book I give a variety of resources (Web sites and toll-free numbers) so you can also get up-to-the-minute information before you make a financial decision.

Congratulations! By reading this book, you've taken the first step on the road to controlling your financial fate. Let's get started.

SIMPLE
MONEY
SOLUTIONS

Jump-Start Your Finances

Have you ever tried to take charge of your finances? Even if you only toyed with the idea, you may have gotten discouraged by the fact that most people who try, don't succeed—at least not the first time. Why? They unwittingly set themselves up for failure by sabotaging themselves from the start. But you can learn from other people's missteps. Here are the top four ways people sabotage their financial efforts and simple ways you can avoid making the same mistakes:

- *Sabotage 1 They don't set any goals.* What does it mean to say, "I'm going to take charge of my finances?" Without setting specific goals, you have no way to plot your course or to measure your progress. Those who do succeed at shaping up their finances have one thing in common: They're motivated by a long-term goal (or goals), such as paying for their children's college education, buying a house, starting a business, or paying off their credit card debt.
- *Sabotage 2 They set unrealistic goals.* If you're earning $40,000 a year and resolve to save $20,000, that's probably not going to happen. A better option is to start with smaller goals—goals that you can meet relatively quickly, then build on your success to set and reach larger ones.
- *Sabotage 3 They are doing it to please someone else.* Most people who attempt this at someone else's request (typically a spouse or an accountant) can't go the distance. You'll only succeed if you are ready and willing to make life-improving financial tradeoffs that will put money in your bank account.
- *Sabotage 4 They don't see themselves succeeding.* Just seeing yourself reaching your goals is not enough to make it happen, but if you don't believe you *can* reach your goals, unconsciously you'll sabotage your progress. You may be intellectually ready, but you have to be emotionally ready and willing to succeed. Some people just aren't ready—yet. But when you are, nothing will hold you back from setting goals that are important to you and putting some creative plans in place to reach them.

In this first of ten solutions, I will show you step-by-step simple and proven ways to free up cash, end self-defeating money habits, and boost your money IQ. And while you can do a lot of this yourself, there are times that a little one-on-one professional help, with an objective financial planner or tax adviser, could be a good money move, so I'll also show you how to find the best professional advisers for your individual situation.

Chapter 1

Get the Money Mindset and Put an End to Yo-Yo Money Diets

Taking charge of my money is a snap. I've done it a thousand times—I just can't stick with it.

—Charlie, a classic yo-yo money dieter

If you're like most people, when you think about your credit cards, your kids' college education, or saving for your own retirement, your heart may start to race a bit, your hands may get a little clammy, and feelings of queasiness or even dread may come over you. Those are normal reactions. But the important question is: What do you do next, to allay your nerves and to initiate the steps you and your family need to take?

Worrying is extremely draining to your mind and body. When worrying occupies your thoughts, it closes you off to opportunities. You can't see the forest for the trees. You're so busy trying to figure out how to deal with your day-to-day money concerns that you can't make long-term plans to reach the goals that matter to you and your family.

Martha's Story

Every New Year's Eve, for the past six years, Martha has been setting the same resolution. "Come midnight, I vow to take charge of my money, and each year I get off to a great start," she says. "I'm really motivated, so I come up with all sorts of ways to spend less money." She cuts out every expense that's not a necessity: eating lunches out, going to the movies, buying a cup of coffee at a pricey coffee bar on her way to work, and so on. She packs a brown-bag lunch every morning and, to avoid temptation, she leaves her credit cards at home.

"For a while, everything is great," she says. "Then something always happens that I haven't counted on. In two of the last six years, I discovered that I owed a lot more money on my income taxes than I had thought. In another year, my college roommate asked me to be her bridesmaid, so I had to spend a couple of thousand dollars on a wedding gift, a plane ticket, and an ugly dress I'm sure I'll never wear again."

Despite these monetary setbacks, each year Martha would stick with her resolution for several weeks. "Then, without warning, I'd hit the wall," she recalls. "I could be walking by a nice restaurant and the aroma of the food would be so seductive that I would walk in and end up ordering the most expensive item on the menu. Or, I would stroll by a department store and spot some shoes in the window and, I swear to you, they would be calling my name! So I'd go in just to try them on, but I couldn't pull myself out of the store without buying something expensive—much more expensive than I would normally buy. And there went my resolution and all my hard work.

"After I broke my resolution, I'd get my credit cards out and go on a spending spree. I'd tell myself that I was entitled to a little reward for my hard work," Martha recalls. "Then I would feel really guilty and start the whole sacrifice thing again. Whether I was sticking to my resolution or spending like crazy, I couldn't get past one fact: I was a failure. I couldn't even stick to a simple New Year's resolution."

But Martha wasn't a failure. She was a yo-yo money dieter. After breaking her promise to herself by cheating on her resolution, she faced a dilemma that is familiar to everyone who wants to improve his or her quality of life. "I wondered what difference it would now make if I cheated a little more," she recalls.

STEP 1 SET UP A PLAN THAT YOU CAN LIVE WITH.

Let's face it, making any changes to your lifestyle takes work. Temptation is everywhere. No matter how strong your resolve is when you start, a momentary lapse can cause you to revert to your old habits. Getting back to your resolution can be harder than starting it in the first place.

What you do at this crossroads—and even how you describe yourself—can spell the difference between success and failure. Here are five common money types. Do any of them sound familiar?

- Money Type F: *The self-described financial failure*. You get out the credit cards and buy whatever you want. You've already gone off your money diet and you'll never take charge of your finances, so what's the point of even trying?
- Money Type B: *The bucks binger*. You start spending more because you feel you're entitled to a reward—or two, or ten—after making such huge sacrifices.

- Money Type M: *The money martyr.* You start out as a bucks binger but then guilt sets in. You feel that you are not worthy of the things you bought. Your closets are lined with pricey clothes you have never worn or costly electronics items that have never been taken out of the original boxes.
- Money Type P: *The penny purger.* You're a bucks binger but when your feelings of guilt take over, you decide to get rid of your purchases by giving them away to friends or to a charity. You get rid of the goods, but you're still on the hook for the credit card bills, which may take years to pay off.
- Money Type C: *The cash compromiser.* You cut yourself a little slack. By sticking with your money diet, you have made a lot of progress. You feel it's okay to reward your hard work occasionally and in moderation. But you pay for your treat with cash because you don't want to rack up any new credit card charges while you're still paying off old ones.

STEP 2 UNDERSTAND THAT YOUR DAY-TO-DAY CHOICES WILL SEAL YOUR FINANCIAL FATE.

How can you keep the yo-yo syndrome from ruining your plans? You need to do seven things:

1. Set and prioritize realistic goals—goals that are attainable and are important enough to make the sacrifices worthwhile.
2. Give in to an occasional urge to splurge. Build some inexpensive treats into your spending plan, such as lunch at a nice restaurant with a friend, or a new shirt, or whatever gives you some joy and makes your other sacrifices seem worthwhile.
3. Boost your money IQ so that you won't be chasing investments that aren't right for you.
4. Understand the tax consequences before you make any money moves.
5. At fixed intervals, measure your progress toward reaching your goals.
6. Recruit your family for help with your work in progress, as well as for emotional support.
7. Have the determination to "get back on the horse" if you fall or are thrown off.

Remember, you're in this for the long haul. If you stay on a money diet 100 percent of the time, all you'll think about is forbidden treats. An occasional treat is not a sign of weakness. You can consider yourself weak only if you fall off your new plan and refuse to get back on it.

LLOYD'S LAW

Your little decisions—the ones you make day in and day out— will seal your financial fate. It's the decisions you may not give a second thought to that determine whether you will ever reach your goals and lead the life you want. The life you could have.

STEP 3   UNCOVER WHAT PUSHES YOUR SPENDING BUTTONS.

Almost all of us, at some time, have tried to fill a void in our lives with something material. And credit cards are often used to pay for it. But saying "Charge it" isn't going to bring you true happiness. It may give you a quick spender's high, but, trust me, it won't last long. The high is guaranteed to be ended by the time the bill arrives. The agony of paying the bill—and the accompanying finance charges—will last much longer than the temporary morale boost.

"I hadn't put two and two together, but maybe my little foray in the shoe department wasn't an accident," says Martha. "Looking back now, it's kind of clear what caused it. I had just been passed over for a promotion earlier that week, and while I pretended I didn't care, I *did*. My boss had told me that I wasn't ready for the promotion. 'You're not mature enough,' she said. So I guess that when I looked in the department store window, I thought that a new pair of shoes might make me feel better. Maybe my clothes were making me look too young, so if I came into the office wearing a very expensive, chic pair of shoes, maybe my boss would reconsider and give me the promotion after all. It seemed reasonable at the time.

"I wore the shoes to work the next day. My cubicle mate said that she liked them but asked, 'We both earn the same amount and I could never afford those, so how can you?' I shrugged and said in a low voice, 'They were on sale.' But of course they weren't. Later that day, while I was waiting for the elevator, Marjorie, the woman who got the promotion instead of me, stared at my feet for a long time. She rolled her eyes and sneered, 'You know, those shoes don't go with your outfit.' When I got home, I put the shoes in their box and I haven't taken them out since. But I'm still paying for them."

STEP 4 — LEARN TO BOUNCE BACK.

What should you do if you have a momentary money lapse? Don't condemn yourself over occasional stumbles. Instead, commend yourself for all the times when you didn't crumble—the times when you stayed on or got back on your financial plan. But if you feel your resolve slipping:

- *Avoid spending triggers.* If times, places, or people you are with lower your resistance, ask yourself why, and then steer clear of those temptations.
- *Run your own race.* Don't try to keep up with the Joneses or impress someone else. Make purchases for the right reasons—because you *need* something.
- *Don't shop to drown negative feelings.* If you were passed over for a raise, had an argument with a spouse or relative, or are just feeling icky that day (or week or month), stay out of the stores. Instead, acknowledge your negative feelings. Then do something that will make you feel better, such as volunteer work or exercise.

In the next two chapters, I will show you more ways to stay motivated and reach your goals without feeling cheated.

Chapter 2

Free-Up Cash Each Month and Break Your Self-Defeating Money Habits—Without Having to Live Within a Budget

Does money keep slipping through your fingers? You don't have to fear the dreaded "B" word—Budget. The good news is that most people don't need to live within the constraints of a budget, but it can be a real eye-opener to see how much you spend on certain things. If your income is big enough to cover your expenses, including your income taxes, you won't need to make any serious changes.

Any time invested in taking charge of your money is time well spent. Planning and a little sacrifice—or at least some delayed gratification— are the keys to reaching your financial goals or your life's dreams. Focus your energy and attention on the methods that will get you the biggest— and fastest—results.

Chalk up your past money lapses as learning experiences. You can't change the past, but you can take control of your financial fate. This chapter gives you five easy steps toward that control.

STEP 1 UNDERSTAND WHERE YOUR MONEY GOES.

Several times a day, each of us comes face to face with the same choice. We can either spend or not spend our hard-earned money on one of the thousands of services or products we're offered. Some expenses—food, shelter, clothing, and transportation to get to work—are necessary. Others, such as the morning newspaper, a three-dollar cup of espresso, or a first-class vacation in the Bahamas, might be nice, but you'd be hard-pressed to call them life-or-death necessities. Whether you're earning $25,000 a year or $250,000 a year, you have only a fixed amount of money. What you choose to do with it is up to you, and you get to make that choice over and over, day in and day out.

"I know that bill is here somewhere. . . ." Have you ever uttered that phrase? I have, more times than I care to admit. Over the years, I'll bet I have spent a total of one month of my waking hours looking for bills and other papers. I ultimately do find them, but I should have been able to put my fingers on them right away. Misplacing any important papers can be time-consuming and annoying, but doing it with bills can also be very costly. It can even ruin your credit rating.

From credit card companies to utility suppliers to department stores, a growing number of billing departments have no qualms about adding finance charges to an overdue balance. And these days many creditors are also quick to slap you with a late-payment penalty of $29 each time your payment is received even one day late.

So what can you do? I bought a very inexpensive, wicker basket into which I place every bill as soon as it arrives. (If a basket doesn't suit you, consider a file folder or a large manila envelope.) Organize the bills by date. On top, place the bill that is due the soonest, then the one with the next due date, and so on. Even a simple system like this one can fail if you keep moving the basket (or folder or envelope). So you need to establish one set place to store your collection of unpaid bills, such as the top drawer of a designated kitchen cabinet or desk or bedroom dresser for a folder or envelope—near where you sit when you pay your bills.

When bank interest rates were high, paying bills very close to the due date was a good strategy. That way, you (instead of the creditor) got to collect the interest accruing during those extra few days that the money stayed in *your* bank account. But with so many creditors charging late fees and finance charges when payments are received even one day late, as well as placing negative marks on your credit report, that strategy can cost you plenty.

> ## Lloyd's Law
>
> *Paying bills only once a month is no longer often enough. If you miss a due date by even one day, you're apt to get hit with finance charges and late payment penalties. You may also find that the creditor has put negative marks on your credit report for being a slow payer.*

Bill paying is just one part of money management. Next, take a snapshot of your current financial situation. Here's how to add up what you're spending and what you're saving, and what to ask about before you move your finances online:

1. Track your spending for one month.
2. Determine how much money, if any, is left at month's end.
3. Consider tracking your money online (on a home computer, not in your company's system).

Do you frequently flex your financial muscles by regularly investing part of your paycheck, paying off your credit card balance (at least most of the time), and keeping impulse purchases to a minimum? Or are you a self-described financial couch potato who sits back and hopes everything will work out someday? Well, someday is *today*. Now is an ideal time to launch a fitness program for your finances.

Kyra and Paul's Story

"I was at the ATM all the time, yet I always seemed to be low on cash," says Kyra. Like many people, Kyra and Paul had come to rely on their ATM card for a needed cash infusion several times a week. When their bank added the debit card feature, allowing them to use the card to pay for merchandise, they began paying for almost everything, from groceries to gasoline, with plastic. At first, this cut down their need for cash. But later, each time Kyra or Paul swiped the debit card to make a purchase, they would also take out extra cash. "The sad part is, when I look back, I can't recall what I spent the money on," Paul says. "I have nothing to show for it."

Tracking Your Expenses

It's easy to get started tracking your expenses. For one month, carry a small notepad and pen with you everywhere you go, and jot down every cent you spend (cash, check, credit card, or debit card). Include all the little items, such as the newspaper you buy at the newsstand or the coins you feed into the gumball machine.

Don't forget ATM or debit card surcharges that are taken from your bank account when you use a plastic card at the gas station, supermarket, or cash machine. (In Chapter 5, I will show you how to rein in runaway bank fees.)

At month's end, total your expenses in each category and copy the totals onto the form on page 11.

To arrive at a monthly amount to put aside for vacations and other occasional items, set a yearly goal for those categories, and divide by 12.

Spending Plan for _____ (mo/yr)

Housing (mortgage/rent)	$ _____
Utilities (electric, gas, water, phone)	_____
Taxes	_____
Credit card	_____
Student loans	_____
Obligations you must pay (alimony, child support)	_____
Bank fees (ATM, late-payment and other penalty fees, others)	_____
Insurance (health, home, car, life, disability)	_____
Medical/Dental	_____
Food (meals, snacks)	_____
Clothing (purchases, dry cleaning)	_____
Transportation (car payments, gas, tolls)	_____
Magazines, newspapers, books	_____
Gifts, charities	_____
Personal (toiletries, allowances)	_____
Entertainment	_____
Sports and hobbies	_____
Vacation	_____
Repairs	_____
Other	_____
Total Spent	$ _____

Determining How Much, If Anything, Is Left at Month's End

That is your savings—money you could start investing without making any other changes. Try to save at least 10 percent of your pay. If that's too hard, start by saving five or three percent. Then increase the amount every six months until you reach 10 percent.

To calculate your savings amount, subtract your "Total spent" from your total monthly pay (and any other sources of income). If the result is a negative number for that month, you have spent more than you took in. You are living beyond your means and this pattern cannot go on indefinitely.

Sign up for an automatic savings plan at work or at your bank, and designate a fixed sum to be withdrawn each month. If you don't see that money, you won't be tempted to spend it!

As a general rule, it's good to have a cash cushion equal to three to six months of your expenses. That way if you were to lose your job or become seriously ill or injured, you could still meet your obligations. This money needs to be easily accessible, so keep it in savings accounts, short-term certificates of deposit (CDs), or money market accounts. Verify that your bank deposits are insured by the Federal Deposit Insurance Corporation (FDIC).

Tip: If you have a good line of credit (credit cards and other sources) and you haven't already tapped these credit lines, consider keeping just three months' income as a cash cushion.

Tracking Your Money Online

If you have a computer, consider using a software package to track your spending and keep the rest of your financial life in one place. Quicken and Microsoft Money are both big sellers, and either will do the trick— and could make your tax prep easier. (More on this in the next chapter.) These days, you can often download your monthly financial activities, such as your bank statement, credit card statement, mortgage statement, mutual fund statement, and utility bills.

LLOYD'S LAW

If you don't own a computer, don't put your financial information on your computer at work. Many financial advisers urge consumers to do this, but they fail to point out that an employer is legally entitled to see everything on a computer in their workplace. So keep your finances to yourself.

You can also arrange to pay many, if not all, of your bills online through your bank. But before you make this move, be sure to ask about all the fees you will be charged for this convenience and how long it will take for your bills to be paid. Some "automated" bill-paying plans aren't as automated as they sound, and bills are not paid electronically. Instead, even though the money may come out of your bank account immediately, the bill-paying service may physically cut a check that is then forwarded (often by snail mail) to your creditors. This manual procedure can add days to the bill-paying process, so it may take longer to pay this way than if you write a check and mail it yourself. Also be sure to ask about your bank's online security procedures for keeping strangers from getting access to your personal finances.

STEP 2   START POWER SAVING.

Throughout this book, I'll show you many ways to trim your expenses painlessly. Once you get the hang of it, spending less gets easier and requires less thought, and you can start using your newfound money to reach your true goals. As an added bonus, you'll feel better because a weight is being lifted from your shoulders.

If you are saving less than your goal of 10 percent of your pay, go back to your spending plan and identify places where you could pinch pennies painlessly. Here are some belt-tightening strategies that have worked for others:

- Kick the soft drink, bottled water, and coffee bar habits. The money you save will go a long way to pay off credit card debt or student loans or toward funding an IRA or 401(k) plan.
- If you need cash, avoid the surcharge some cash machine owners levy on ATMs at a supermarket entrance. Use your ATM card at the checkout instead.
- Use coupons you print from Internet Web sites to cut the cost of your routine purchases. Coupons aren't just for cents off at the supermarket anymore. I've been using coupons posted by my car dealer to get everything from free state auto inspections to big discounts on oil changes, lubes, and expensive body work.
- Buy a late model used car instead of a new one, and drive it longer. After you make the final loan payment, keep writing a check—to yourself—on the same schedule. When you need a replacement car, you will have money on hand for a down payment, or perhaps enough to pay the full ticket price.
- Raise your insurance deductibles, and ask for insurance discounts (for instance, accident-free discounts on auto insurance; discounts for burglar alarms in your home or car; multiple-policy discounts if you have more than one policy from the same insurance company; or a discount for taking a defensive driving course).
- Challenge your real estate taxes. Errors in property tax records are not uncommon. Also if your neighbors have been sprucing up their property with pricey improvements, you may be a victim of

guilt by association. It's vital that you inform the tax department that you live more modestly and should be taxed accordingly. Contact your local government's tax assessment unit for details.

- Fertilize your lawn only twice a year (fall is the best time in many parts of the country). Check with your local government's extension office for free, cost-saving tips for your lawn and garden.
- Maximize your tax deductions. If you don't qualify for itemizing your deductions each year, consider lumping two years' deductions (charitable contributions, medical expenses, and so on) into one year and itemizing them. In alternate years, when your deductions are too low to itemize, take the standard deduction.
- Cancel any credit card life insurance or mortgage life-and-disability coverage. Chances are you can get better, less restrictive, and less costly coverage elsewhere.
- Say "No" to extended warranties on electronics products, automobiles, and so on. To avoid products with reliability problems, research your purchases before you buy.
- Ask your mortgage lender to cancel your private mortgage insurance (PMI) as soon as your equity reaches 20 percent of your home's value. This could save you about $1,000 or more each year.

As you can see, amassing money is all about trade-offs. You can spend money on something that gives you pleasure, or you can save that money, invest it, or spend it on something that is now more important to you. The choice is yours.

To stop letting money slip through your fingers, try doing the following:

- Pay yourself first. Many people find it easier to stick with a savings plan if the entry on the first line on their monthly spending plan is the dollar amount they want to save.

Tip: If an emergency eats up some of your savings one month, get yourself back on track the next month. Start saving again, right where you left off.

- Post a photo of your goal where you can't help seeing it. Whether it's a dream house, a boat, a college education, or an exotic travel destination, it will remind you what your sacrifices are for. The refrigerator door is a good spot for it, but stroll through your home to find other places that may call out to you, such as above the television set, near the computer, or posted to the bathroom mirror.

- Reward yourself occasionally. Taking charge of your money is not supposed to be a punishment. A small splurge from time to time can make the difference between staying on a money-smart plan for life or falling off the debt diet wagon. Don't dwell on what you are giving up. Instead, focus on what you will do with all the newfound money—and on your feelings of freedom and accomplishment.
- Make it harder to get to your credit cards. Wind two thick rubber bands several times around each credit card. It will be harder to get the cards out of your wallet, and you'll have to spend time unwinding the bands before you can use a card. The extra few seconds may give you a chance to come to your senses and resist the urge to splurge.
- Leave your credit cards at home. Avoid temptation—or a way to pay that's too easy. Take your credit cards out of your wallet.
- Start a *Non*spending journal. You spent a month tracking the money you were spending; use that information to track what you are *resisting* spending your hard-earned money on. Create a Nonspending journal by carrying a small notebook and pen, and jotting down all the things that you used to spend your money on, but no longer do.

  Jot down what these items would have cost you (including tax). At the end of each day (or week or month), tally all the money you DIDN'T spend. You'll see the amount quickly adding up.
- If seeing your savings on paper isn't enough motivation, get yourself a piggybank. (No, they're not just for kids!) Add up the money listed in your Nonspending journal, count out the amount in bills and coins, and put this money in your piggybank. I find the sound of the new coins hitting the ones already in there (*ca ching, ca ching*) very satisfying. You can see the money growing in the bank and you can touch it. Once a month, count it out. Every few weeks, take your newfound savings and put it to use to pay down your credit card balance or other debts.

Credit card debt—or rising credit card costs—is the main drain on many consumers' cash. The next two steps show you how to pay off your debt sooner, and how to shop for better credit card terms. (An in-depth discussion of debt and credit cards can be found in Chapter 4.)

STEP 3   PAY OFF CRUSHING CREDIT CARD DEBT SOONER.

(Note: If you aren't carrying a credit card balance, skip to the fourth step.)

If you tracked your spending for a month, you may have been shocked to discover how much your credit card has been costing you. For many consumers, crushing credit card debt is one of the biggest budget busters. Containing your credit card costs could yield the biggest financial and emotional or psychic return on your effort.

You will never get wealthy—in fact, you will always be teetering on the brink of disaster—as long as you are carrying credit card debt month after month, year after year, or decade after decade. The sooner you can pay off your credit card debt, the sooner you can reach your long-term financial goals. Here are some ways to rein in your rising credit card costs and pay down your debt.

Tally Your Total Debt and Manage Your Monthly Payments

Add up all your credit card balances, not just the minimum monthly payments. Creditors know what you owe, and so should you.

If for some reason you're unable to make the minimum monthly payment, call the creditor to work out an alternate payment plan *before* you default, so you can avoid a negative mark on your credit report. Explain *why* you can't make your scheduled payment. For instance, if you (or someone in your family) have had a costly illness, or if you've been laid off at work, the creditor may agree to suspend interest—or even the required payments—for a few months.

If the first person you speak with won't help, ask for his or her supervisor or request a meeting. Ask for confirmation of the new terms (revised payment schedule, reduced interest rate, or suspended interest charges) in writing, along with a promise that no negative marks will be placed on your credit report. If your request for a written confirmation is refused, send your own note to the creditor, confirming your conversation. Keep a copy of all correspondence in your files.

Take a Credit Card Breather

If you can't pay your balance in full, consider putting your credit cards away for a while. Your entire monthly payment will then go toward paying down old debt.

Pay Off Your Balance(s) Once and For All!

If you're sick and tired of carrying a credit card balance year after year, and you want to pay off your credit card bills as quickly and inexpensively as possible, what's the best way to go about it? Which card should you pay off first—the one with the highest balance or the one with the highest rate?

LLOYD'S LAW

If you pay off your balances in the wrong order, or pay too little to one or more creditors in any month, you could end up paying hundreds of dollars more than necessary.

Pay off the card with the highest interest rate first; when that's paid off, move on to the one with the next highest rate. Here's how to do it:

- Arrange your bills in sequence, from the *highest interest rate* (not the highest balance) to the lowest interest rate.
- Try to refinance your debt by transferring your high-interest-rate balance(s) to a card that offers a much lower interest rate, so that your monthly payments will pay off your total balance(s) more quickly. (See Step 4 below for Web sites where you can search for better terms.)

Tip: Before you sign up for any new card, make sure that you understand all the fees and other terms. For instance, some cards charge a fee of 1 to 3 percent of the transferred balance. (This fee could more than offset your savings.) Look for a card issuer that will waive that fee. Double check that the lower interest rate applies to balance transfers and not just to new charges.

- Make more than the minimum monthly payments whenever you can, until your card with the highest interest rate is paid off. Then start making more than the minimum payments to the card with the next highest rate.

Tip: Always make at least the minimum monthly payment on *all* your cards, to avoid penalties.

- Make your payment well ahead of the due date. It lowers your "average daily balance," so (with most cards) it will cut your finance charges and allow you to more quickly pay down your outstanding balance.

- If you've got a low "teaser" interest rate that's good, typically, for six months, don't forget to refinance again before the rate expires, or you could easily blow your hard-earned savings. Or, if your card issuer raises rates or fees (they can do it with just 15 days' notice), ask the "retention department" to continue your old terms. Even if you're carrying a balance, some lenders will agree to retain your account and keep you from defaulting. If they refuse, begin to search again for a lower-rate card.

Tip: Some cards now charge a hefty fee for closing an account within 6 months to a year of opening it, so get all fees confirmed in writing before closing an account.

Could this "quick fix" cause long-term problems? (Or, what you better know about home equity loans before you take one out.)

Marc's Story

"Nicole and I had been carrying credit card debt for years, and paid at least the minimum payment every month—more, any month we had extra money. But frankly, it didn't seem like we were making a dent on our balances, which were hovering around $12,000," says Marc Miller. "When we saw the ad on TV saying that we could refinance our high-interest credit card debt with a low-cost home equity loan, we looked at each other and it was like a light bulb had gone on over our heads."

The Millers contacted the lender, and, after filling out a lengthy loan application, they transferred their credit card debt (with an average 16.7 percent interest rate) to an 8.3 percent home equity loan. "We even took out an extra $9,000 to get some needed plumbing and roof repairs on our house. The best part was that, with the lower interest rate, our monthly payments were just a few dollars more than we were paying on our credit card bill," recalls Marc. "After the house repairs were done, we had close to $3,000 left over, so we went on a little cross-country trip and visited some relatives. To be on the safe side, we left our credit cards home so we wouldn't be tempted to start charging them up again."

When the Millers returned home, a gray storm cloud seemed to be hovering over them. "First, my car was stolen while it was parked outside the building where I work, and I got almost nothing from the insurance to buy a new car with," says Nicole. "Then Marc's mom got ill, and we had to give her almost $7,300 to cover some of her medical costs and to pay for some in-home health care. The last straw was when the company where Marc works went through a rough patch and said that they would be 'holding onto his sales commissions until their financial picture improved.' To make a long story short, we suddenly couldn't pay our bills. The home equity lender even sent a letter to us saying that unless we sent them our missing payments, plus several hundred dollars in late fees and extra interest, they would begin foreclosing on our house."

Faced with these unappealing choices, the Millers started using their credit cards again "just to put food on the table," explains Marc. "We also had to take out a cash advance to pay the utility bills and to make a big payment on our home equity loan."

The credit card cash advance did not come cheap. "It ended up costing us over 20 percent when you add in all the fees they charged us. In addition to the $21,000 home equity loan, we're also carrying over $8,500 in new credit card debt. And since we missed a few payments along the way, our credit cards are now costing over 21 percent. So the home equity loan, which seemed like a low-cost lifesaver for us, has become a steel anchor, and we are literally drowning in debt."

The Millers were forced to learn a hard lesson about home equity loans: If you fail to make timely payments on them, the lender has the legal right to foreclose on your home. That is why transferring "unsecured" credit card debt to a "secured" home equity (mortgage) debt is not something to enter into lightly. You are literally betting your home, and you could be forced to sell your home if you fall behind on your payments.

LLOYD'S LAW

Transferring credit card debt to a home equity loan is much riskier than many homeowners realize. Even if you can get a lower interest rate (and may be able to deduct interest payments on your taxes), only switch your (unsecured) credit card debt to a (secured) home equity loan if you are absolutely certain you will not start racking up new charges on your credit card. To avoid temptation, if you switch to a home equity loan, cut up the cards and cancel the accounts by writing letters to the credit card companies.

STEP 4 — SHOP FOR BETTER CREDIT CARD TERMS.

Whether you carry a balance or pay your bills off in full each month, small differences in terms from one credit card to another can mean a big difference to your wallet. Even some of the most innocuous sounding credit offers can carry some hefty hidden costs. These days, it's not a bad idea to scrutinize offers you've already accepted, and to keep an eye out for better credit card terms.

Check for Ticking Credit Card Time Bombs

Did you sign up for a credit card offer that sounded good but will soon explode in costly finance charges? Two popular offers are: deferred billing plans and teaser rates.

- Deferred billing plans lure you with promises of no finance charges for three, six, or twelve months. Pay off your balance before the offer expires, or you'll be hit with retroactive interest from the date of purchase.
- Teaser interest rates entice you with a low introductory interest rate that expires after six months. Shop for another low-cost card or call your current card issuer's "retention department" to negotiate an extension of favorable terms. Read on for some card-shopping tips.

And beware of sudden changes in terms. By law, all credit card terms (interest rate, fees, and so on) can change with just 15 days' notice. Read the fine print in the credit card inserts immediately, and if the terms suddenly change, complain. Call the "retention department" and say you're not going to pay new penalty fees or jacked-up interest rates. Many issuers will comply, to keep your business. Ask for confirmation of your agreement in writing. If they refuse to improve the terms, be prepared to cancel the card (but not until you have another credit card with better terms in hand) and transfer your balance to your new card.

Make Companies Pursue You

The credit market is saturated, so card issuers will often cut deals to keep business. Here's how you can benefit:

- Call your credit card issuer and ask for better terms. Stress your loyalty, longevity, or prompt payment history—whatever applies.
- Even if you're behind in your payments, your credit card issuer may still give you better terms so you won't default and they won't have to write off your balance.

- Shop for a credit card and bank package together. The more business you offer, the more bargaining power you'll have. (Banks love direct deposit of payroll checks.) Review your bank statements for the past six months to see what services you use—ATM, checking account, overdraft, and so on. (I give more tips on cutting bank costs in Chapter 5.)
- Contact three local banks or credit unions, and ask for their best terms on the services you use. Then go back to your current credit card issuer and ask for a deal that beats the competition.

On the Web, you can comparison shop for a better credit card at www.bankrate.com and www.cardtrak.com. Lists of credit card rates are provided at both Web sites.

Before you transfer an outstanding balance to another card, be sure to comb the fine print for hidden fees. Some credit card issuers treat balance transfers like cash advances and add on a fee of 2 or more percent.

Beware of Penalties

Penalties include bumped-up interest rates, and fees of up to $30 for paying less than the minimum or for being as little as one day late. Even if your card came with a fixed interest rate, the card issuer could push your rate up as a penalty for paying late.

Make more than the minimum monthly payments when you can, and always pay off the highest-interest-rate cards first. Always make at least the minimum monthly payment on *all* cards, to avoid penalties. If you're carrying a balance, make your payment well ahead of the due date; it lowers your "average daily balance" and (with most cards) your finance charges will be reduced, and you can more quickly pay down your outstanding balance.

Read Up on Rebate Rules

Consumers who were counting on big rebates (cash back, merchandise, or frequent flyer miles) based on card use got a reality check when issuers began curtailing the size of rebates and the length of time consumers could bank them before cashing them in. Why the change? Some consumers were working the system to their advantage by putting huge charges on their rebate cards but either paying the balances off each month or transferring them to lower-interest-rate credit cards. The issuers got less interest income than expected.

"Use it or lose it" is good advice for many rebate cardholders, but before you ante up cash to redeem a rebate, comparison-shop for the merchandise (airplane ticket, car, whatever) to be sure you couldn't do better independently. (More advice on getting a grip on your credit is given in Chapter 4.)

STEP 5 SEE HOW MUCH YOU OWN AND OWE.

Before you can get where you're going, why not see where you stand? Once a year, calculate how much you're worth. Your personal balance sheet will be a first step toward charting your financial progress. Besides, you'll need this calculation if you plan to apply for a mortgage, a car loan, or student aid for your children, and for estate planning purposes.

A worksheet is provided on page 23. Here's how to begin. In Column A, list the value of all of your assets (everything you own and earn), including stocks, bonds, bank accounts, pensions, and your home's equity (its market value minus your mortgage balance).

In column B, list all of your liabilities (what you owe), including the balances on your mortgage, car loan, and credit cards. An accurate picture of your net worth is only possible if you're thorough about including every asset and liability, so be sure to go through the list carefully.

Gather and review your financial documents, such as pay stubs and year-end statements from your bank, credit card issuer, and mutual funds. Ask your bank to determine the market value of any savings bonds you're holding (the market value is different from the face value).

The easiest time for many people to calculate their net worth is right after filling out their income taxes. Their records are all assembled, and they are up to speed on their investments. But whether you're getting around to this in April, August, January, or whenever, the important thing is that you do it. Take this snapshot of your personal balance sheet, to see where you are and to help you get to where you want to be.

For many people, just going through the process of filling out their personal balance sheet, along with a one-month spending plan, can be a real eye-opener. It fills in a lot of holes in their financial lives and helps them plot a course to improve their financial situation.

After Kyra and Paul completed the steps in this chapter, they admitted it was worth the effort. "Now that it's down on paper, we have a much clearer idea of where our money is really going. And we've spotted several places where we can cut back and not feel that our lifestyle will be seriously crimped."

Worksheet

Column A   Current Assets: What You Own
- Cash $_____
- Bank account balances (checking, savings, money market) $_____
- Life insurance (cash value) $_____
- Mutual funds, stocks, bonds, CDs $_____
- Retirement savings [401(k), IRA, vested pension] $_____
- House and other real estate (equity amount) $_____
- Car (resale value) $_____
- Personal property $_____
- Money you are owed $_____
- Jewels, precious metals, collectors' items $_____
- Salary (annual gross) or pension $_____
- Other $_____

Line A: Total Assets $_____

Column B   Current Liabilities: What You Owe
- Mortgage(s) $_____
- Credit card balances $_____
- Student loans $_____
- Auto loans/leases $_____
- Other loans $_____
- Federal, state, and local taxes (owed or estimated) $_____
- Taxes due on investments if cashed in $_____
- Other obligations (tuition, leases) $_____

Line B: Total Liabilities $_____

Total Assets (Line A) $_____
Less: Total Liabilities (Line B) $_____
Net Worth $_____

Kyra adds that completing their personal balance sheet made them confront a few other things. "First, we own more (in the asset column), than we thought, so, at a minimum, we need to update our wills and do some serious estate planning so that our family would be taken care of if something happened to either of us." (Information on wills and estate planning is given in Chapter 12.)

"Second, our older daughter, Melanie, will be applying to colleges in a couple of years, and to go to a good college she is going to need financial aid. It turns out that this was the right time for us to start getting familiar with the process. If we make some changes in our finances (our credit card debt and even our own student loans) in the next few months, Melanie can qualify for more money. If we hadn't done this now, Melanie would have had to settle for less financial aid than she is eligible for, and probably would not have been able to afford the college she really wants to attend." (Information on qualifying for financial aid is in Chapter 31.)

Chapter 3

Boost Your Money IQ on Your Own— or with Some Professional Help

It's *your* money. Nobody else is going to care about it as much as you do. Many financial advisers and tax planners are qualified and honorable, others are unscrupulous. They may *say* they care about you and your money, when all they really care about is how much money *they* will make off your money. What should you do? Increase your money IQ because the more you know about money, the better decisions you will make now and for the rest of your life.

LLOYD'S LAW

The real challenge facing you is figuring out ways to not only make more money, but to keep more of your money after taxes.

Boosting your money IQ is not something you do in a week. For most people, it may not be a total do-it-yourself job. To get up to speed in a hurry, you may want to consult a professional, *objective* financial planner who can help you understand your options and guide you toward the best financial decisions for *your individual situation.* But how do you find the right financial planner for you and not pay more than you have to?

And where money is involved, taxes inevitably seem to follow. If your financial situation has suddenly changed (perhaps you've received an inheritance, or you are getting married or divorced, or you'd like to start a business), you may want to consult a tax planner. He or she could lay out some financial options for you *before* you do something that could result in a huge tax bill. If you're like most people, you may not know how much tax planning and tax preparation help you really need. Will a national tax preparation chain give you enough assistance? Would consulting a tax attorney be overkill and too costly?

In this chapter, I will show you simple ways you can boost your money IQ. I will also help you determine how much financial and tax-planning advice you need, as well as how you can go about finding the right person for your individual situation without overpaying for the advice.

Keith's Story

"I went to one of those weekend financial planning seminars a few months ago," recalls Keith. "I figured that, since it was free, the most I would be out was a few hours of my time, right? The seminar was an eye-opener. The instructor introduced himself by saying that he had been a financial planner for over twenty years, and he really seemed to know what he was talking about.

"'Do any of you think you're paying more than your fair share in taxes?' is how he began. Of course, everybody in the room raised their hands. He then went on to show how many of us were paying more in taxes than we even realized. The seminar was taught like a good college course and was loaded with information I didn't know.

"While the morning session was low-key, things really heated up in the afternoon as the instructor began taking apart some of the most popular types of investments. He said, 'Life insurance policies and mutual funds are overhyped and oversold, and are not good investments.' He then compared the returns on insurance policies and mutual funds to those on a variety of tax-deferred and totally tax-free investments. He cranked out the after-tax numbers and brought home the fact that most of us could slash our tax bills by going with these other types of investments.

"I had doubts, so I asked a lot of questions and was really impressed with the answers. By the time the seminar ended, I was sold. [When the instructor circulated a sign-up sheet] I, along with everyone else there, put my name and phone number on a list of people who wanted to receive more information. Monday morning, the instructor called. He said how 'insightful' my questions were. That should have tipped me off, but my ego fell for the flattery.

"Then he had another financial planner in his office send me sales brochures and testimonials from 'other satisfied clients.' I called a few of the clients, and they raved about the instructor and his firm. Within the next six weeks, the second planner kept calling to say, 'You could get much better returns and pay much less in taxes by swapping your life insurance policies and mutual funds for a combination of tax-deferred investments and retirement savings plans.' When I finally said okay, she arranged to have a broker she knew make the purchases.

"I never really understood what the investments were that I was buying, until my tax preparer started looking over my financial statements and explained that the so-called 'tax-saving investments' I was sold were nothing but insurance policies. And I had paid a bunch of fees to sell what I already had and buy the new stuff! First, I owed a 'surrender fee' to cash in my old insurance policies. Second, I owed taxes on some of the money I got back from my old policies. Third, they didn't even have the decency to tell me that the financial planners who ran the seminar made $7,670 in bonuses—money that came directly from my pocket—for referring me to their friend, who bought these products. So much for 'free investment advice.'

"My tax preparer and a new financial planner he recommended say that these new investments aren't even appropriate for us. But I can't afford to unload them because I will owe huge 'surrender fees' if I sell them within the next seven years.

"So what have I learned? That there's no such thing as free financial advice. The 'free' financial planning seminar I attended has already cost me thousands of dollars and will continue to cost me money for years to come. Financial advisers should be required, up front, to tell you what *all* the costs will be for an investment they are touting."

This brings me back to my original point: Nobody else—no financial planner, no stockbroker, no accountant, and no insurance salesperson—will ever care about you, your family, or your financial security as much as you do. It's in your best interest to learn as much as possible about money (1) so you can make good financial decisions yourself, and (2) so you can assess knowledgeably the advice you get from professional financial advisers or others.

Even if you choose to hire a financial planner to help you manage your money, you have a responsibility to yourself, and to your family, to learn as much as possible about making and investing money. Otherwise, how will you be able to tell whether the advice you are being offered is right for you, or too risky? And how can you assess the accuracy of the projected earnings, or the safety of the proposed investments? It's a big responsibility and one you cannot afford to give entirely to anyone else. Here are three steps to help develop your own expertise.

STEP 1 BOOST YOUR MONEY IQ.

Bone up on some money basics, and stay up-to-date on money news that could affect your investments, your job, your credit cards, and your home's value.

- Take a course. Look into personal finance classes taught at a community college. These classes can be an inexpensive way to get up to speed quickly. Steer clear of "free" financial seminars because, as Keith learned too late, most instructors are actually insurance salespeople, financial planners, accountants, or stockbrokers who hope to make money by selling specific financial products that— not coincidentally—they are probably touting during the seminar.

- Subscribe to a personal finance publication. *Money, Kiplinger's Personal Finance,* and *Smart Money* are just a few of the popular personal finance sources that even novices find easy to read. Check out the personal finance information in the business section of your local newspaper, or visit these financial information Web sites:

ABC News	www.abcnews.com
Barron's	www.barrons.com
Bloomberg	www.bloomberg.com
Business Week	www.businessweek.com*
CBS Marketwatch	www.cbsmarketwatch.com
CNBC	www.cnbc.com
CNN/financial network	www.cnnfn.com
Consumer Reports	www.consumerreports.com*
Forbes	www.forbes.com
Fortune	www.fortune.com
Fox news	www.foxmarketwire.com
ivillage	www.ivillage.com
Kiplinger's	www.kiplinger.com
Money	www.money.com
Moneycentral	www.moneycentral.com
Morningstar	www.morningstar.com
Motley Fool	www.fool.com
Newsweek	www.newsweek.com
New York Times	www.nytimes.com
Oxygen network	www.ka-ching.com
Quicken	www.quicken.com
Reuter's Moneynet	www.moneynet.com
SmartMoney	www.smartmoney.com
The Street.com	www.thestreet.com
Time	www.time.com
USA Today	www.usatoday.com
US News and World Report	www.usnews.com

---

* These Web sites charge a subscriber fee to access some or all of their information.

Valueline	www.valueline.com*
Wall Street Journal	www.wsj.com*
Washington Post	www.washingtonpost.com
Women's wire	www.womenswire.com
Worth	www.worth.com
Yahoo	finance.yahoo.com
Ziff-Davis	www.zdnet.com

 STEP 2 CONSIDER HIRING A FINANCIAL PLANNER.

You need to understand all the financial decisions you make, but with the growing array of financial products from which to choose and the increasing complexity of tax laws, from time to time it might make sense to consult a financial expert who can shed some light on your options. Here are some instances when hiring a professional financial planner could be a smart move:

- You have come into some money, through an inheritance or other lump-sum payment.
- You are contemplating a lifestyle change, such as starting a family, retiring early, or starting your own business.
- You don't understand the tax consequences of some investments that you are considering or that you already own.
- You are being kept up at night by the gyrations of the stock market.

The quality of financial advice and the fees charged for it vary greatly. Virtually anyone—regardless of training, education, or even a criminal past—can hang out a shingle and call himself or herself a financial planner. So how can you know whether the products being touted are in your best interest and not just chosen to give the planner the biggest commission or sales bonus?

Financial planners are often compensated in ways that create inherent conflicts of interest. You probably know that even if you buy a financial product from a no-fee financial planner, you will pay for that recommendation. The planner isn't giving advice just to be nice. He or she will be getting a commission and/or bonus for selling you a product, and that can taint the advice you are given. (Is the planner recommending a product because it's good for your bank account or the planner's?) The amount that the financial product is "marked up" (to cover a commission and/or bonus) can end up costing you much more than if you had paid the financial planner strictly for advice (by the hour or a flat fee) and bought the product elsewhere.

Here's something you might not know. Financial planners who bill themselves as "fee-only" or "fee-based" may also be receiving bonuses, or other "goodies" such as free trips, in exchange for selling specific financial products. Those perks can taint their recommendations. When you're searching for a financial planner, your goal is to find someone who has at least ten years' experience giving advice to people who are as much like you as possible in income, age, financial goals, views on risk, and so on. You can start your search by asking friends, relatives, and coworkers for referrals, or by calling the Institute of Certified Financial Planners, at (303) 751-7600, or the Registry of Financial Planning Practitioners, at (800) 945-IAFP (4237).

Before you hire any financial planner, be sure you understand how he or she is compensated and the services that will be performed. Ask prospective planners:

- How are you compensated? Is your fee determined by the hour, as a flat fee, or as a percentage of my assets?
- Do you receive any commissions, bonuses, or other rewards for selling specific products?
- What, if any, financial or other business arrangement do you or your firm have with any companies whose products you recommend or sell?
- How much do you expect this service will cost me? What will I receive for my money—an individualized financial plan, trades, or other financial transactions?
- If you refer me to another business (such as a broker or dealer) for advice or to purchase a product, what remuneration will you receive for that referral or subsequent business?
- If I decide not to implement your proposals, how much will I owe?
- How many and what types of clients do you have?
- What services do you provide? Do you only make recommendations, or do you want to actively manage my money and coordinate the purchases and sales of financial products? (Note: Additional services will cost more, and it may not be wise to hand over so much control.) How will you help me implement a plan?
- Can I see a sample financial plan for a client in a similar situation? (Check that the client's name has been removed.)
- What schools did you attend and what degrees have you earned? What courses have you taken since graduation?

- What do you specialize in, and what qualifications do you have in that field? Do you have any professional designations, such as CPA, CFP, or CFA?*
- How many years of experience do you have in the following areas: tax and estate planning, investment planning, retirement planning, insurance planning, or any others?
- Will I be working with you or a subordinate? What training and experience does the other person have?
- Are you registered or licensed as an Investment Adviser? With which state(s)? With the federal government?
- Is your company registered or licensed as an Investment Adviser? With which state(s)? With the federal government?

Ask the planners for names of satisfied clients. Don't assume that good referrals guarantee an honorable planner. The testimonies may be coming from paid friends or relatives, or even from actors hired to sing his or her praises. But steer clear of any financial adviser who *cannot* provide names and numbers of at least three satisfied recent clients. Obviously, the planner should have asked the clients' permission before giving out their names to you or anyone else, and your name should not be given to another prospective client without your permission.

When you begin a background check (some sources are listed below), here are some questions to ask:

- Has the planner ever been convicted of a crime or disciplined for any unlawful or unethical actions?
- Is a copy of the planner's disclosure document (Form ADV) available for you to see? It includes information about the financial planning firm's investment and billing methods, and its services. Investment advisers who are registered with the Securities and Exchange Commission (SEC), or with state securities agencies, must supply a copy of Form ADV, or the state equivalent, if you ask for it.
- Is a Schedule D for this person available? The firm must file one for each financial adviser it employs. It itemizes the planner's background and any disciplinary actions taken. Firms are not required to show clients this form, but if a firm refuses, you might wonder what it might be hiding.

---

* Certified Public Accountant, Certified Financial Planner, or Certified Financial Adviser.

- Contact your state attorney general's office and your local consumer affairs office to check out the firm's disciplinary record and any outstanding complaints.

Here are some sources for checking up on a prospective financial adviser:

Certified Financial Planner Board of Standards
(888) CFP-MARK (237-6275)
www.cfp-board.org

National Association of Insurance Commissioners
(816) 842-3600
www.naic.org

National Association of Securities Dealers
(800) 289-9999
www.nasd.com

Securities and Exchange Commission
(800) 732-0330
www.sec.gov

North American Securities Administrators Association
(888) 84-NASAA (846-2722)
www.nasaa.org

After you have decided how much you want the planner to do—or not do—on your behalf, ask to have your agreement spelled out in writing. It will cut the chances of a later misunderstanding. Include the services to be performed (and those you want excluded), as well as how the fee will be determined. List the steps you must take to terminate the relationship. File this document where you can find it easily for later reference.

STEP 3 WEIGH THE PROS AND CONS OF HIRING A TAX PROFESSIONAL.

Did you know that filing your own tax forms without thoroughly understanding the current tax laws, or without triple-checking your math, can cause you to pay more tax than you actually owe? You may not be aware of allowable deductions or new changes in the tax laws. Preparing your own taxes can also be very stressful for you and your loved ones. So a little professional tax-planning or tax-preparation advice could save you time, aggravation, and money.

What Can the Right Tax Pro Do for You?

In addition to filling out your tax forms, a good tax adviser can help you organize your records for the current year, offer tax-saving investment advice for the next time you must file, and determine how much, if anything, you should pay in estimated tax during the year.

Keep in mind that the quality of the tax advice you will get, and the amount you will pay for it, can vary greatly. Since tax laws keep changing, you want someone who is up on the latest rules. Paying more for tax assistance is no guarantee that you will get better advice.

Could You Benefit from Professional Tax Help?

If you've gone through any of these significant lifestyle changes since last year, some professional tax advice might help you:

- Gotten married or divorced, or become widowed.
- Given birth or adopted a child.
- Started supporting an elderly parent or other family member.
- Bought or sold a house.
- Bought or sold rental property.
- Started or sold a business.
- Sent a child off to college.
- Made a significantly larger sum of money than in past years, at work, or through investments that differ from those made in previous years.
- Made less money, so you may be eligible for tax breaks that you couldn't get before.
- Made new or complex investments.
- Recently retired or are about to retire.
- Inherited money.

If you can foresee any of these life changes, waiting until after the event to consult a tax expert can be a very costly mistake. For instance, once you've elected a lump-sum withdrawal of a retirement savings plan (instead of receiving annual payments), or once you've started to invest a windfall, you're locked into irrevocable tax consequences. By meeting with a tax planner or accountant *before* the event, you may be able to avoid owing a substantial amount of taxes.

Like your financial planner, your tax pro should have a lot of clients whose incomes, types of jobs, and financial goals are similar to yours. Why? Because you want someone who knows the deductions you are entitled to, and who asks the right questions before starting to prepare your forms. He or she should also know the answers to the tax questions you might have. Ask friends, relatives, coworkers, your financial planner, or your banker for referrals of tax preparers.

I identify five general types of preparers:

1. Certified Public Accountants (CPAs). CPAs are tested and certified by the state in which they work. The American Institute of Certified Public Accountants (AICPA) can give you more information on the qualifications and experience of its members and can be reached at (201) 938-3100. Plan on paying $75 to $300 per hour when you hire a CPA. He or she can represent you if you are called in for questioning by the Internal Revenue Service (IRS). A CPA is available year-round and can give you tax-planning advice.

2. Enrolled Agents (EA). EAs have either worked for the IRS for several years or passed a rigorous IRS tax exam—or done both. The National Association of Enrolled Agents can give you information on its members. You can call (301) 212-9608 or (800) 424-4339. An enrolled agent can also represent you at an IRS meeting.

3. National chains such as H&R Block and Jackson and Hewitt. Preparers working for big chains must demonstrate some basic skills in tax preparation and, typically, must pass a yearly test. If your tax situation is simple enough to allow you to use Form 1040 EZ or 1040A, these chains may be your most cost-effective option. They tend to be fairly conservative regarding deductions, and most don't give tax-planning advice. If you own a business, real estate, mutual funds, or more elaborate investments, you might do better with a CPA or enrolled agent.

4. Tax attorneys. For most taxpayers, hiring a tax attorney to fill out IRS forms is overkill, and they would pay dearly for this service. But if you are starting or buying a business or considering a divorce, you might want to consult a tax attorney to avoid making any irrevocable decisions or costly avoidable errors. If you are

called in for an audit and hire a tax attorney to represent you, you may end up paying the tax attorney more than the amount that is being questioned by the IRS.

5. "Drugstore cowboys." These tax preparers ride into town at the beginning of the year, set up shop in the local drug store or a similar temporary place of business, and are gone as soon as the tax season ends. They are very risky as tax preparers because they swoop into town and hang out a shingle in January, but vanish on April 16. Steer clear of them. Instead, look for a tax preparer who's a year-round expert and will be available if the IRS decides to audit your return or asks for additional information regarding how your tax forms were filled out.

The National Association of Tax Practitioners includes CPAs, enrolled agents, accountants, tax attorneys, and other preparers. More than 1,400 members are listed on the tax practitioners' association Web site: www.taxprofessionals.com.

After you've gathered a list of referrals, start interviewing prospective tax preparers. Here are some questions to ask:

- What do you charge? What services do I get for my money? Do you charge by the form, by the hour, or a flat fee?
- Will you give me a written, binding estimate? Under what circumstances would I be charged extra, and how is the higher rate determined?
- What (if any) tax planning or financial planning advice do you offer to clients?
- What access to tax-law research do you have?
- What happens if I am audited by the IRS or receive a request for additional information? What help will you provide, and how much will it cost? Will you accompany me to the audit, or go alone, as my representative?
- Where can I find you after the tax season is over?
- Will you pick up the cost for penalties or interest if an error you made causes me to owe more taxes?
- How many years have you been preparing taxes?
- What types of clients do you have? Are their income levels, types of income, and investments similar to mine?
- What is your educational background? What degrees do you hold from what institutions, and how recently did you earn them?
- What continuing training (if any) have you had?

- What state or IRS exams have you passed, and how long ago?
- Can I speak to some current clients, including a client who has been through an audit?
- Who will actually prepare my form—you, or a lower-level associate?
- Will my forms be reviewed by more than one member of the firm? (This is especially important if you have a complex financial situation.)
- What will you expect me to provide or do?

Watch for these red flags when you're choosing a tax preparer:

Guaranteed refund. Promises a refund before seeing your records, or boasts in advertising that he or she can get a bigger refund than other preparers.

Fees based on refund size.   Charges fees based on the size of the refund he or she claims you will receive, instead of based on the work done.

Questionable deductions.   Advises you to take deductions you know you are not entitled to, because "All my clients take them." Remember, *you* will be on the hook if the IRS questions your tax moves.

How Can You Work Most Efficiently with a Tax Pro?

If you will be hiring a tax professional, you can make the experience more pleasant, and possibly less costly, if you do some preparation before your meeting. A growing number of clients has discovered that they can cut their tax-prep bill (and sometimes get their taxes prepared more accurately) by presenting their preparer not just with receipts but also with partially completed tax forms. To make this first stab at your tax forms easier, consider using a tax-prep software package, such as TurboTax or TaxCut. These packages have gotten easier to use and now rely on a question-and-answer interview format that resembles working with an accountant. Just hearing these questions may remind you of deductions (business, medical, educational, and so on) that you may have forgotten. If you've been using a money-management software package, such as Quicken or Microsoft Money to store your financial information, you can download this information directly into most tax-prep software packages, so you don't have to key in the information again.

Here are some more tips for working efficiently with a tax pro:

- Get organized. Even if you've merely been shoving receipts into a shoebox all year, you'll get better help (and probably spend less) if you organize the receipts before you plop them on your tax preparer's desk. Arrange your records so that your W-2s and other income statements (including 1099s) are in one place.
- Make copies of all your documents before handing over any originals to a preparer.
- Review your last two years' tax forms to see what deductions you took. Did you (or your preparer) add notes about special circumstances in either year?
- Bring a copy of last year's return if this the first time you are using a preparer.
- Don't be timid. Volunteer information that you think will make the tax preparer's task easier.
- Ask questions that may have arisen while you were going over your records or trying to figure out the forms yourself.
- Ask your tax preparer to write a letter detailing any judgment calls he or she made in gray areas of the tax law. The letter should be annotated with references to IRS rulings or legal precedents.
- Tell your preparer to contact you for any clarifications or additional information that may be needed to prepare your tax forms.

It's vital that you read and understand your return before signing it. If you have questions, be sure to get them answered to your satisfaction. You may even insist that the form be revised before it's ready for you to sign and send to the IRS. And insist that the tax preparer sign the completed form so that he or she thinks twice about any questionable judgment calls that may have made on your form.

Are You Aware of the Free Tax Filing Help the IRS Offers?

If you need answers to specific questions, or some other tax filing help, you can consult with the IRS, but don't wait until just before taxes are due, because it will be very hard to get through. The IRS offers several ways to ask for tax forms or advice, or to track the status of a refund:

- IRS Helpline, (800) 829-1040, to speak with a real person.
- IRS TeleTax, (800) 829-4477, for automated refund and tax information help.

Turn to the IRS only for relatively straightforward questions, not complicated situations or gray areas of tax law. A myriad of IRS publications are available free of charge. Publication 17, a comprehensive booklet, is revised every year.

And of course the IRS can provide tax forms, so choose your medium:

- Internet: www.irs.gov
- Phone: (800) TAXFORM
- Fax: (703) 368-9694

Local libraries have replaced post offices as the places to pick up forms. If the forms you want are not in stock, you can copy them from the library's master forms book.

If you want to consult detailed tax-prep books, I suggest these annually revised tax guides:

- *Ernst and Young Tax Guide*
- *J.K. Lasser's Your Income Tax*

What Are the Best and Worst Ways to File and Pay Your Taxes?

Should you pay your taxes with a credit card? You can now pay your tax bill with a credit card, but this convenience does not come cheap. The IRS is passing on a surcharge of 1½ to 2½ percent of your tax bill (that's the part that would normally be paid by the merchant if you were using the card at a store). Add to that surcharge any interest you will have to pay if you can't pay off this charge in full when you get your credit card bill. If you don't have the cash to pay your tax bill, paying with a credit card is better than not paying at all—and probably less expensive than working out a payment plan with the IRS. But first, try to borrow the money elsewhere, at a lower total cost (interest plus any loan fees).

If you can't come up with money to pay your taxes, and you don't have a credit card, what should you do? Even if you don't have the money, it's important to file your tax return on time—or, file an extension to avoid being charged a late filing fee. Attach Form 9465,

"Request for an Installment Agreement," to the front of your tax return with a statement explaining why you can't pay. A $43 processing fee, plus interest and penalties on any overdue amount, will be added to your tax bill.

What should you do if you have the money, but you can't fill out your tax forms by the due date (documentation is missing, or there is not enough time to complete the form)? File for an extension using Form 4868, which is simple to fill out. Send it (by mail or otherwise; see below) by April 15 (or whatever date taxes are due that year). You still owe the IRS money when you file an extension form. You must send a good-faith estimate of what you will owe when you file (you had better be within 90 percent of your ultimate tax bill). You then have a four-month extension, to August 15, for filing your tax return.

What if you still can't file your tax return by the extension date of August 15? You can request an additional two-month extension, but you need a good excuse, and the IRS makes the judgment call.

If you mail your tax forms and payment to the IRS and the packet gets lost or arrives late, how do you prove that you sent it on time? With standard mail, you have no leg to stand on. If you want proof that you sent it on time, you have several options. You can mail it via the U.S. Postal Service, using certified mail, return receipt requested. Or, you can use one of the overnight delivery services: FedEx, Airborne, UPS, or DHL. Before you choose one of these carriers, verify your choice with the IRS. Each service offers several delivery options (prices vary greatly) and the service you choose may not be on the approved IRS list.

Are You Paying Through the Nose for Fast Cash?

Need your refund in a hurry? Don't waste your money on refund-anticipation loans. Despite how it sounds, it's not a cost-effective way to get your refund sooner. It's actually a loan from a bank. You receive the money in a couple of days, and when your refund arrives from the IRS, you repay the bank. If you file electronically, you should be able to pay the bank back within a month (or six weeks, if you file the old paper-and-pencil way), but you'll pay through the nose for this very short-term loan. For instance, a $50 charge to get a $1,000 refund a month early is the equivalent of more than 100 percent interest per year (depending on the size of the fee and the size of the loan). You can cut as much as three weeks off the arrival of your refund by having the refund deposited electronically into your bank account.

How Would a Tax Pro Handle an Error or Tax Change?

You spot an error on your form after you file your taxes, or you get a revised W-2 or 1099. What can you do? You can usually file an amended tax return (Form 1040X, if you filed Form 1040 originally) within three years of when the original was due or filed, or two years from the date the tax was paid—whichever is later. You'll need to fill out an amended form (see page 38 for the phone and fax numbers and the Web site). Follow the directions carefully, and, in an attached note, explain succinctly any changes you made. The change in question may require you to recalculate any deductions that were based on a percentage of your adjusted gross income—for example, medical expenses, miscellaneous deductions, and Social Security contributions or benefits. Be sure to include documentation (an amended W-2 or 1099) to support your revised calculations. You will also need to file a revised state (and local) tax form. Ask your state and local governments' tax offices for forms and the required time for filing.

What Should You Do—and Not Do—If You Get Audited?

First, don't panic. Just because the IRS is auditing you, it doesn't automatically mean that you will owe more taxes. Tax advisers do say that what you say, how you say it, and how prepared you are for the audit can spell the difference between owing additional taxes, penalties, and interest, and owing nothing extra. Here is some specific advice from tax professionals:

- Stay calm.
- Be professional and courteous but not chummy toward the auditor.
- Bring only the documentation that supports the audit item in question.
- Don't blurt out additional information. What you say, however innocently, can end up triggering questions on tax matters other than the one currently being audited.
- Take your time answering questions. "One client came to me only after he was audited," explains one accountant. "His problem was that he was so efficient and quick at finding the documentation that the auditor was able to ask several additional questions on

other areas of his tax form that weren't originally included in the audit notice. If this client hadn't been so well organized, the auditor would have run out of time, and my client would never have been asked about the things that resulted in additional taxes plus interest and penalties."

Remember, you don't have to go to an audit alone. You can bring along a tax attorney, CPA, or enrolled agent to speak for you at the meeting. In fact, you don't even have to show up yourself. You can have one of these tax experts go in your place.

Improve Your Credit and Slash Your Bank Fees

With smaller banks being gobbled up by bigger ones, truly good credit card offers, as opposed to those that just appear good in the advertisements or pre-approved credit card offers, are getting hard to come by. Do you know how to separate the credit card deals from the credit card duds? In this solution, I will show you what to look for—and look out for—when sizing up your current credit cards, shopping for a new credit card, or even weighing the pros and cons of debit cards.

Whether you're applying for a loan to pay for a car, a home, or college costs, or even looking for a job, you can bet that the lender or potential employer, the person who will determine your financial fate, will check your credit rating. Do you like what he or she will find? Do you even know what is there? Since your personal credit is one of your most valuable assets, there are some steps you need to take now to get your credit report shipshape before anyone else takes a peek.

For several years now, banks have been posting record profits, but what's good for a bank's bottom line may not be good for yours. Bank fees keep climbing and interest rates paid on deposits have stayed relatively low. A growing number of consumers are literally paying their banks to hold their money. When was the last time you perused your bank statement to see what services you use and exactly how much you are paying for them? In this solution, I will also show you some simple ways to slash bank fees.

In Chapter 2 we talked about several quick ways to get on top of your credit card bills. Taking charge of your credit can be a monumental task so in this chapter I give more detailed information on many new issues and potential problems facing consumers.

Chapter 4

Take Charge of Your Credit

Vicki's Story

"'Two-point-nine percent interest rate!' That's what the credit card mailer screamed, in big, bold letters," recalls Vicki. "They even sent me 'convenience' checks so that I could transfer my credit card balance from my old 8.9 percent credit card to the new one. Anyhow, I figured that I'd be saving money by making this switch, but that's not quite how it turned out. While it didn't say it anywhere that I could see, that low interest rate only applied to new purchases. Interest on my balance transfer came in at a steep 12.9 percent. On top of that, they added a 2 percent fee for transferring my balance. The checks may have been convenient, but they sure cost me plenty."

The rules used to be so simple. If you carried a credit card balance, you chose the credit card with the lowest interest rate. And if you paid off your credit card balance each month, you carried a card that charged no annual fee. But choosing a credit card based on interest rates or annual fees alone will no longer get you the best deal. You also need to compare fees, grace periods, and how finance charges are calculated.

If your mailbox is brimming with unsolicited credit card offers boasting "Low Interest Rates," "No Annual Fees," or "Rebates with Purchase," beware! With hidden fees and convoluted finance charges, you could end up paying hundreds of dollars more than you'd pay with competing cards—money that would be better spent paying off (or at least paying down) your credit card balance.

Some credit card issuers are even punishing consumers who have used their card too much (or too little), or who have had the audacity to accept a card from a competing company. The stiff penalties include doubling the interest rate on outstanding balances, levying staggering new fees for a variety of "infractions," and closing credit card accounts with no notice.

Be proactive about choosing any new credit cards. See how you score on the quiz in Step 1, then absorb the good advice in Steps 2 through 6. Advice in this chapter can not only save you money, but also turn your so-so credit report into one that's squeaky clean.

LLOYD'S LAW

The squeaky wheel gets the best credit card deal.

STEP 1 TEST YOUR CREDIT CARD KNOW-HOW.

Do you know the best ways to choose and use a credit card? Here's a quiz to see how savvy you are. The answers offer tips for cutting your credit card fees.

Question 1: If you carry a credit card balance of $1,750 on a card that charges 18 percent interest, how long will it take to pay off the bill, and how much interest will you pay if you make only the minimum monthly payments (2 percent of the outstanding balance)?

    (a) 3 years + 2 months; $627 interest.
    (b) 7 years + 9 months; $1,129 interest.
    (c) 16 years + 4 months; $2,189 interest.
    (d) 21 years + 11 months; $3,647 in interest.

Answer 1: (d) 21 years + 11 months. You'd spend almost 22 years and $3,647 in interest to pay off $1,750. (That's $2 interest for each dollar of purchase!).

    Tip: By paying an extra $25 per month, you could wipe out the balance nearly 19 years earlier and pay only $588 in interest—a saving of $3,059.

Question 2: If you are only one day late with your payment, your credit card issuer may:

    (a) Assess a late payment fee of up to $30.
    (b) Boost the interest rate on your card.
    (c) Cancel your credit card.
    (d) Any of the above.

Answer 2: (d) Any of the above. Fees are rising. Credit card companies are boldly changing terms and canceling cards to punish consumers who don't use their cards in the ways the issuers would like. Credit card issuers can change terms (including interest rates or fees) with just 15 days' notice. Read the insert that comes with your monthly bill.

Be prepared to switch to a cheaper card if the terms on yours become unattractive.

Question 3: True or False? If you accept a "preapproved" credit card offer with a $5,000 credit limit and a 13 percent interest rate, you may only get a card with a limit of $250 and an 18.6 percent interest rate.

Answer 3: True. Bait-and-switch occurs in unsolicited offers. Typically, you'll get a much lower credit limit and/or a higher interest rate. There are disclaimers in the fine print, but card issuers count on consumers' taking whatever card they get. Cut up the undesirable card without using it, and call the company to close the account.

Question 4: True or False? If the card issuer raises the interest rate, it will apply only to new purchases.

Answer 4: False. Most rate increases also apply to outstanding balances. But if you make no new purchases on your card, a few states prohibit card issuers from raising the rate on the existing balance. To qualify, you must notify the card issuer about your plans to discontinue using the card for new purchases. Know when any "teaser rates" expire (the bank won't notify you), and switch to another card before the expiration date, or ask your bank to continue the lower interest rate.

Question 5: True or False? Cards that offer rebates (cash back, frequent flyer miles, and similar perks) based on your card usage are great bargains for most consumers.

Answer 5: False. Unless you're a heavy credit card user (charging more than $5,000 per year), fees may exceed benefits and are only a good deal if you pay off your balance each month and use your cards frequently. (These cards typically charge the highest interest rates allowed. If you don't pay your monthly balance in full, you'll pay more in finance charges than the rebates are worth.) Most cards charge high annual fees (often $50 or more), so, for most consumers, the fees will exceed the value of the rebates. Count on long waits for big payoffs, and be aware that awards can be changed or rescinded with little or no notice.

Question 6: True or False? Taking a cash advance on a credit card that charges 13 percent on purchases may cost you the equivalent of 40 percent or more in interest and fees.

Answer 6: True. This is an expensive way to get cash. First, most cards charge a higher interest rate on cash advances than on purchases, and they don't have to disclose the rates in the bold or the fine print. Second, card issuers often assess fees (typically, 2 percent of the cash advance), so look for a card that caps cash advance fees at no more than $10. Third, there is no grace period. Interest typically begins from the date of the cash advance, even if your account is paid in full.

Question 7: True or False? Paying for merchandise with a credit card "convenience check" (which bills the check amount to your credit card) is the same as paying with a credit card.

Answer 7: False. You may be hit with a big fee for writing a check, a higher interest rate than on credit card purchases, or interest charges that start sooner than with credit card purchases. Plus, you may not get other benefits, such as extended warranties and consumer protection against defective merchandise or mail-order merchandise that never shows up. Before you write a convenience check, ask about the fees and the interest charges, and find out when the interest starts accruing.

Question 8: True or False? Department store credit cards offering "deferred billing," with no finance charges for six months, will charge retroactive interest if you don't pay off the balance within six months.

Answer 8: True. Interest is due from the date of purchase. The store will forgive the interest *if* you pay off your balance before the offer expires (within six months, in this example). Otherwise, you'll owe interest from the date of purchase, and many store cards charge the highest interest rates allowed by law. "Deferred billing" is only a good deal if you pay off your balance before the offer expires.

Question 9: True or False? If your credit card issuer sends an offer to "skip a payment," you won't owe finance charges for that month.

Answer 9: False. These offers are sent to customers who usually pay their bills in full, to induce them to carry a balance from month to month. Finance charges, of course, begin the day a payment is overdue.

Question 10: True or False? If you carry a balance, you'll pay less in finance charges if you make your payments earlier in the month.

Answer 10: True. Make your payment as soon as the statement arrives. Most finance charges are based on the average daily balance, so the earlier you make a payment, the lower your average balance will be, and therefore the lower your finance charges will be. (More of your payment will go to reduce your balance, not just to pay interest.)

Question 11: As few as one in five consumers who apply for a low-cost credit card is accepted. The main reason for rejection is:

(a) Applications for more than two cards within six months.
(b) A credit report that contains errors.
(c) A job change within the past two years.
(d) All of the above.

Answer 11: (d) All of the above. Get a copy of your credit report before applying for a low-cost card. (See Step 3: Check your credit report.)

Question 12: True or False? If your credit card is tied to your home's equity and you miss payments, the bank can foreclose on your house.

Answer 12: True. For these cards, your credit limit is based not on your credit history, but on the value of your home's equity (your home's market value less your mortgage balance). If you fall behind on your payments, the bank can foreclose. If you have credit cards that are tied to your home's equity, save them for important purchases (such as home improvements or tuition), not vacations, restaurant bills, or anything that will be used up before you're finished paying for it.

STEP 2 · LEARN HOW TO DECIPHER THE FINE PRINT AND SPOT THE RED FLAGS.

What they give in the bold print, many credit card offers take away in the fine print. Get out a magnifying glass and scrutinize the offer. Watch for these credit card red flags:

◀ **High annual percentage rate.** Over 12 percent for purchases and/or cash advances. Avoid cards that charge higher interest on cash advances.

◀ **Annual fee.** Any fee. If you ask them, many card issuers will waive annual fees.

◀ **Short grace period.** Less than twenty-five days for new purchases. With a shortened grace period (the time between the billing date and when finance charges start), you'll likely pay finance charges even if you pay your bills in full.

◀ **Method of computing the balance.** "Two-cycle billing" or "Including new purchases." If you sometimes carry a balance, two-cycle billing lets issuers charge retroactive interest, so it's impossible to compare cards. If you pay finance charges, you'll pay less with a card that computes balances "excluding new purchases."

◀| **Uncapped transaction fee on cash advances.**   Two percent or more of the amount of the cash advance, but not less than $10. Along with transaction fees, most cards charge a higher interest rate on cash advances than on purchases, and they are not required to show rates in print. Look for a card that caps the fee under $10.

◀| **Hefty fees for exceeding the credit limit or paying late.** More than $10. Shop around for a card with low penalty fees.

The Credit Card Issuer Went Thataway

Roger's Story

A few minutes after Roger Lucas pulled out his credit card to pay for a restaurant meal, he was surprised and embarrassed when the waiter handed the card back saying it had been rejected. "It must be a simple mistake," he recalls sheepishly telling his date. "I never carry a credit card balance, and I had just paid the last bill two weeks earlier. Fortunately, I had another credit card and paid for the meal with that one." The next day, he called the credit card company that had rejected his card and was told that his card had been canceled, not by the company that issued his card, but by the new bank that had purchased his and hundreds of other credit card accounts. Still, if he paid his card on time, why was his account closed? "The new bank said I hadn't been using the card enough," he said, shaking his head in disbelief.

Can you be punished for following consumer advocates' advice to credit cardholders—to pay off your credit card balance each month? Finding out that your account has been closed because your card is not being used enough may sound extreme, but it happens. And that may not be the only threat lurking.

A growing number of consumers are discovering that their credit card accounts are being sold to other banks, and when the name on their credit card bill changes, changes in their card terms are often quick to follow. If your card is sold, what should you do? Even if your account remains where it started, you need to know about any new or changed credit card terms. Keep your eye on the fine print.

Tens of millions of consumers have had their accounts sold or traded to another financial institution, and tens of billions of dollars in credit card balances were moved with them. After they pay to acquire credit card accounts, the acquiring banks are often holding their new cardholders to more stringent profitability standards than the prior card issuer did.

How do credit card accounts generate revenue for the issuing bank? Credit card companies can make money from their cardholders by charging:

- A finance charge (interest charge) on the outstanding balance.
- An annual fee (which many consumers get waived these days).
- A fee (paid by the merchant) each time you use the card.
- A penalty fee of up to $30 for each infraction, such as paying as little as one day late, exceeding the account's credit limit, or paying less than the minimum.
- A fee for the sale of extra—and overpriced—services, such as credit life insurance, job loss protection, and credit card registries.

By increasing the revenue in any these areas, a credit card issuer can significantly enhance its bottom line.

What typically happens if your credit card account is traded to another bank? Your account is scrutinized to see how much revenue you are producing from your credit card and from other financial services, such as bank accounts, insurance, and other investments that you have bought (or are likely to buy) through the bank's financial services branch. If your account is among the least profitable, it may be terminated. Two groups in particular are likely to lose:

1. Out-of-town customers are often the first to get canceled. They may like to keep the credit card account open, but, unlike local customers, they are less apt to sign up for other bank services.
2. Customers with low "teaser" interest rates or other favorable terms are often dumped next. Statistically, these customers are less loyal to the card issuer and more apt to leave when their terms are changed.

Next among the losers are the "convenience users," those who rarely, if ever, carry a credit card balance. They don't pay interest because they are not carrying a balance. With the credit card market saturated, few convenience users are paying an annual fee, and these cardholders rarely (if ever) pay penalty fees (because they don't pay late, or send in less than the minimum). Some banks have canceled these customers' accounts with little or no notice. Even if your card isn't canceled, you could be hit with an "inactivity" fee for each month in which you don't use your card. The inactivity fee does one of three things: (1) it generates additional revenue for the credit card company; (2) it may spur cardholders to use the card more; (3) it encourages closing the account to avoid the fee.

If you pay your balances in full each month, beware of another change. To generate more revenue, some card issuers are shortening the grace period or eliminating it altogether. The grace period has traditionally been twenty-five days between when your bill is sent and when payment must be received. During that time—if you aren't carrying any balance—you will be charged no interest. But if your grace period is shortened, and you didn't notice the change, you may get hit not only with a finance charge, but also with a "late payment" penalty fee of up to $30.

How much notice does a credit card issuer have to give about changes in terms? When I conduct person-on-the-street interviews, almost everyone tells me they think they are entitled to 30 or 60 days' notice, but the correct answer is 15 days' notice. The moral is: You must read the little insert that typically comes with the bill (but may come separately) and peruse the bottom of your statement for any notice of changes. Because they are often printed in very tiny type, many consumers find it hard to wade through these details. But you need to spot them quickly, and if you don't like them, call your credit card company's retention department and ask if you can keep your old terms.

"Guaranteed" rates can go up even during the guarantee phase. For instance, although a credit card with a "teaser" interest rate of, say, 5.9 percent, may have stated that you could keep that rate for six months, there was a caveat that you may not have noticed: If you pay your bill late, your interest rate can be jacked up. For some consumers, the increase is above 20 percent!

If your interest rate goes up and you don't use the card again, will you still continue paying the old, lower interest rate? No. They can jack up the rate on your existing balance. A few states have laws that allow consumers to keep the lower interest rate if they notify the bank that they are closing the account (not making any new charges), after the newer terms are imposed.

Most financial advisers tell consumers to carry fewer credit cards. I'm telling you that many people are in danger of carrying *too few*. Always carry at least two cards. You need a backup so that if your card is not usable due to a computer glitch or *cut off* (a cancellation without notifying you, or because you've reached your credit limit), you have another one ready to go. By the way, you could reach your card's limit while traveling and not know it. Rental car companies (and some hotels) often place a big hold (hundreds or thousands of dollars) against your credit card to cover estimated future charges, as well as any possible damage you *might* cause to their property, even though your auto insurance would likely pay for the actual damage. Consider checking in at a hotel or rental car company with one card (the one that will have the hold on it), and then use the other card to pay for purchases while you travel.

STEP 3 CHECK YOUR CREDIT REPORT.

If you are in the market for a new job, a mortgage, an apartment, a car loan, an insurance policy, or a lower-cost credit card, chances are your credit report will be thoroughly combed before you are given the green light. Black marks on your credit report, caused by your defaulting on loans or paying bills even a little late, can keep you from getting approved.

But what if those black marks were not posted as a result of your own actions? For years, consumer advocates have been complaining that errors on consumers' credit reports are far from uncommon.

Until recently, regulations governing how consumers' credit histories are reported were anything but consumer-friendly. In fact, the burden of proving that a report was incorrect was on the consumer, instead of on the credit bureau or creditor.

What can you do to protect yourself? Several weeks before you apply for a new job, a mortgage, an apartment, an insurance policy, or a car, carefully review your credit report for accuracy. To get a copy of your credit report, call or write to one of the three national credit bureaus listed below. Typically, you will be charged $8 or more for a copy of your report, but consumer laws in a few states allow lower fees.

If you spot a significant error in the report you order, pay to get a copy of your report from the other two bureaus as well. Here's how to contact them:

Equifax
(800) 685-1111 or (800) 997-2493
www.equifax.com

Experian (formerly known as TRW)
(800) 682-7654 or (888) EXPERIAN (397-3742)
www.experian.com

Trans Union
(800) 916-8800 or (800) 888-4213
www.transunion.com

If information on your report is inaccurate, write to the credit bureau immediately and explain in detail why you believe the information is wrong. For instance, does the credit card listed under your name actually belong to someone else? Or does the file show you made late payments in the past, without indicating that you are no longer delinquent? Send *copies* (not the originals) of documents that support your claim, and keep copies of all your correspondence.

If you have been turned down for a job, a loan, or an insurance policy because of something written on your credit report, you are entitled to a free copy of your report. Ask the company that turned you down for the name and address of the credit bureau that issued the report, and contact that bureau within 60 days for your free copy.

If the credit bureau agrees with your claim and corrects its file, it must also send a notice of corrections to anyone who received your report during the past six months (up to two years, if your credit file was used for employment purposes). If the investigation does not resolve the dispute in your favor and the credit bureau refuses to change its information, you can request that your report include a statement of up to 100 words, written by you, explaining why you believe the information is incorrect.

But this strategy can backfire. Many companies that look at credit reports rely on the so-called "credit score" (the rating's number given to your history by the credit bureau and used to determine your creditworthiness or risk). The recipients may never see your written comments. And although most negative marks will be removed from a credit report within seven to ten years, your written statement can stay there forever and may raise unnecessary questions later. If you add a comment to your report, be sure to tell the credit bureau to remove it when it is no longer applicable. Then verify that it has been removed.

GET THE LOWDOWN ON DEBIT CARDS. (BANKS LOVE THEM, BUT SHOULD YOU?)

Rick's Story

When $3,000 was siphoned from Rick's bank account, the bank said he was a victim of electronic theft. "But the bank also told me that unless I could *prove* I hadn't given out my debit card number, I would be out the full $3,000, plus $128 in bounced check fees!" recalls Rick. "Tell me, how do you prove a negative? If I'd known that I could be out so much money, I never would have accepted my bank's offer to swap my perfectly good credit card for this debit card. Why aren't the banks required to tell consumers about the differences?"

Debit cards look like credit cards and are accepted in almost as many places, but they levy no finance charges. Think of a debit card as an enhanced ATM card; it can be used to withdraw cash from your bank account and to purchase merchandise.

But because many debit cards can be used without a PIN number, they are riskier than standard ATM cards. Many debit cards, like credit cards, carry a VISA or Master Card logo, but that's where the similarity ends. They offer less federal protection and they differ from credit cards in other ways, yet debit card issuers don't like to acknowledge any differences.

Each month, thousands of consumers are discovering that their ATM card was replaced by a debit card without their knowledge or approval. Why are the banks pushing debit cards so strongly?

First, the credit card market is saturated, so many banks have turned to debit cards as a way to increase their market share. Second, debit cards allow a bank to shift risk and costs to consumers in ways that are not possible with a credit card.

By law, if your credit card number is used fraudulently, you have 60 days to notify the bank, and the most you'll be out is $50. With debit cards, you must notify the bank within *two business days* to limit your loss to $50. Wait three days, or up to 60 days, and you're liable for $500. Wait longer and you could be out your *entire bank balance plus your overdraft line.*

But haven't VISA and Master Card voluntarily begun offering similar protection for debit cardholders? "It doesn't go far enough,'" says consumer advocate Ed Mierzwinski. "Since it's not a federal law, VISA or Master Card can cancel it at anytime. And if you write bad checks because you don't know a thief drained your account, you'll be hit with bank fees and maybe negative marks on your credit report. Banks should pick up fees resulting from fraud." Let's look at some other drawbacks of debit cards.

No Grace Period, No Float

If you typically pay your credit card bills in full, with a debit card you'll lose the "float"—the one to two months between making a purchase and paying for it. With a credit card, you won't get billed for up to 30 days, and you have a 25-day grace period before payment is due. During that time, the money stays in your bank account and you get interest. With a debit card, the money is taken out right away, so you get no interest.

More Fees

Merchants can add surcharges for purchases made on debit cards, and they may not post them. Ask merchants about fees before you pay. Banks often charge debit cardholders a transaction fee, membership fee, or monthly fee.

Not Accepted in Many Places as Credit Cards

Debit cards, unlike credit cards, do not show creditworthiness. Some rental car agencies, for instance, will accept payment but not rent you a car if you only show a debit card (they have no assurance you could pay for damages to the car).

Should you consider a debit card? Only if you can't qualify for a credit card or if you're paying hefty finance charges and don't have the discipline to pay off your balance. With a debit card, money is taken from your account within days of a purchase, so you can't carry a balance and you won't pay finance charges.

STEP 5 — BOUNCE BACK FROM BAD CREDIT.

If you can't make at least the minimum monthly payments on your bills, don't hang your head in shame, take action.

"Call your creditors *before* you default, to avoid negative marks on your credit report," advises bankruptcy attorney Robin Leonard. "If the first person you speak to won't work out a better payment schedule, ask for his or her supervisor or try to meet in person if [your creditor is] a local bank." Ask the issuer to confirm the new terms in writing. If your request is refused, send a letter yourself, confirming your conversation. If the agreed-on terms aren't carried out, you'll have documentation to support your case.

What if you're already behind in your bills? First, look out for scams. Here are some common fixes that aren't fixes at all—they can actually make your credit problems worse:

- *Credit repair companies.* They say they know the "secrets" to getting negative information removed from your credit report, and, for a few hundred dollars, they'll share them. Their typical advice—to use someone else's Social Security number—can get you into legal hot water and does nothing to improve your credit rating. Credit repair companies can't do anything you can't do yourself, and creditors are more willing to work with consumers than a for-profit intermediary. For help negotiating with your creditors, call the nonprofit organization, Consumer Credit Counseling Services, at (800) 388-CCCS (388-2227).

- *Debt consolidation loan.* Consider a debt consolidation loan only if it will lower the interest rate on your debt. If you're already late with your payments, this loan probably won't help much—and it may be almost impossible to get. Call your local consumer affairs office (in the blue pages of your local phone book) before handing money to anyone other than your original creditors.
- *Sham secured cards.* If your applications for credit cards keep getting turned down, consider a secured card. It would give you a credit card with, say, a $500 limit, in exchange for opening a bank account with a $500 deposit. If you fall behind on your bills, the card issuer can take payments from your bank account. If you pay on time, the credit card issuer should report your prompt payments to the credit bureaus so you can later qualify for a regular credit card. But beware of these red flags with secured cards:

◀ **Hefty application fee.** Some secured cards make their money from application fees, but they rarely, if ever, issue cards. Look for a card that charges no application fee. Before signing anything or sending money, check out a secured card company with your local consumer affairs office.

◀ **High account fees or no interest.** Some secured cards charge exorbitant annual fees or other fees to maintain the account, or they pay no interest on your bank balance. Comparison-shop. Look for low fees and competitive interest payments.

◀ **No reporting to a national credit bureau.** Even by paying on time, you won't be improving your credit report if your record is not sent to a credit bureau. Ask your bank if it offers a secured credit card that reports to at least one of the three major credit bureaus, so that eventually you can get an unsecured card.

◀ **"Secured card" is on the card's face.** Embarrassing, and unnecessary. Get a list of consumer-sensitive secured card issuers from www.bankrate.com or www.cardtrak.com.

◀| **Not accepted at stores.**   Some secured cards are only usable for overpriced merchandise offered through catalogs the card issuer operates. Make sure that it's not just called a "gold" or "platinum" card but that it has a nationally accepted name such as VISA or Mastercard on it.

STEP 6 — AVOID PRICEY PLASTIC PERKS.

Credit card companies make a lot of money selling additional services. That's why most monthly bills are filled with glossy brochures promoting extras they say cost "just a few dollars a month." If you're offered these extras, save your money and just say no.

- *Credit card life insurance.* It pays off your outstanding balance if you die, but it's costly. Instead, buy a lower-priced term life insurance policy from an insurer. It costs less and gives your family flexibility.
- *Credit card disability coverage.* This sounds like it will pay off your credit card balance if you become disabled. But it will only make the minimum monthly payment. It's costly, and there are long waiting periods and other restrictions before you can collect. Get disability insurance through your employer or an insurer.
- *Credit card "job loss" protection.* If you lose your job, only the minimum monthly payment is paid, not your credit card balance. If your union goes on strike, or you're unemployed frequently, or your issuer thinks you deliberately got fired, you won't collect. Skip it altogether.
- *Credit card registries.* For a fee, all your credit card issuers are notified if your cards are lost or stolen. Instead, keep all your card and phone numbers in a safe place, and report any loss yourself.
- *Platinum or gold credit cards.* With these cards, you may get frills like rebates on purchases, extended warranties, or free accidental death insurance or collision damage coverage on a rental car, but the snob appeal may cost you dearly. Resist the urge to pay for these "precious metals" unless you are certain that the benefits you will use outweigh the costs. They don't advertise it, but some credit card issuers will upgrade consumers to one of these cards free of charge, just for the asking.

Chapter 5

Slash ATM Fees, Mortgage Costs, and Other Bank Fees

Banks have been posting record profits for years, but what's good for a bank's bottom line may not be good for yours. Bank fees keep climbing, and interest rates on deposits have stayed relatively low. A growing number of consumers are literally paying their banks to hold their money. When was the last time you perused your bank statement to see what services you use and exactly how much you are paying for them?

Frank's Story

"I bounced a couple of checks last year," confessed Frank. "I made an honest mistake while trying to balance my checkbook, so it turned out I had less in my account than I thought. While bouncing the checks was embarrassing, it was also costly. I got hit with a bunch of fees: A $30 fee for bouncing each check and a $25 fee for falling below my required minimum balance for one day. (I made up for the shortfall by making another deposit the next day.) Even though my average daily balance was twice the required minimum amount, because of that one gaffe I paid the bank more in fees than I earned all year in interest on that account."

As banks continue to unbundle their services, many consumers are now getting charged for services that used to be free. Watch for an additional fee:

- To verify your balance.
- If you forget to bring a deposit slip with you.
- For depositing coins—even in rolls—or exchanging coins for paper money.
- For making a copy of a check or sending a duplicate bank statement.
- To have a customer service rep help you balance your checkbook or explain discrepancies (often, a *big* fee).
- For servicing of no-frill accounts.

- To use an ATM not owned by your bank. (Here, you may pay twice. You get hit with a charge from your bank and a surcharge from the owner of the ATM.)
- For speaking with a bank teller (depending on the type of account you have).
- To close your account (in addition to any other fees); sometimes, this fee only applies if you close the account within six months or a year of opening it.

To trim the costs of banking, take the eight steps described in this chapter.

STEP 1 CHOOSE THE RIGHT BANK ACCOUNT FOR YOUR NEEDS.

You can save money by shopping for banking services the same way you would shop for a new car. You can negotiate better prices—lower fees, and better interest rates on loans and certificates of deposit (CDs)—by accepting only the services you know you will use. You can also refuse to pay for overpriced extras, such as credit life insurance and costly home-equity lines.

A low-cost bank account for one customer may be a high-cost account for another customer, so here are some tips on getting the best deal.

Tip 1: Examine your bank statements for the past six months. What services did you use: checking account, ATM transactions, overdrafts?

Tip 2: Comparison-shop for these services at three banks or credit unions. Here are some things to ask for:

- Free checking (in exchange, you may have to agree to direct deposit of your paycheck).
- Free checks.
- A no-fee ATM card. (You may still get hit with a "foreign bank" fee if you use an ATM that is not owned by your bank.)
- A no-fee, low-interest-rate credit card.
- Free upgrade to a platinum or gold credit card.
- Free traveler's checks.
- Lower account fees or higher interest rates on deposits if you do your banking or pay your bills via the Internet.
- Better terms on loans.

Tip 3: Meet face-to-face with the branch manager where you do your banking. Bring along any flyers or newspaper ads featuring better terms at other banks, and ask your bank to match or to beat the competition.

Tip 4: Before you open a new account at another bank, and before you close your present account, be sure to ask whether there are any fees to close the account. If so, do they apply at any time, or only if you close the account within six months? Ask both banks to waive any fee for switching banks. Some banks will waive the fee if you close one type of account they offer and switch to a more appropriate account at the same bank. (A new account might cost you less, depending on how you utilize a bank's services.)

If you decide to switch banks, be aware that it's harder than it used to be. In the old days, you calculated your balance in the old account, subtracted the amount of the outstanding checks that still had to clear for payment, and your old bank handed you a check to close out your account. Nowadays, with automatic deposits and automatic bill-paying services, you have to allow enough time for these services to be stopped at your old bank and started at your new one. To avoid bouncing checks or paying penalty fees, it's a good idea to keep both accounts going for a few months.

 MAKE THE MOST OF A BANK MERGER.

If your bank is taken over by another bank, what should you do? Take your time. Don't immediately jump to the new bank. Call competing banks; many will give favorable terms to lure away competitors' customers. Realize that whether your bank has merged or not, the more business you can bring to it, the stronger your negotiating position becomes. Consider shopping for a credit card and a bank at the same time. Will your bank give you a better deal if you sign up to have your paycheck or Social Security check electronically deposited into your account? Include credit unions and small banks in your comparison shopping. They often charge lower fees than bigger banks for the same services.

 BANK BY THE NUMBERS.

If you understand the way your bank calculates your interest and fees, you can highlight big differences between accounts. Be sure to:

- Know your annual percentage yield (APY). Interest rates don't tell the whole story. In June 1993, the Federal Truth in Savings Law took effect, forcing all banks to compute interest the same way—on your entire balance and for each day your money is on deposit.

(Previously, some banks lured customers with high interest rates but actually paid much less. Banks paid interest only on the lowest monthly balance, or they computed interest less frequently—for example, monthly instead of daily.) Now you are able to compare accounts within and between banks because each bank must post its APY—the amount of interest an account with a $100 balance would earn in a full year. An account with a 3.96 percent APY would pay $3.96 in interest—one penny more than for an account with an APY of 3.95 percent. (This law applies only to bank deposits, not to loans or credit cards. For those accounts, you have to read the fine print to compare bank offers.)

- Choose a bank that assesses fees based on *average* monthly balances. Avoid banks that base their charges on *minimum* monthly balances. If your balance dips below the agreed-on amount—say, $500—for even one day, you could be socked with a fee. And when you are calculating your average monthly balance, ask your bank to include *all* your accounts—savings, CDs, and any mutual funds purchased through the bank's brokerage firm.

- Avoid overdrafts if possible. With overdraft protection you won't bounce checks, but the protection could cost you several times the bank's advertised interest rate. Here's why. When the bank activates the overdraft (moves money into your account to cover a check you wrote), it may round *up* to the nearest $100. If your account is, say, $110 short, the bank can charge you for a $200 loan, even though you never touch the extra $90. This almost doubles the interest you pay. If your bank charges a fee each time you overdraw, you're charged even more. Pay off any overdrafts as quickly as possible, to minimize the interest charges.

- Look for a bank that does not charge for automated teller machine (ATM) use. Now that so many of us are hooked on the ease and convenience of twenty-four-hour banking, many banks charge a fee ($1 to $4) for each ATM transaction. If your bank has such a charge, ask it to waive the ATM fees. If it won't, cut your fees in half by taking out, say, $100 once a week instead of $50 twice a week. And stick to ATMs owned by your bank, to avoid surcharges. (For more on ATMs, see the section that follows Step 8 in this chapter.)

- If you don't generally need your canceled checks, cut your costs by switching to a "truncated" account. Your checks will be listed on your monthly statement, but only those checks you request when you need proof of payment will be returned.

- Save money by ordering checks by mail. Some banks claim to have experienced problems processing these checks; to avoid the hassle, ask your bank to match the mail-order price.

STEP 4 CUT MORTGAGE COSTS.

A mortgage payment may be the biggest drain on your bank account, but rushing to refinance your mortgage can be a costly mistake. Before you spend thousands of dollars in application fees and closing costs for a replacement mortgage, try to strike a better deal with your current lender. Consider doing the following:

- Renegotiating your existing mortgage. If your bank still holds your mortgage, a loan officer could reduce the interest rate, which would lower your monthly costs while keeping the balance and term of your original loan. It's simple, and you avoid closing costs.
- Locking in a fixed interest rate. If interest rates have dropped since you took out the note, consider switching from an adjustable mortgage to a fixed-rate mortgage. If you expect to own the house at least two years longer, or if you think interest rates are headed up, locking in a fixed rate can be a wise money move.
- Increasing your monthly principal payments. If you can pay off your mortgage sooner, you will pay less in total interest, and your home's equity will grow faster. But just making an additional principal payment (or paying more than your required monthly payment) can be a costly mistake because some lenders charge their customers a prepayment penalty. The prepayment penalty—typically, 1 or 2 percent (but can run as high as 5 percent) of the amount paid early—is usually tacked on at the end of the loan, and many consumers don't realize that they're being charged a penalty until years later. Before you pay even one dollar more than your payment schedule requires, check with your mortgage lender (and read your mortgage agreement) to see whether your mortgage has a prepayment penalty clause. If it does, ask the lender to waive the penalty in writing before you make any additional payments.

If refinancing still seems like the best way to go, here are some more ways to keep your mortgage costs down:

- Ask your bank to give you better terms (lower closing costs or a lower interest rate) if you have other accounts or investments there.

- Consider a 15-year instead of a 30-year mortgage. The rate may be ¼ to ½ percent lower, so your monthly payment may be just a few dollars more than on a 30-year loan, but you'll save tens of thousands of dollars in interest payments and pay the loan off in half the time.
- Don't refinance for a longer term than your existing mortgage. (If you have, say, 23 years left on a 30-year mortgage, don't take out another 30-year loan.) Your monthly payments will go down, but you will pay thousands more in interest during the life of the loan (30 − 23 years = 7 additional years in this example).
- Beware of adjustable rate mortgage "teaser" rates (introductory rates prominently displayed in advertisements). They usually go up within a year. Choose an adjustable rate mortgage (ARM) that can't rise more than two points in one year or five points over the life of the loan.
- If you plan to sell your house within the next few years, opt for a higher interest rate instead of paying points up front.
- Avoid balloon mortgages, which amortize payments as those on a 30-year mortgage do, but in three, five, or seven years demand the whole balance be repaid. If you can't refinance when the balloon is due, you could be forced to sell your house. Similarly, avoid a mortgage with a "call" provision. It allows the bank to demand early repayment of the loan, at a time when you may not be able to refinance at favorable terms, if at all.
- Ask a new lender if you can use your old survey. If your land boundaries haven't changed, why should you have to pay for a new survey?
- Ask the title insurance company for a discount. If you use the same title insurance company that wrote your current policy, you will need only a shorter, updated search, not the full title search that was done when you bought the previous policy.
- Ask the lender if you can use the original appraisal of your home. Unless you've had remodeling done since you took out the current mortgage, you may not need an updated appraisal.

For more mortgage tips, see Chapter 24.

STEP 5   TAP YOUR HOME EQUITY WITH EXTREME CARE.

When you are comparing annual percentage rates (APRs) on home equity loans, home equity lines of credit, and consumer debt, don't forget to add in all points, loan origination, application, and activation fees. When these fees are included, home equity lines may cost more than other debt and might even negate any tax savings. Here are some other caveats:

- If you made a small down payment on your home (less than 20 percent of the home's value), your lender is probably charging you for private mortgage insurance (PMI). When your equity in your home exceeds 20 percent of your home's value, ask your bank to drop this added insurance, so you can stop paying the fee.
- Avoid home equity loans larger than 95 percent of the value of a home. Some homeowners have been forced to turn down promotions to higher-paying jobs in other cities because they couldn't come up with enough cash to pay off their home loans.
- Home equity loans may be less expensive than equity lines of credit. Loans may carry a fixed interest rate and may not have an activation or application fee, but you will be paying interest on the full amount of the loan even if you don't currently need all of the money. With a home equity line, however, you pay interest on the money only when you've tapped it, but a variable-rate line can become quite pricey if interest rates rise.
- If you're requesting a second mortgage that makes your borrowed amount exceed 80 percent of your home's value, many banks will raise your interest rate for the full amount of your loan. Ask for two separate loans or a "blended" rate. You will then pay the lower rate on most of the loan and the higher rate only on the amount that exceeds 80 percent.

STEP 6 **AVOID THESE LOAN PITFALLS.**

- If your bank demands early repayment of your loan or line of credit, don't just hand over the money. Ask for an early payment discount. The bank may be eager to get loans like yours off its books.
- If you have to close out a CD prematurely to pay off a loan, most banks will waive the early withdrawal penalty. Be aware that you can also get cash at a relatively low interest rate by borrowing against your CDs.
- If you're late making a loan or credit card payment, you may find that your other accounts at the same bank have been raided, without your permission, to offset the overdue amount. That's why

some bank officers tell their friends and family not to keep bank accounts or other assets at the institution that has issued their credit cards.

STEP 7   SAY "NO" TO OVERPRICED EXTRAS.

"Credit life insurance is a terrible rip-off—you should never get it," says Robert Hunter, Insurance Director for the Consumer Federation of America, and former Texas Insurance Commissioner. If you died while carrying credit card debt, credit life insurance would pay off your outstanding balance. Similarly, mortgage life insurance would pay off your mortgage balance. But credit life insurance and mortgage life insurance are far less flexible than a term life policy, which allows your beneficiary to use the money to pay off these debts, or for other purposes, as he or she sees fit. With credit or mortgage life insurance, the money can only be used to pay off the debt.

Banks love credit and mortgage life insurance. Why? Because they know your loan will be paid off if you die, and these policies are very profitable for the banks. The costs of these insurance plans vary widely from state to state. Mortgage and life insurance policies are rarely required to get a loan. If they're added to your loan documents, ask to have them deleted before you sign.

If a lender insists that you get life insurance in order to obtain a mortgage, don't buy the insurance from the bank. It's cheaper to buy a term policy from an insurance company.

STEP 8   CHECK FOR COMMON, COSTLY BANK MISTAKES.

By catching these errors quickly, you can save money:

- Miscalculation of the new payment on your adjustable rate mortgage. Did you know that when adjustable rate mortgages (ARMs) are recalculated, they are often done incorrectly? A small mistake made one year compounds into a larger, costlier error over the life of the loan. Calculation errors typically occur when banks recalculate the payment on the wrong date, use the incorrect index rate, exceed the loan cap, or put too much money in escrow for taxes and insurance. You can try to check it yourself (at least verify that the right index was used) or, for a fee, these companies will do it for you: Loantech (800) 888-6781 or the American Homeowner's Foundation (800) 489-7776.

- Overstatement of your escrow requirements. Even on fixed-rate mortgages, banks can miscalculate escrow accounts (these accounts hold your real estate taxes and insurance premiums until your lender pays them for you). A good time to check your escrow account is during the month after the bank pays your property taxes. Your escrow account will then be at its lowest point for that year. Call the customer service department and ask for a copy of the statement. Demand a refund of any excess money.

- Incorrect computation of the interest on your bank accounts. Banks can also make errors in computing the interest on deposits. For instance, they will post a deposit a day or two after you made the deposit (so you don't earn interest on those days), or they will calculate the interest based on a lower interest rate than the posted one. [This can even happen on bank certificates of deposit (CDs)]. The Truth in Savings bill originally required banks to provide enough information to verify the interest amount, but the banks balked at the paperwork. If you can't check the interest yourself, ask a bank officer to show you how it was calculated. Your bank should not charge for this service.

- Improper posting of deposits or withdrawals. Banks can make mistakes when they post deposits and withdrawals. Keep your check stubs and receipts until you verify that they were posted correctly. If you find an error, call your bank's customer service department immediately (definitely within 60 days of the transaction). If the matter is not resolved quickly, send the bank a certified letter explaining the error. Include copies of the relevant deposit or withdrawal slips. (You keep the originals.)

When an ATM Fails to Deliver Your Money, Satisfaction May Not Be Near at Hand

When Sam Willis tried to withdraw $100 from an ATM that was in his bank's network but was owned by another bank, he got back his ATM card and a receipt confirming the withdrawal. What the machine didn't dispense, however, was his cash.

Willis picked up the courtesy phone at the ATM, "but no one from the bank would even come out to look at the machine," he says. "They told me that if I wanted my money, I would have to file a complaint with my own bank."

Rod Finch regularly deposited his paychecks at his bank's ATM and never gave his account a second thought. "I didn't realize until I looked at my bank statement several weeks later that one check was never credited to my account," he says.

An ATM that Renny Smithe used shortchanged him by $200. When he asked the bank that owned the machine for restitution, he was told to pursue a claim within his own credit union.

In 1998, consumers used automated teller machines 11 billion times to check their account balances, make deposits, and/or withdraw cash. From time to time, mechanical failure or human error causes a problem.

Transactions also can go awry when dealing face-to-face with a bank teller, but the resolution procedures are fast and obvious. If you are given too little cash versus your withdrawal slip (or too little credit for a deposit), you catch it right away and correct the error before leaving the bank. If a transaction is later posted to your account incorrectly, you have a withdrawal (or deposit) slip in hand to prove your case.

As Willis and Smithe discovered, when things go wrong at a "foreign" ATM (an ATM not owned by your bank), you won't be able to resolve it on the spot. A federal law known as Regulation E requires you to try to resolve the dispute with your own bank.

With the evidence still intact, why not let a consumer and an ATM operator try to resolve it then and there? "You don't have a relationship with the operator of the ATM, so requiring the bank that holds the customer's account to resolve a dispute seems to make more sense," says John Wood, a senior attorney at the Board of Governors of the Federal Reserve System.

Smithe immediately filed a complaint form with his credit union and says, "I got my $200 back the next day." Willis promptly filed a complaint with his bank, but no quick resolution followed. When ten business days had passed, his bank issued him a provisional $100 credit, as mandated by law. But after six weeks, the bank said that the documentation supplied by the ATM owner did not support Willis's claim, so it took back the $100 credit it had issued.

If a cash machine fails to dispense the money you request, presumably, at the end of the day, the ATM drawer, when balanced, would have a surplus equal to the amount you are owed. The bank should reimburse you that amount.

But if the drawer balances because the next customer got your money along with his or hers, and kept it (or because the teller who emptied the drawer had sticky fingers), you could have an uphill battle. The dispute will come down to your word against the bank's—and the bank can decide the outcome.

Don't count on viewing a videotape of your transaction to prove your case. Videotape equipment is there to deter crime, so it's usually focused on customers, not on where the cash is dispensed. To keep costs down, some banks don't even use real cameras. They install realistic-looking toy cameras that record nothing.

Even deposits made at your own bank's ATM are not without peril. They can disappear before they get credited to your account. Tenacious customers, like Rod Finch, often find a missing check still nestled inside the envelope used to make the deposit. If you don't get full credit for a deposit you make at an ATM, insist on seeing the envelope. (Banks hold them for at least two months.)

Finding a missing deposit may not be the end of your problems, however. If you've written checks against a missing deposit, you may have been assessed penalties for bounced checks, and possibly other fees for falling below a minimum balance requirement.

"If it's the bank's fault, they should reimburse you for all actual and consequential damages," says Ed Mierzwinski, consumer program director of the U.S. Public Interest Research Group, a nonprofit watchdog organization. "This includes reversing all the false charges, sending letters of apology to the recipients of any bounced checks, paying any late fees to credit cards, etc., and contacting check verification and credit bureaus to ensure that no negative entries appear on your credit report. Ideally, consumers should also be able to recover additional penalties against the bank."

Finch says that when his deposit was misplaced, his balance was high enough that he didn't incur any fees, but the problem concerned him so much that for a while he stopped using the ATM. "I'm using it again, but monitoring it closely," he says. "I look carefully at each statement as soon as it arrives and immediately compare it with the deposit and withdrawal slips."

If you get shortchanged at the ATM, here's how you can try to resolve the problem:

1. File a complaint with your bank right away. Send copies of documentation; you keep the originals.
2. Insist on seeing the documentation that the "foreign" bank (cash machine owner) provided to your bank. You may spot something that the bank overlooked.
3. If you are a long time customer and have never filed a complaint, let the bank know. As Sam Willis discovered, many banks will give

a customer the benefit of the doubt—and a refund—to keep his business.

4. If you still don't get the money you're owed, file a complaint with your local consumer affairs office and your state attorney general's office.

5. Send a letter explaining your problem, along with copies of documentation, to one of the organizations listed below, depending on what kind of bank or credit union was involved:

- If your bank is state-chartered and a member of the Federal Reserve System: Board of Governors of the Federal Reserve System, 20th and C Streets NW, Washington, DC 20551; (202) 452-3000.
- If your bank is state-chartered but not a member of the Federal Reserve System: Federal Deposit Insurance Corporation, Office of Consumer Affairs, 550 17th Street NW, Washington, DC 20429; (800) 934-3342.
- If your bank is a national bank (has "National" in the title or "NA" after its name): Comptroller of the Currency, Customer Assistance Group, 1301 McKinney Street, Suite 3710, Houston, TX 77010; (800) 613-6743.
- If your bank is a savings bank or a savings and loan (S&L) institution: Office of Thrift Supervision, Consumer Programs, 1700 G Street NW, Washington, DC 20552; (202) 906-6237 or (800) 842-6929.
- If your account is with a federally chartered credit union: National Credit Union Administration, Office of Public and Congressional Affairs, 1775 Duke Street, Alexandria, VA 22314-3428; (703) 518-6330.

6. Never deposit cash at an ATM. If it disappears, you'll have no way of proving your loss.

What's Sold in a Bank Is Not Always Insured

Banks aren't just for checking and savings accounts anymore. These days, your bank may be more than happy to sell you a mutual fund or an annuity. Not that there's anything wrong with that, but studies have shown that consumers have many misconceptions about the products their banks offer.

Many consumers mistakenly believe that all products sold in their bank are federally insured and that they cannot lose money by buying a product there. They're wrong. A mutual fund, for instance, can go up or down whether you buy it at a bank, through a stockbroker, or directly from the mutual fund company. (For more information on buying mutual funds, see Chapter 27.) Also, some banks are tacking on fees for mutual funds that you might not have to pay if you bought the same fund elsewhere. So you need to know the costs before you buy mutual funds, insurance, or annuities from a bank or any other source. Bank reps selling these products at a desk in your bank's branch office (next to a bank employee) may be employed by an investment subsidiary, not by the bank itself.

Maximize Your Pay
and Perks at Work

In the first two money solutions, you learned the basic financial building blocks. You've boosted your financial knowledge, saw where you stand, and found creative ways to negotitate better terms with your credit card company and your bank. You've also found (or begun your search for) some good financial advisers who can help make your money grow, as well as help you minimize your tax bill.

Don't stop there. The fun and rewards are just beginning. Believe it or not, where you work is the next place to turn to improve your finances. Your employer *could* play a large part in helping you reach your financial goals. In this solution, I will show you how to maximize employer-paid benefits, position yourself for a raise, find a better-paying job, and even keep an unexpected layoff from ruining your family's future. In other words, we'll find ways to free up more of your money so that you can reach your goals that much sooner.

Chapter 6

Make the Most of
Employer-Paid Benefits

To become wealthy or even financially self-reliant, you not only need to make good investments, you also need to avoid selling yourself short by settling for too little pay or too few employee benefits. In the next four chapters, I will show you creative ways to make sure you're not leaving money on the table at work. Landing a raise or finding a better-paying job would put more money in your bank account, but those are not the only ways to improve your financial picture.

Another way to boost your net worth is to stop paying for things out of your own pocket if someone else (namely your employer) is offering to pay for them for you. Another way is to take advantage of all tax breaks that you are entitled to as an employee. Either way, you should be keeping more of your hard-earned money so that you can put it toward reaching your other goals.

Would you be interested in a 30 to 40 percent raise? That's how much employer-paid benefits could be worth. Does your employer pay all or part of your insurance premiums (such as life, health, or disability insurance)? Are you able to use pretax dollars for bills you would normally pay with after-tax dollars, such as child care and out-of-pocket medical costs, which aren't covered by your health insurance plan? Too many workers leave money on the table. Why? Here are some common reasons:

- When you first started working at your firm, the benefits coordinator probably gave you a rundown of available benefits. But if you were hired young (maybe you were unmarried and without dependents), you may have felt indestructible. The idea of paying for life insurance or disability insurance may have seemed like a complete waste of money. It isn't.
- Your employer may have changed the benefits originally offered to you, but you didn't hear about the new benefits package. Or, you heard about them but didn't understand them and never bothered to get more information. Retirement savings plans and flexible

spending accounts are among the least understood and most underutilized benefits. But they can save you money big time.

- When you got married and had your kids, or when you got divorced, you may have forgotten that you could get low-cost insurance through work. You're now paying for higher-priced insurance on your own. Hey, it's not too late to reassess your choices.
- At a growing number of companies, some of the best employee benefits are not available to new employees. When you became eligible on your first or second anniversary, did you forget to sign up for these valuable bennies?

You've got to get past the past. Here's how you can start making the most of your employee benefits from now on.

STEP 1 FUND YOUR FLEXIBLE SPENDING ACCOUNT ACCURATELY.

The program allows you to use *pretax* dollars to pay for a range of things, from child care costs to attorney's fees to health care deductibles and out-of-pocket expenses (such as eyeglasses).

Tip: Most plans cap the benefit at $5,000 a year. You will forfeit any money left at the end of the year, so use this year's expenses to determine next year's contribution.

STEP 2 MAKE THE MAXIMUM CONTRIBUTION TO YOUR COMPANY'S 401(K) RETIREMENT SAVINGS PLAN.

The money will grow tax-deferred, so you won't be taxed until you withdraw (probably after you've retired, when you may be in a lower tax bracket). Some employers will match all or part of your contribution. Give serious consideration to fully funding this plan. For many workers, this will be the only postretirement income they will get from their former employer.

In a company that offered a traditional retirement plan (called a "defined benefit" plan), your employer might have promised to pay you a pension (say, $46,000 a year for life) based on your length of service and preretirement wages. Years before you retired, your employer, for planning purposes, should have provided you with a good estimate of the annual benefits you would be receiving. But most of these plans have gone the way of the dinosaur as many employers have learned that they are more costly than other types of retirement plans—most notably, the 401(k) plan.

A 401(k) plan, by comparison, is a "defined contribution" plan. You (and possibly your employer) put in a certain amount of money. This *contribution* (not the eventual benefit) is known ahead of time. The amount you'll get at retirement will depend on where the money was invested (and how the investments performed), and you won't know that amount until you retire. Your goal is to outpace inflation, so, in your 20s, 30s, and 40s, you should be heavily invested in stocks. As retirement nears (and you have less time to recoup following a drop in the market), begin switching to less risky money market funds and bonds.

Tip: If you have a retirement saving plan or a pension plan at work, be sure to check the accuracy of your records with those of your benefits coordinator. And every three years, verify your Social Security records by calling (800) 772-1213. Errors in these records are not uncommon, and you are the only one who will lose if too little income is posted to either of these accounts. The sooner you catch a mistake, the easier it will be to get the information verified and corrected.

Most 401(k) plans have a provision for borrowing from them, but this type of loan can be costlier than others. Even though you pay the interest to yourself, the money that is on loan is not compounding, and that standstill will greatly curtail the growth of your retirement savings. And, to avoid owing taxes and penalties, you should plan on repaying any loan within five years or when you leave the company. Look into a low-cost credit union or bank loan instead. (For more information on 401(k) plans, see Chapter 30.)

Note: If you work for a nonprofit organization, or for the government, you may be eligible for other retirement savings programs. Ask your benefits coordinator at work for details.

STEP 3 LOAD UP ON "FREE" COMPANY-OFFERED LIFE INSURANCE.

Comparison-shop if you need supplemental coverage, beyond what your employer is offering at no cost. The rule of thumb is that families need to be insured for five to eight times their gross income. If you are in good health, you may get a better deal through a union or professional organization than through your employer.

For more advice on life insurance, turn to Chapter 13.

STEP 4 SIGN UP FOR DISABILITY INSURANCE AT WORK.

This insurance would replace some income if you are unable to work. It is especially important for single people, parents-to-be, and one-income families who don't have access to another source of income or funds. A typical policy covers 65 to 70 percent of gross income.

For more advice on disability insurance, read Chapter 14.

 ### MAKE THE MOST OF HEALTH CARE CHOICES.

You'll typically get better coverage for less money by signing up for group coverage at work instead of individual coverage on your own. Ask when the employer allows you to change health plans, what is known as open season. Then work the numbers and talk to plan participants to see which of your employer's plans would be best for your family's needs.

For more tips on health care plans, see Chapter 16.

 ### TAP EMPLOYEE TUITION PLANS TO MOVE UP THE CORPORATE LADDER.

Under these plans, you train for a better job with your current employer or elsewhere, but on your employer's nickel.

 ### ASK ABOUT ADOPTION ASSISTANCE.

Some employers will pick up the tab, up to $5,000 or $10,000.

 ### COAX YOUR EMPLOYER INTO MATCHING YOUR CHARITABLE CONTRIBUTIONS.

Many companies will give one or two dollars for every dollar an employee contributes to a qualifying tax-deductible organization. In effect, you'll be giving a raise to your favorite charity.

OPTIMIZE YOUR STOCK OPTIONS.

More workers are being granted stock options as part of their compensation package. Under the right circumstances you could use these options to generate profits for you by buying your company's stock at a below-market price. Here's how it works. You might be offered, say, 100 options at $25 a share, so if the stock price rises to say $65 a share, you could exercise your options and buy 100 shares at $25 ($100 \times \$25 = \$2,500$). Since the price of the stock has risen to $65, your $2,500 purchase would be worth $6,500 and you would have earned a profit of $4,000.

You will owe a tax on that $4,000 profit in the year you exercised the options and you will likely be taxed at your ordinary income tax rate, not at the lower, long-term capital gain rate.

Timing is everything when it comes to making money with stock options. For one thing, if the stock price goes up, you first must decide when to exercise the option: now or should you wait, and hope, that it rises further? Conversely, the stock price could drop instead of going up, in which case you'd let your options expire without exercising them. But a more common way that many workers leave money on the table with stock options is by forgetting to exercise them *before* they expire. So even if the price has gone up, and you could have made a bundle, once the options have expired, they are worthless. Don't expect your employer to notify you before your options expire. Keeping track of them is your responsibility.

If you leave the company you will likely have to exercise the options within a short amount of time or not at all, so check with your employer before you retire or quit. Finally make sure you understand the vesting rules: how many years do you have to be with a company before the options, and any ensuing profits, are yours to keep? And does your current company have a non-compete clause that would force you to give up your options, or refund any gains you have realized, if you head off to one of its competitors?

Chapter 7

Position Yourself
for a Raise

Another way to increase your net worth is by getting a pay raise. Contrary to what many people think, asking a boss for a raise out of the blue, and getting it on the spot, is not the norm. Positioning yourself for a raise or promotion usually takes months or years.

Matt's Story

Matt Turner had not gotten a pay raise in 23 months. At the end of his annual performance review, he decided to broach the subject with his boss. "The review had gone well, so I mustered my courage and asked for more money," he recalls. "But my boss dismissed the subject immediately, saying, 'This isn't a good time to ask.' He then stood up, opened the door, and left for lunch. I don't know how to interpret this. I've been avoiding my boss because I don't know what to say or what he's thinking. Was he signaling that I should start looking for another job?"

STEP 1 — FIND THE BEST TIME TO ASK FOR A RAISE.

When you ask for a raise can affect not only your chances of getting one, but also the amount you will get. If your company's earnings are good, there will be one less reason to turn you down. But if downsizing plans have just been announced, put off asking for more money until your company's financial situation improves.

The best time to ask for a raise is when you've accomplished something that has had a positive result on the organization—for instance, you just made a big sale or brought in a new client.

STEP 2 — GET—AND STAY—FOCUSED ON YOUR GOAL.

When you ask for a raise, be assertive. Let management know you're serious, and strengthen your case by pointing to your specific accomplishments. Keep the discussion focused on you and your achievements at—and for—your company. If your boss suggests postponing the discussion until another time, ask him or her to pick a time and date.

Avoid Clichés if You Hope to Get a Raise

The way you phrase your request can doom your chances. Here are some show-stoppers. Employers hear them often, but they will likely doom your chances of getting more money. So, don't say:

- "John is getting $3,000 more than I am, for the same job." You may not know the full employment arrangement your boss has with your coworker.
- "I have three kids at home and can't pay my bills." Personal financial problems are irrelevant.
- "If you don't give me this raise, I am going to leave the company." Never threaten something unless you're prepared to follow through. Even if you have a written offer in hand from another company, using it as leverage may not be in your best interest. Many employers will match a competitor's offer, but this approach may yield only a short-term win. You could be labeled as a "traitor." And most employees who stay with a company after delivering such an ultimatum end up leaving within two years.

STEP 3 BECOME YOUR OWN PUBLICIST.

Larger companies, and a growing number of smaller ones, base pay increases on their employees' yearly performance evaluation. To get the results you want, don't wait until the last minute. You should be having ongoing conversations with your boss about what he or she expects of you, and what you are producing for your employer.

Many workers make the mistake of assuming that their boss knows *and remembers* what they have accomplished. Think back: Can *you* remember, in detail, what you accomplished over the past month, let alone year? Probably not.

So how realistic is it to think that your boss can remember not only what he or she accomplished, but also what each staff member accomplished?

You can get a leg up by keeping your boss informed via a one-page "Highlights List" each month. Itemize your completed accomplishments and update your progress on your ongoing projects for the month and for the longer term.

What kinds of accomplishments could bolster your case? Anything that affects your employer's bottom line or gets favorable publicity for your company. For instance:

- Did you do something to increase your company's profits?
- Did you find a way to lower your company's costs?
- Did you get many thank-you notes from clients?
- Did a professional organization elect you to an office?
- Did you get written up in a newspaper or trade publication?

Send your boss a copy of anything that shows what a valuable employee you are—or anything that just makes you and your company look good. Remind your boss of times when you took on some additional responsibilities, especially if your work avoided the need to hire another employee.

JOG YOUR BOSS'S MEMORY *BEFORE* HE OR SHE PUTS PEN TO PAPER.

Three or four weeks before your appraisal, have a friendly, casual review with your boss, to remind him or her what you've accomplished. This will simplify the chore of writing up your appraisal, and will make you stand out in contrast to your peers (who are sitting passively by, hoping that the boss says something nice about them).

STEP 5 UNDERSTAND WHAT'S EXPECTED OF YOU.

How do you really know what your boss wants or expects you to accomplish? It helps to get this in writing. Many companies are leery of lawsuits, so their written objectives in a job description (sometimes called a performance plan) may be cryptically phrased.

Don't leave this to chance. Delve for understanding. And since no one works in a vacuum, and teamwork is encouraged in most companies, it's a good idea to compare your objectives with those of your teammates.

LLOYD'S LAW

Job #1 for you is to make your boss look good.

It's also wise to see how your objectives feed into the goals your boss is working toward. Learn how *he or she* is being measured, in addition to how you are. Most bosses do not volunteer this information, but don't leave it to your imagination—your imagination could very well be wrong. Instead, ask your boss how his or her performance is measured. "It's a refreshing change when someone on my staff asks how they can help me, instead of telling me what they want me to do for them," says Joseph Baker, a manager at a large communications industry corporation. "It's not always easy for me to talk about this, but I appreciate getting the opportunity. In many ways, I'm just like the people on my staff: I have a boss and a performance plan, and I am expected to accomplish certain things in the course of a year. And I can't do it alone, so I like the idea that we're all in this together."

Don't wait until the last minute (or two weeks before your appraisal/ job evaluation is scheduled) to have this discussion with your boss. It's better to have some lead time—say, one year—to find out exactly what your boss needs to do in order to succeed. You can't do much in two weeks.

STEP 6 TELL YOUR BOSS WHAT YOU EXPECT IN RETURN.

If you don't get a raise, should you start looking for work elsewhere? Not necessarily. Maybe you didn't get a raise because the company is in financial trouble. Or maybe your boss thinks a pat on the back and verbal "atta-boy" are sufficient.

You need to sit down with your boss at least a couple of times a year, so that he or she can say, "This is what I expect of you." You then get your chance to say, "This is what I expect from you in return." Describe what you would like, from more responsibility, to additional training, to a promotion and/or a raise.

If you are going to ask for a raise, it's best to go armed with information—for instance, salary grids showing what similar employees in your field are getting. The business room of your local library, professional organizations, and trade papers can often point you to these numbers. If you can get specifics about the salaries (and other perks) coworkers in your company are making, that's even better.

Point to the numbers and say, "I certainly feel I'm accomplishing [fill in the blank, preferably with some *quantifiable* results] and I deserve at least $_____." It's harder for someone to say no when you have the facts on your side.

Tip: Don't squander a hard-earned raise. One of the easiest (least painful) ways to increase the amount you save—and your total wealth—is by saving all or most of a pay raise. You're not used to having or spending that money, so you won't miss it. If you're carrying credit card or student loan debt, use some of your raise to pay down this debt sooner. Pay off your highest-interest-rate debt first (but, to avoid penalty fees, always make at least the minimum monthly payments on all your debts).

Chapter 8

Land a
Better-Paying Job

What are you really worth as an employee? To become wealthy or even financially self-reliant, you need to not only make good investments but also avoid selling yourself short by settling for too little pay or too few employee benefits. Even if you managed to snag a raise lately, you might want to stick your toe into the job pool to see what dollar amount another company would place on your services.

The grass may really be greener on the other side of the fence.

As much as you would like to think that your current employer appreciates your contributions and the sacrifices you make for your company, getting the money, benefits, and recognition you deserve aren't necessarily going to come your way at your present company. To get the renumeration and future career growth you want and need, it might be time to punch up your resume and pound the pavement in search of a more appreciative employer.

Even if you feel that everything is going great at your current company, a few exploratory interviews can be a good morale boost. You may realize that you've got a good deal where you are and you may have been taking it for granted. But you'll never know for sure unless you test your wings in the open market.

At this point you may be wondering, what this has to do with your personal finances? Here's the thing: you can achieve personal wealth by spending less, by making good investments, or by earning more at work. You can boost your earnings by getting a raise, switching to a better paying job, or having your employer pick up the tab for benefits such as insurance, health care, or child care. If you have great skills and a lot to offer to an employer, you need to get that message across. A well-crafted resume and a carefully honed presentation about your work experience and the expertise you bring to an employer are initial steps toward getting the salary you deserve and building your personal wealth.

LLOYD'S LAW

Before you spend any time sending out resumes and going to job interviews, get yourself in a job-hunting mindset. You must be ready to persuade interviewers that you are the best person they could possibly hire. Since sincerity is hard to fake, you need to persuade yourself first. If you can't do that, postpone the job search until you are ready, willing, and able to declare yourself the best candidate.

Roger's Story

"Harry came to the job interview looking well groomed, and his recommendations were glowing," recalls Roger, a department manager at a midsize company. "My staff was very impressed by Harry during his last round of interviews, so by the time I met him, the job was almost his to lose."

Then came the fateful question. "I asked him, 'In one sentence, tell me: Why should I hire you?' He could have gone a lot of ways with his answer. For instance, he could have talked about his experiences at his current company or how he understood the competition we were now facing and what kinds of aggressive marketing we would need to keep growing our business. But he didn't. Nope. Instead, Harry said, 'I'm a hard worker, a loyal employee, and I think I'd like working here.' He paused, adding, 'If I can convince my family that we should pick up roots and move.'

"I've been sitting across the desk from job hunters for decades, and I feel like I've heard it all. And I always thought there was no wrong answer to that question, but Harry blew it."

What *does* Roger look for? "After we've gone through a candidate's qualifications and ability to do the work and to fit into the organization, there comes what I call the mating dance. It's a ritual, but it needs to be played out. We have a good company that I am very proud to be a part of. I think that anyone would be lucky to work here.

"So I want prospective employees to realize that. I want them to tell me they really want to work here—that they would appreciate the opportunity. It's ego on my part and, in some ways, a validation of what I've chosen to do with my life and where I've chosen to work. So I don't want them to hesitate. I want them to sell me on why they are the best person for the job."

What about candidates' hesitating after they get an offer—not jumping to accept it? "In a strange way, that almost makes me want that person more," says Roger with a grin. "I've invested time and put my credibility on the line with my bosses to get an offer. So I want him [or her] to jump at the chance to work here. That's the time I am most vulnerable and willing to give more—more money and, especially, benefits. *That's* the time for an applicant to play hard-to-get, not during the interview."

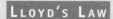

LLOYD'S LAW

At most companies, pay increases are figured as a percentage of your yearly salary, so time spent negotiating a higher starting salary, before you take a job, is well worth the effort. Think of it as a gift that can keep on giving to you year after year.

The workplace has been undergoing a series of changes recently. Job-hunting skills that worked just a few years ago may not even get you called in for an interview now. Successful job hunters are learning to package themselves in new, more creative ways, to grab a potential employer's attention. Here are two things the interviewer wants to know about you, but probably won't ask you directly: Can you do the job? Will you fit into the organization?

Whether this is your first job or you've been in the workplace for decades, the nine steps in this chapter describe some simple things you can do to maximize the number of job offers you get.

STEP 1 TARGET YOUR JOB SEARCH.

Sending out 100 resumes almost at random won't cut it anymore. Savvy job searchers target a few specific companies before they send out any resumes. Your goals are to identify the challenges facing those particular companies and to come up with ways you could help to address them. In other words: *The company has a problem, and you can deliver the solution.* How do you accomplish this? By doing some research and networking.

Did you know that by the time many job openings make it to the employment section of a newspaper, people with connections (friends of current employees, and clients of headhunters) may have already made bids for those jobs?

By networking, you can get yourself into the loop and be accepted among the people you would like to call your peers. Professional associations and alumni groups can be invaluable sources of information about job openings, corporate cultures, and salaries, so if you aren't already a member, start joining.

Consider doing some volunteer work. Beyond your donation of public service, the rewards will be improved self-esteem, and opportunities to rub elbows with employees, and even senior management, of local corporations.

Next, explore in depth a handful of companies that interest you. Read their annual reports (available at libraries, through stockbrokers, by contacting the companies' public relations offices, or by surfing the Internet). Find out as much as you can about salary ranges for jobs at each company and in the industry as a whole. Be sure to visit corporate Web sites. You can often find job postings, press releases, and other valuable information about a potential employer.

Who are these companies' competitors? Do an online Nexus search to be on the lookout for any recent news articles about planned expansions or problems the company may be facing. Find out what charitable organizations the company supports. This research will pay off during an interview.

STEP 2 · WRITE A FOCUSED RESUME.

Do you know the real purpose of a resume? If you think it is to get you a job offer, think again.

> ### LLOYD'S LAW
> *A resume is intended to pique a potential employer's curiosity, so that the response is: "We must invite this person in for an interview."*

How do you achieve this? By writing a short, but focused, resume. Think of it as a sales pitch, and you are the product. Organize it so that the best things you have to offer almost pop off the page to a potential employer. Emphasize teamwork.

Tip: Keep it brief—no more than one or two pages—or interviewers may only skim it and could miss your key strengths (especially if they're buried in the middle of page three).

From your research, you should have uncovered some problems or other challenges facing the company. Your resume should show ways that you previously have solved similar problems.

Identify key accomplishments, and quantify your results. Don't say, "I was responsible for managing 25 employees." Instead, say, "I managed the marketing staff that increased revenues 14 percent over three years."

Stay away from gimmicks, and keep your presentation focused. "Resumes that are overproduced turn me off," says Art Moore, Director of Programming, WABC-TV. "If they're selling that much, they're probably covering up something. And if they have that much time and money to spend, they may not be good in a budget-minded environment."

No matter how cleverly you've crafted your resume, it won't get you in the door unless it's read by the right person. When you're responding to an ad, how do you get past the mailroom clerk who does the initial screening?

"In the cover letter, use the exact language of the ad, followed by a specific accomplishment," advises Barbara Collins, Managing Director, New York office of Drake, Beam, Morin, an outplacement firm that helps laid-off workers find jobs. "If the ad says, 'Strategic planning for retail operations,' respond with 'Strategic planning for retail operations: Worked with $50 million retail chain in the area of strategic planning for five-year operational plan.'"

LLOYD'S LAW

Never send your resume to the name listed in the ad. Call the company and get the name of the director of the department you're applying to (finance, marketing). Send your letter to that person. And triple-check the spelling and title of the person you're writing to.

STEP 3 USE THE INTERNET WITH CAUTION.

Sending a resume over the Internet is akin to nailing your resume to a tree in the town square. Resume-posting sites often swap resumes with other sites, so you never know where your resume will end up—perhaps on the computer screen of your current employer! Like the "blind" want ads that supply only a post office box and no corporate name, you don't know who will see your resume.

There are personal risks as well. To minimize them:

- Include your e-mail address and possibly your home phone number.

- Don't include your home/street address, salary history, or Social Security number. (Your Social Security number should *never* be included on any resume—paper or electronic.)

In general, the earliest you should consider disclosing personal information is when you have visited a company for an interview. Before you go for the interview, be sure to check out the company.

For more detailed help in launching an online search, here are a few Web sites to visit:

- *Career Mosaic:* www.careermosaic.com
- *Fortune Magazine:* www.fortune.com/careers
- *Career Builder:* www.careerbuilder.com
- *USA Today:* www.usatoday.com/careers/careers.htm

STEP 4 REHEARSE YOUR RESPONSES BEFORE THE INTERVIEW.

Having the right skills and experience is one thing, but being able to impress or persuade a potential employer is another. You cannot go into a job interview cold. Do a dry run in a safe environment, preferably with a friend who can critique your verbal delivery and your answers to questions.

"You need to articulate what you're good at, and think in terms of sound bites," says Collins. "The interviewer will probably take you through your resume, and you'll have to address every single item in one or two sentences."

Practice your answers in front of a mirror, or videotape a mock interview. Take a critical look at your appearance and your clothes. How does your voice sound? Are you making good eye contact? Are you sitting up straight? Are your clothes neatly pressed and your shoes shined?

Find out about the company culture before the interview. Your goal is to fit in, so dress like the employees do.

Tough Questions: Smart Responses

With the cost of hiring employees rising, and because employers fear lawsuits if they make a bad choice, many interviewers are becoming amateur psychiatrists and part-time sleuths.

Are you prepared for an onslaught of questions? Many of the queries you will be asked should be fairly obvious, but if you haven't given them a thought before the interview, they can quickly become showstoppers.

Be honest with your responses, but don't volunteer information or comments you might later regret. Here are seven typical questions and some professional ways to answer them:

1. "Tell me about yourself." This is an icebreaker, and your answer should take one to two minutes. This is not the time or place for you to tell your life's history, starting with your first day at kindergarten. "I would [briefly] tell where I'm from, where I went to school, and what I studied, and give a brief chronology of my work experience," advises Collins.

2. "What's your ideal job?" Before you start interviewing, you should do some self-analysis, according to Collins. What did you like (or not like) in past jobs? What kind of an environment allows you to thrive (or stifles you)? Do you like to be managed closely (or given a lot of autonomy)? Identify your people skills, technical skills, or any other specific skills that would be useful to an employer.

3. "Where do you want to be five years from now?" The correct response is a truthful description of a goal that you feel comfortable with and that is realistic within your profession. Two wrong answers: "In the same job" (indicates lack of motivation) and "president of the company" (shows unrealistic expectations).

4. "Can you give me an example of a weakness?" "Saying I don't have any isn't an option," says Collins. "You need at least two nonfluffy ones. Couch them as follows, 'I have a tendency to be too detail-oriented, but I'm working with my manager to talk about more global issues.' You leave the interviewer thinking you're not apologizing or defensive." *Don't* offer a laundry list of reasons not to hire you.

5. "Why should I hire you?" This is asked at the end of the interview. Collins advises referring back to your interview notes and saying, "'Based on our discussions, here are the challenges that I perceive you are having. My experience for this problem is such and such."

6. "Are you married? Do you have kids?" If you tell the interviewer these questions are illegal, you'll probably kill your chance of getting the job. "Don't give details," advises Collins. "Just say, 'Rest assured, I'll be here every day.' That's all they really want to know."

7. "How much money do you want?" Avoid the urge to respond by asking, "How much does this job pay?" Or, "How much can I make by working at this company?" This question may sound like it's only about a salary figure, but it may be a surrogate for more. Several employers have told me that they are using this question

(along with others) to test a prospective employee. They want to find out how much research an applicant has done about their company and the industry they're in, and what an applicant knows about his or her true worth in the workplace.

Your response to the money question depends how it's worded. If a prospective employer asks, "What are you making?" reveal your total compensation (salary plus bonus). Be honest; they may ask to see your W-2. Of course, if you're currently getting a fabulous benefits package that would be costly to replace, you can also mention that, but separately.

"If the question is, 'What [amount] are you looking for?' try to postpone answering it until a later date—after you have more information about the company and the job," says Collins. "If they won't let you, then give a narrow range." The employer will negotiate down from your bottom number, so don't start too low. How do you find that range? By networking, and by researching compensation and benefit surveys (available at the library).

When an offer is made, don't accept on the spot, no matter how good it seems. In most companies, you get one shot to negotiate more money or perks (vacation days, a bigger office, free parking, free health club membership). Articulate why the job *with you in it* is worth more, and then follow up with objective reasons.

STEP 5 — REALIZE THAT ANYTHING YOU SAY CAN (WILL) BE USED AGAINST YOU.

As an IBM manager, I often interviewed job applicants. One promising candidate asked to use my phone to call her office. "I signed out to my customers because I've used up my vacation days," she told me. "I don't want my boss to know I'm looking for another job." We rejected her because of her lie—and her obvious poor judgment. The lesson: You're being observed throughout the entire interview process, so act accordingly.

Some interviewers test applicants for loyalty to their current or former employers. Don't fall for it: Never divulge proprietary information or bad-mouth an employer.

STEP 6 — COACH YOUR REFERENCES.

Can you recall in detail what you did two or three years ago? Neither can your references. To get them to sing your praises, you must prepare them.

Send an annotated resume and go over your accomplishments with them. "Don't forget to tell them one or two areas where you could use a little improvement," says Collins.

Should the reference be someone you reported to or someone you worked with? At least one of your references should be someone you reported to, because the interviewer wants to know what you were like as an employee.

 ## STEP 7 PICK UP ON THE INTERVIEWER'S CUES.

As your meeting ends, listen carefully to what the interviewer says about your chances of getting the job and what follow-up (if any) the company or you will make. "I know what I want to do and when," says Moore. "If I say I'll let them know in three weeks, I will. I don't want them calling every week."

What if you get turned down before you leave? "Be upbeat," advises Moore. "I know it's hard, but you must try. You could be terrific but not right for the job. If you leave a positive impression, we might hire you next time." Whatever happens, don't forget to send a short, polite thank-you note within five days.

 ## STEP 8 ASK FOR THE JOB.

Do it politely and with enthusiasm. But do it. Many interviewers complain that applicants lose interest before the interview ends. If you're not comfortable asking directly, Collins suggests saying, "It was a fascinating discussion. I'm very interested in pursuing it further."

STEP 9 SET THE STAGE FOR A GLOWING, NEW-EMPLOYEE JOB APPRAISAL.

A little forethought can help you maximize the performance appraisal at the end of your first year on the new job. Before you accept any job offer, be sure you've come to a meeting of the minds with your soon-to-be new employer. Agree on specifics: What you are expected to accomplish in that first critical year and how you will be appraised, based on quantifiable results. Get it in writing! (*Note:* This is in addition to the offer letter, which should include salary, the work-start date, benefits, and any other conditions of employment.)

Breaking Up Is Hard to Do

After you've landed a new job, you'll have to give notice to your current employer. Two weeks still is common, but, if possible, allow enough time to finish outstanding projects.

By the way, your employer may tell you to hit the road then and there, so pack up your belongings *before* you announce your exciting, new plans.

If your employer tries to entice you with an attractive counteroffer, don't succumb. After you've shown that you are entertaining outside offers, you may be viewed as a traitor. Many workers who accept a counteroffer leave within two years—often at the employer's request and on a timetable that could devastate your search for a replacement job.

Whether your employer is happy or sad to see you go, write an upbeat letter of resignation. After all, you may want to consider rejoining this company when you're pursuing your next career move and salary increase. "Tell them about the good things you learned and how you respect your coworkers and the company," advises etiquette expert Letitia Baldrige. "The letter will stay in the file and, who knows, if you come back years later, they'll read the letter and decide 'We must hire this person back.'"

Beware of Unscrupulous Headhunters

If you're looking for a job, you might be tempted to call a headhunter for help. Ironically, many headhunters will refuse to work with people who contact them. They only work with clients who are referred by others. The best way to get referrals is to network—get involved in professional organizations and community volunteer work.

If a headhunter contacts you, resist the urge to confide your salary or personal information to a stranger. If the call comes out of the blue, say you will call back. "I answered questions from a headhunter last year and wish I hadn't," recalls Erin. "The woman on the phone sounded sincere. She said she was representing a new company moving into the area and it needed to make some quick hires. A week later, I found out she wasn't a headhunter at all, but someone who worked for my then-employer to test my loyalty and see what I would say about my boss. I don't think I said anything bad about my employer, but I got called into my boss's office and was given a choice: I could accept a transfer to a lower-paying job at a location that would double my commuting time, or I could leave the company."

LLOYD'S LAW

Steer clear of headhunters who charge you a fee to rewrite your resume or sell you a list of "hot" job prospects. Reputable headhunters only charge the employer, not the job applicant. And "hot" lists are often names merely copied from a phone book.

Erin's situation is a bit extreme and, hopefully, most employers wouldn't resort to such tactics. But it brings home a point: Don't speak to a headhunter until you've gathered your thoughts. And no matter how intriguing a prospective job sounds, if you don't personally know the headhunter, do a background check before divulging any information. If the headhunter and the job opening are on the level, your cautious judgment will be appreciated.

Chapter 9

Negotiate a Bigger Severance Package and Find a New Job Faster if You're Laid Off

You hope it won't happen to you, but in this time of corporate mergers and across-the-board cost-cutting initiatives, the chances have never been higher that you may be downsized and offered some kind of severance package to quietly leave your current employer.

Many workers make a big—and very costly—mistake at this stressful time: They settle for their employer's first offer. Besides being devastating to your psyche and your bank account, settling too quickly can hinder your search for a new job.

Ross's Story

"I got called into my boss's office on a Friday morning and was told that my department was being consolidated with another one and my job would be eliminated at the end of the month," recalls Ross. "My manager said that I would get a week's pay for each year I had worked at the company, and I could get an extra $10,000 if I would sign a form, then and there, saying that I would not sue the company for any reason."

If you are being downsized, don't jump on your employer's first offer. Many issues need to be considered. What should you ask for, and when should you settle? How can you keep from losing your health insurance? Are there other employer-offered benefits you should ask to take with you? What's the best thing to do with the lump-sum severance money to minimize your taxes and make it grow without taking undue risk? How can you increase the chances of quickly landing a new job and getting your downsizing employer to give you a glowing reference?

Negotiating a severance package that will meet your individual needs takes time, research, and a strong stomach. Your employer may be counting on your accepting the first severance offer. Be prepared to have it presented as though the company is doing you a favor and you must accept, but stay noncommittal until you have weighed your options. Chances are you can ask for and get more money and additional benefits.

If a lot of money is involved, or if your employer is asking you to sign a release stating you will not sue, consider hiring an attorney who specializes in labor law. Ask the lawyer to at least look over the severance document or, possibly, to negotiate on your behalf. (See Chapter 12 for tips on finding a lawyer.)

The steps in this chapter highlight some areas you (or your attorney) should negotiate.

 ### ASK FOR MORE SEVERANCE PAY.

Most workers can expect one to two weeks' salary for each year worked at a company. Folks in top management can often get three to four weeks' pay per year of employment. Always ask for more, but have realistic expectations.

 ### HOLD OUT FOR BENEFITS YOU NEED.

You may be offered some benefits that don't cost your employer a lot and that you don't really need. Instead of accepting, try to trade them for benefits that can help you find another job quickly. You'll need to approach your search as though it were a full-time job, so consider asking for:

- Office space.
- Secretarial service.
- Phone number and long-distance calling privileges.
- Copier and fax machine privileges.
- Professional outplacement assistance.

STEP 3 MAKE SURE YOUR HEALTH CARE PLAN DOESN'T LAPSE.

Medical expenses can eat up your savings, so if you're near retirement, ask your employer if you can keep your health insurance going until you're eligible for the company pension, or at least eligible for Medicare.

If retirement is a long way off, you'll be on your own. Your first possible solution may be health plan coverage offered by your spouse's employer. If you're single or your spouse is not employed, be aware that a federal law known as COBRA allows most laid-off workers to keep their corporate health insurance for eighteen months. You will have to pay the premiums, and they will be much higher than while you were with the company (perhaps $200 a month instead of $40), because you will be charged the employee premium and the employer portion, plus an administrative fee of about 2 percent. Since employer plans usually offer better coverage than you could get on your own, and at lower costs than an individual policy, check into this option immediately. You have sixty days to sign up for this health care coverage, and if you miss it, even by one day, you'll be out of luck. Pursue this option vigorously so that all the papers are signed by you and received by the issuer before the due date.

STEP 4   ASK FOR OTHER BENEFITS.

If you are eligible to retire with a full pension from the downsizing company, you may also be entitled to employer-paid life insurance and other benefits. But you *must ask.* If you are under age 65 but are eligible for early retirement, you'll likely be better off financially if you wait out the extra few years and can then receive full monthly pension payments. Crunch the numbers both ways (or have your employer calculate them for you). Remember, you'll get a reduced monthly pension payment if you retire early, and this monthly payment will *not* increase when you turn 65.

STEP 5   WEIGH LUMP-SUM PAYMENTS CAREFULLY.

Whether retirement is close or decades away, don't be lured by a lump sum equal to the current value of your pension, until you (and your tax adviser and financial planner) have crunched the numbers. Why? Because that money has to last until you and your spouse die. If you're a novice investor or you make investment choices that are very conservative, it's probably smarter to leave the money with your employer, where it will be professionally managed, until you are old enough to start drawing your pension.

STEP 6   UNDERSTAND THE TAX CONSEQUENCES BEFORE TOUCHING ANY MONEY.

Resist any urge to spend the money you've invested in your company's 401(k) plan. You'll owe taxes on the money, plus a 10 percent penalty if you're under age 55. (*Note:* The eligible age is not 59½ in this situation.) Instead, consider rolling it over into an IRA or a retirement plan offered by your new employer. Even if you are rolling it into another plan, DO NOT touch the money. If you do, 20 percent will be withheld for taxes. Unless you make up that withheld money by adding new money yourself, you will owe taxes plus a penalty. [For more information on 401(k) plans, see Chapter 30.]

Tax Tip: Insist on a "direct rollover." Your old employer will then send the money directly to your new account. In that way, as long as you don't touch the money, no money will be withheld and no tax bill will be generated.

If you convert to an IRA, where should you invest it? At the beginning, while you're still looking for a job, go for security and easy access, so that you can get the money in a pinch. Consider a no-load, money market mutual fund. (For more information on IRAs, see Chapter 30.)

STEP 7 DON'T LEAVE THE BUILDING WITHOUT A GOOD REFERENCE IN HAND.

A good reference is a very important part of a severance package. It's very hard to get a job without a reference, yet most laid-off workers don't think to ask for one. If you've been laid off, you can often negotiate a good reference from your immediate supervisor. That person may be happy to help you, but have no idea what to say in the reference, so, draft an appropriate letter yourself. Send a copy to your soon-to-be former boss, along with an annotated resume that states your accomplishments and good points. In most cases, he or she will be happy to go along.

Ross's Story

"Losing my job was bad enough, but it's been sixteen years since I looked for a new job, and the prospect is scary," says Ross. "What am I supposed to tell a prospective employer about why I'm currently unemployed? If I say that I was laid off, doesn't that raise a lot of unnecessary questions about me and the quality of my work?"

Finding Another Job After Being Laid Off

Before you seriously start looking for another job, do a little self-assessment. You'll find it easier to ace an interview, or to write a resume, if you know what you're good at and what you love to do. You also need to think about what kind of environment or employer allows you to thrive.

You may not be able to do this on your own. Consider consulting friends, former coworkers, or an employment adviser for help.

How can you increase your chances of finding another job? If you've been pounding the pavement without a job offer in sight, it may be time to reassess your job-hunting strategy. Here are some time-tested suggestions.

- *Don't begin your search until you are ready.* Getting laid off is emotionally and physically draining, so don't start looking for a new job until you have completed the mourning period over the loss of your last one.
- *Hold out for a good fit.* Don't try to force-fit yourself into a job that is not right for you. Holding out for a job that is a good fit is a better strategy in the long run.
- *Learn to speak in sound bites.* If you haven't looked for a job in a while, you may be surprised at some of the changes in interview techniques. These days, a job interview is not much different from a television interview. You have a short amount of time to describe your strengths and convince a potential employer that you are the best candidate. So go through your resume and start thinking about how to express your accomplishments in the form of *sound bites*—concise phrases. You want to state the situation briefly and give a specific action you took, and describe a measurable result— or, even better, give the quantified results. For instance, "Sales in my department had been lagging, so I sent my sales team out on 15 percent more sales calls, and they boosted sales by 23 percent."
- *Make the most of want ads.* The odds of getting a job from a want ad are slim, but if you've been laid off, and are less tapped into your industry's grapevine than you used to be, you may need to rely on ads more than other job-hunters. So here are two ways to increase the chances of getting called in for an interview for a job listed in the want ads:
  - Use the same wording in your cover letter that appeared in the ad—it makes it easier for the person sorting the mail to put you into the "potential" pile.
  - Don't respond too quickly. Wait a few days so your resume won't get lost in the crowd.
- *Dust off your Rolodex and start to network.* Make lists of people you know—even if you don't think they are in a position to hire you. A good job lead could come from anyone who knows you and

is aware that you are in the job market. Plan on coming clean to these people about why you left your last job.

Don't cross the etiquette line when you're networking. It's okay to ask a person you are meeting with to look over your resume and to help you expand your network by suggesting other people for you to talk to, but it is taboo to ask such a person to hire you. Seek advice and counsel on your resume and on how you come across. You also want them for suggestions of other people to call and other places that might be able to use your skills.

- *Don't bad-mouth the boss.* "My first job interview after being laid off was going great until I was asked, 'What didn't you like about your last job?'" says Ross. "My response was polite at first, but, before I knew it, I was on a tirade about how unfairly my former employer treated its workers after the merger. My pulse raced as I spoke, and I began to sweat. Needless to say, I didn't get that job. Thinking back on my rage-filled response, if I were in their shoes I wouldn't have hired me either."

Being laid off is unfair, and anger toward your former employer may be justified. But a job interview is not the place to vent it. Many strong candidates sabotage their search by bad-mouthing their former employer, so resist that urge. If you're not sure that you can control yourself, put off your interviews until the rage has passed and you can present yourself— and your pink slip—in a nondefensive way. Don't dwell on it, and don't apologize for it. Don't lie, either. Stick to the truth as closely as possible.

- *Rehearse your references.* Under the best of circumstances, you never know what your references will say about you. But if you've been laid off, it's vital that you not leave your references' comments to chance. Prepare them for the tough questions a prospective employer might ask. Send your references a resume that you have annotated with answers to potential questions, including why you are not currently employed. Prospective employers try to learn as much as they can about a job candidate before they take the costly plunge and hire anyone. Talk up your strengths, and include examples of things you do especially well. Don't overlook areas where you need to improve your present skills or develop new ones, and be sure to include some specific ways you are working on them.

Stop the Squabbling (or Break the Family Silence) About Money

Whether you come from a family that was rolling in dough or your family could barely make ends meet, home is where you picked up your first money lessons. At a conscious level, or an unconscious one, there's something about major life milestones, such as marriage, birth of your first child, even the aging of your parents, that tend to bring out the money lessons we learned as kids.

So wouldn't it be better to come to terms with your childhood money lessons—what you learned at your parent's knee—than to go on autopilot and perpetuate things that you may have partially picked up as a child, or that you may not have fully understood? By coming to terms with money you can begin to make smart financial decisions based on your own beliefs and income and then can plot a realistic course to reach your goals.

Chapter 10

Make Smart Money Moves at Life's Major Milestones: Marriage, Birth of Children, Divorce, Death of a Spouse, Aging Parents

This chapter takes a close look at the major milestones that are common among adults. For each milestone, I offer some easy to follow steps to protect you and your loved ones, and to stay on track to meet your long-term goals. This reference list will quickly direct you to topics that may be of special interest—now or in the future:

Milestone	*Steps*
Marriage	1–5
Birth of a Baby	6–11
Divorce	12–20
Death of a Spouse	21–26
Aging of Parents	27–33

The Marriage Milestone: Merging Your Money After Saying "I Do" to Your Honey

Lynn's Story

"Tom and I met during our junior year of college. He sat behind me in psych class. We dated a few times during our senior year, but after graduation we went our separate ways. Two years ago, on New Year's Eve Day, we bumped into each other—literally—while skating at the Rockefeller Center ice rink. We started going to lunch together, then dinner.

"We had so much to talk about. We came from big families, and both of our fathers died while we were in junior high. We talked about our hopes and dreams. We wanted the same things in life, all the way down to the number of kids—three. Soon, we stopped dating other people. In March, we got engaged. In June, we got married.

"Tom came into the marriage with no credit cards—in fact, no credit history at all. 'Cash is better,' he would say. Still, I always believed that, in a marriage, 'What's mine is yours and what's yours is mine,' right? So I added his name to my credit card accounts and got him his own cards, just in case he needed money in a pinch.

"The pinch came right after we bought a little fixer-upper home. Those small repairs added up to some big money, and Tom didn't like to scrimp. When picking out faucets, tile, and whatever, I would have bought decent quality, but not the best. Tom insisted on buying the top of the line, for everything, and he would sometimes use the credit cards to pay for materials. Of course we both wrote checks against our joint checking account.

"Then, one day, our casual money system nearly cost me my job. I had taken a new client to lunch, and when I tried to pay with my credit cards, the first card was rejected. And it gets worse. The second card I tried to use got cut up by the waiter, wielding scissors, right in front of my client. I was mortified. I asked to call the credit card company. They informed me that my card was being rejected because they hadn't received a payment in almost three months. When my boss heard about it, he was furious.

"I thought Tom had been paying the bills. He thought I had. So some bills, it turned out, never did get paid. Substantial late fees were regularly being added to our credit card and utility bills. Finance charges were mushrooming, and since neither of us was balancing our checkbook, we also got hit with many bounced-check fees. We never really talked about finances or budgeting before we got married. Looking back, I think we should have."

Are you thinking about getting married? If so, have you discussed money with your beloved? "No," you say, "it's not romantic to talk about credit card debt or prenuptial agreements." Well, how romantic is it to squabble over money after you're married? Besides, isn't it better to have these discussions before you've started amassing joint property?

Picking out china, silver, and crystal patterns may seem like more fun than opening a joint checking account, but making some prewedding financial plans can do more for marital bliss than receiving all the presents on your bridal registry list. Here are some steps you and your fiancé should take before you walk down the aisle.

STEP 1 CHOOSE A DESIGNATED "MONEY PERSON."

Both of you should be actively involved in your finances, but, to avoid confusion and make sure your bills are paid on time, it's a good idea to designate one of you as the family money person. Which of you should do it? Here are some questions to consider: Does one of you like adding up numbers while the other can't be bothered saving ATM receipts? Does one of you do a better job at saving while the other excels at spending? Does one of you have more experience successfully managing your money?

Whoever is more motivated has a better chance of putting in the effort needed to create a solid base for your family finances. But when one of you agrees to pay the bills, keep track of ATM receipts, and balance the checkbook, the other isn't off the hook. Ideally, the two of you should discuss your finances every month—or more often, if you are trying to reach a specific financial goal.

While choosing someone to keep the family books is no guarantee of financial success, it is a vital first step. That way you can avoid later finger pointing where one spouse says, "I thought you were balancing the checkbook!" and the other angrily replies, "No, I thought *you* were." Many couples who later ended up in financial trouble have told me that in hindsight, failing to choose one or the other to manage their day-to-day money matters was a contributing factor in their subsequent breakup.

Tip: To keep track of receipts for ATM transactions and purchases, you don't need an elaborate system. Something as simple and inexpensive as a shoebox will do. Just be sure to add all receipts, checks, and other financial records to your shoebox (or file folders, or whatever you choose), and, if needed, don't forget to pencil in some explanatory notes while you can still remember what the receipts were for.

Next, decide which of you will do the initial legwork before you make big purchases such as major appliances, mutual funds, and retirement savings plans. The best choice for this job may *not* be the designated money person who does the day-to-day bill paying and checkbook balancing. After one of you has done the initial research (gathering product specs and pricing information on any big purchases you're considering), you should discuss the options and make a joint buying decision that you can agree on.

Should you pool your money? Your parents probably had just one joint checking account that each of them wrote checks on. For many working couples these days, that arrangement is too inflexible. Still, a joint checking account can be a good place to pool money you will need to pay for a mortgage, utility bills, and other family obligations. Couples often tell me that sharing this joint account helped them cement their marital bond.

How much should each of you contribute to your joint kitty? If one of you is earning considerably more than the other or if one is a stay-at-home spouse, a "fifty–fifty" arrangement probably won't do. You have to come up with percentages that seem right to both of you. For some couples, one partner is earning one-third of the other's income. The lower earner would then contribute one-third of the amount the other partner chips in. The total joint contribution should at least cover the monthly bills, or ideally, a bit more.

Reality check: Many women need the peace of mind that a little mad money can bring. Divorce, medical emergencies, and sudden death on roads or in airplanes are facts of life today, and women (and men, but less often) need to be able to tap some funds quickly. Supplementing a joint account with separate "his" and "hers" bank accounts can be a good idea after marriage, especially if one partner has significantly more assets or debts, or has children from a previous marriage.

Should you draw up a prenuptial agreement? A prenuptial agreement states how property will be divided if a married couple eventually gets divorced. Many family counselors describe it as an extra strain on an impending marriage because the partners start focusing on their *individual* rather than their joint financial interests.

Tip: If a family business is involved, if there are kids from a previous marriage, or if there are big differences in the partners' individual financial resources, a "prenup" may be worth discussing. Details of the agreement should be agreed on by both parties—and their lawyers—well before the wedding day. All assets must be disclosed before the prenup is set. Failure to do any of these could give a judge grounds to throw out the prenup later.

STEP 2 DISCUSS YOUR DEBTS.

Ideally, you'd like to pay off your debts (credit card, car payments, student loans) before the wedding. If that's not possible, tell your betrothed about the amount of your debts. After you're married, it's a good idea for each spouse to keep one credit card in his or her own name, to maintain individual credit ratings. As with separate bank accounts, you never know when an individual credit card—and an individual credit rating—will be needed in a hurry.

STEP 3 AMASS AN EMERGENCY FUND OF THREE TO SIX MONTHS' LIVING EXPENSES.

As newlyweds, you want to begin stashing some cash together, to establish your financial security as a couple. A joint savings account or a money market account can be a good place to start accumulating your nest egg. These types of accounts won't earn great returns on your money, but your nest egg will be safe. To avoid being tempted to use this money for something else, arrange for an automatic transfer of funds, weekly or monthly, from your joint checking account into this account.

STEP 4 COORDINATE YOUR INSURANCE COVERAGE.

Redundant insurance coverage can be a big waste of money. You can no longer count on your spouse's insurer to pick up the tab for medical expenses not paid by your own policy. Instead, it's becoming standard practice for a spouse's plan to compute what it would have paid for the same claim, and only reimburse a claimant if there's a difference. You could end up paying for excess insurance that you'll never be able to collect on.

You typically have thirty days from your wedding day to add a new spouse to your policy. Do you anticipate having a baby soon? Before you drop either policy, see whose coverage offers better pregnancy and well-baby care. (See Steps 6–11 for more tips.)

- *Eliminate redundant health coverage.* If each of you has health insurance through your respective employers, decide whether each of you should maintain "individual" coverage or convert to "family" coverage under the plan that offers better benefits.
- *Determine whether you need life insurance.* Unless you have dependents, a big mortgage, or other financial obligations requiring two paychecks, you may not need life insurance yet.
- *Load up on disability insurance.* You'll want to receive two-thirds of your current income as a benefit from this policy. If your employer pays for your coverage, any benefits you receive will be taxable. If employer-offered coverage falls short, supplement it with a policy you buy yourself. If you pay the premiums, you won't owe

taxes on any disability benefits you collect. To keep premiums down, increase the waiting period before benefits begin.

 STEP 5 START SAVING FOR LONG-TERM GOALS.

Whether you're trying to save for your first house, your kids' college education, or a comfortable retirement, it's never too soon to start. If your employers offer a 401(k) plan, sign up. Make the maximum contribution, especially if your employer matches employee contributions in part or in full. [See Chapter 30 for more information on 401(k) plans.]

Don't forget to update records, and that includes changing beneficiaries. For instance, you may want to name your new spouse as the beneficiary of your life insurance and retirement accounts. (See Chapter 12.)

The Birth-of-a-Baby Milestone: Giving Birth to a Bundle of Joy Plus Some Great Tax Breaks!

Bill and Shelly's Story

After Bill and Shelly Wall gave birth to their first child, Ben, they decided to keep their out-of-pocket medical costs down by selecting a pediatrician who was on Bill's health insurance plan's "Preferred Providers" list. They were shocked when the insurer refused to pay for most of Ben's visits to the doctor during his first year of life. "They classified the immunization shots and all but one doctor's visit, when Ben had an ear infection, as 'well-baby care' and told me it wasn't covered by the plan," says Shelly. "We pay $263 a month in premiums and rarely submit any claims, so it's not fair that they can just refuse to pay for our baby's medical care. We didn't budget for this."

The arrival of a new baby doesn't have to bust your budget. If you are about to become a parent, or recently became one, take the following steps to trim expenses and ensure that your family's safety net isn't riddled with holes.

 STEP 6 MAKE THE MOST OF YOUR COMPANY BENEFITS.

Are you taking full advantage of the benefits your employer offers? Did you know that many benefits are not taxed, so by signing up for them you can get the equivalent of a 30 to 40 percent pay increase? Here are the key areas to look at.

- *Health care plan.* Traditional health insurance plans, also called indemnity plans, typically pay 80 percent of covered charges (after you meet a yearly deductible, often $150), and you pay the remaining 20 percent. But many of these policies do not pay for well-baby care, such as checkups and routine shots. That's why some new parents switch from a fee-for-service plan to a health maintenance organization (HMO) that routinely covers most baby care during the first few years of life. (See Chapter 16 on health care.) Ask your company's benefits coordinator to explain your options. Carefully analyze your medical bills for the past two years, and estimate the services you might need in the next twelve months. Then compare the projected out-of-pocket costs (including premiums, deductibles, and copayments), under the old plan and under the new one, for each family member.

- *Flexible spending accounts.* If your employer offers this benefit, you can use pretax dollars to pay for a variety of services, such as out-of-pocket health care costs (deductibles and copayments), prescription glasses, and child care. The annual maximum benefit is typically $5,000. Estimate your usage carefully, though, because you will forfeit to your employer any money left in your account at the end of the year. Check your expenses for the past year, and project a likely estimate for next year.

- *Life insurance.* The first time most people need life insurance is when they become parents. If a working parent died, benefits from a life insurance policy could make up for that parent's lost income. A stay-at-home parent may also need life insurance. If she or he died, the insurance proceeds could be used to pay someone for taking care of the children. If your health is less than perfect, it's all the more important that you check into employer-provided life insurance. The coverage will likely cost less than in the open market, if you could buy it there at all.

- *Disability insurance.* During most of your working years, you are more likely to become disabled than to die. A good disability policy could make up for lost income if an illness or injury prevents you from working. The best way to get this coverage is through your employer; you'll likely be offered better coverage, at a lower price than you could get on the open market.

- *Family and medical leave.* If your employer has fifty or more employees, you may be eligible to take time off—with or without pay—to care for your new baby or an ill child (among other reasons).

- *Adoption assistance.* Many employers will subsidize legal and other costs associated with adopting a child.

STEP 7 NEGOTIATE HOSPITAL COSTS.

There's an oversupply of hospital rooms in many parts of the country, so you may be able to negotiate some extras. A few months before your due date, ask your health insurance administrator to give you a list of hospitals you are permitted to use. Then call and tell the patient relations department that you are shopping for a place to deliver your child and would like to visit the facility. Here are some extras to ask for:

- A free upgrade from a semiprivate room to a private room.
- A free second night after you and your insurer pay for the first night. This is easiest to get on weekends, when occupancy rates are typically low.
- An unadvertised discount. For instance, if you bring your own pillow, some hospitals will take $5 off your bill.

STEP 8 REVISE YOUR TAX PLAN.

The federal government gives parents a few good tax breaks, but to take advantage of them your child needs a Social Security number. Ask the hospital to give you a Social Security number application form before you leave.

You're entitled to a tax exemption, worth a little over $2,500 a year, for each dependent child, including a new baby. Instead of waiting for a big tax refund (why give the government an interest-free loan?), adjust your tax withholding down by filing a new W-4 form. Your company's personnel office can supply the form.

If you earn less than $25,000 a year, you also may be entitled to an Earned Income Credit. You can even get your hands on the money (paid into your paycheck) before you file your taxes. To sign up for this advance earned income credit, contact your personnel office.

STEP 9 UPDATE YOUR WILL.

Once your child arrives, you need a will, if for no other reason than to designate a guardian for your child in case you and your spouse were to die. Hire an attorney who specializes in estate planning to write the will. I don't recommend using fill-in-the-blank will forms. If you make a mistake, it may not be discovered until it's too late to correct it.

Don't store your original will in a safe deposit box. (Some states still seal the boxes when one of the owners dies.) Instead, let your attorney hold the original. Keep a copy at home, and tell your family where the original can be found.

STEP 10 START A COLLEGE FUND WITH BABY GIFTS.

The sooner you start saving for your new child's college education, the better. Put away as much as you can afford each month from your pay. Baby gifts are also a great way to start funding a college kitty.

If all you can afford is $4,000 a year, consider a Roth IRA ($2,000 each for you and your spouse). You will have already paid tax on your IRA contribution, so the earnings won't be taxed. Regardless of your age when your child starts college, you can withdraw from the Roth IRA, tax-free and penalty-free, all the money you put away over the years. By your child's eighteenth birthday, you and your spouse will have put away $72,000, if you've regularly made the maximum contribution.

Be aware of the down side of putting any money in your child's name. When he or she reaches adulthood (18 or 21, depending on the state) your child can spend the money on anything he or she chooses—and you will have no say. A college education, or any suggestion you have, may not be his or her choice.

STEP 11 GUARD YOUR BABY'S PRIVACY.

New parents often get coupons for discounts on everything from diaper services to baby portraits or baby food. How do businesses find new parents? Many hospitals, doctors, diaper services, and other sources sell names and addresses of newborns. Some defend this practice by saying, "I've never heard of anyone complain about getting free merchandise."

But security experts and privacy advocates worry that credit bureaus, marketing organizations, and possibly pedophiles are getting access to these lists. Before your child is born, talk to your doctor, hospital, diaper service, and anyone else who has your child's personal information. Tell them that you are concerned about invasions of privacy, and ask them to exclude your name from the lists they sell or trade.

The Divorce Milestone: Dissolving Your Marriage Without Getting Taken to the Cleaners

Becky's Story

"When Scott told me that he wanted a divorce, at first I was sad and angry. But then fear overwhelmed me. After thirteen years of marriage, I didn't know how my three kids and I would get through it emotionally. And I didn't know how we would make ends meet.

"Finding a way to let my kids continue living in the only house they ever knew became my number-one priority. There was no way I could cover the monthly mortgage payments with only my salary. Scott just wanted to get the settlement over quickly so he could marry his girlfriend.

"He made me an offer. He would trade me his share of the house if I would give up my future rights to his pension at work (which he said was worth $89,000). It sounded fair to me. My lawyer said, 'Don't take it!' But I did take it because this would mean my kids and I could keep the house—or so I thought.

"The honeymoon with the house quickly ended. First, the furnace passed away on an 18-degree day. Next, the roof started leaking. Then the refrigerator stopped working. The capper was when the town jacked up our real estate taxes by 13 percent. I asked my ex-husband for help, but he said he was cash-strapped after buying a new house. My only choice was to sell the house, and do it quickly.

"Finding a buyer wasn't easy. It was the middle of a brutal winter, and my real estate agent insisted I disclose all the property's defects. Finally, a buyer offered 18 percent less than I was asking (my asking price was already 8 percent below its appraised value). I had no choice but to take it. After paying off the mortgage and the real estate agent's commission, I netted $3,000.

"My kids and I now live in a two-bedroom apartment. My eldest son was allowed to continue attending his high school, but my two younger kids had to change schools. I now work two jobs to make ends meet. And, worst of all, since I gave up my rights to my ex-husband's pension, I don't know how I ever will be able to afford to retire. My lawyer was right that keeping the family home shouldn't have been a priority in settling the divorce."

Reality check: Fewer than one in four divorced women now are awarded spousal support. You need to have realistic expectations about how much you and your kids will have to live on.

If you are suddenly faced with a divorce, what's the best way to marshall your resources. Here are the steps you need to take to protect yourself, your kids, and your financial security.

STEP 12 CONSULT A TEAM OF EXPERTS.

It's vital that you put together a good team of specialists who can look out for your legal, emotional, and financial future. This means hiring not only a good lawyer who specializes in divorce, but also a well-credentialed counselor or therapist for you and your kids, and a savvy financial planner and/or tax attorney. It also means that if you think your departing spouse may be trying to hide assets, you should also consider hiring an investigative accountant.

Don't waste emotional energy haggling over custody of worthless things you amassed while you were married. Instead, focus on the important, big-ticket items: house, car, pensions, child support, and whatever will affect the quality of your life and your kids' lives now and in the future.

STEP 13 FIND THE MONEY.

As soon as you get an inkling that a divorce might be a possibility, start amassing financial documents and itemizing assets. It's vital that you find *all* the marital assets.

Gather the checkbook ledger and financial statements from the bank, the stockbroker, the mutual fund company, and the retirement savings plans. Make copies of your federal and state tax returns and supporting documentation for the past five years. Then start tallying your debts: mortgage, credit cards, student loans, business loans, personal loans. A financial planner or accountant can help you with this fact-gathering, and the fee for this service is money well spent.

STEP 14 ARRANGE TO CONTINUE YOUR HEALTH CARE COVERAGE.

Keeping health insurance after a divorce has become an increasingly high priority. If your spouse works for a company that has at least twenty employees, a federal law known as COBRA is designed to let a family in your situation keep the spouse's group coverage for up to three years. You have sixty days following a divorce or legal separation to notify your spouse's benefits coordinator that you want to stay on your spouse's plan.

STEP 15   UNDERSTAND THE TRUE COSTS OF PROPERTY BEFORE YOU AGREE TO KEEP IT.

As Becky discovered, although you may wish to keep the house for emotional reasons, there may be stronger reasons to sell it as part of the divorce settlement, and move on. Whether you choose to keep it or sell it, have it appraised by a certified appraiser. Also consider having a thorough home inspection done, so that you have a realistic idea of any costly repairs you might soon be facing.

When you're deciding whether to keep the house, it's important to draw up a realistic budget. List *all* costs to maintain it: insurance, taxes, repairs, and refinancing costs (if you will put your name on the mortgage and have your former spouse's name taken off). Then ask yourself, "Will I have enough money coming in to cover these costs—as well as unexpected costs that could crop up?"

STEP 16   KNOW THE TRUE VALUE OF ASSETS BEFORE YOU AGREE TO GIVE THEM UP.

Get realistic, professional appraisals of all other property. As Becky later discovered, Scott hadn't been forthright about the value of his pension. He showed her the statement from his employer, but it was a very rough estimate as those typically are and should not have been used to make an irrevocable financial decision.

What you need to do is hire someone who can value all of your investments, including pension plans, collectibles, and other assets. Ask how much tax or other penalties you would owe if you sold certain assets. Did you know that 401(k) and IRA plans are treated differently if they are cashed in early? You would pay a 10 percent penalty on an IRA, and a 20 percent penalty for cashing in a 401(k) plan early. Don't assume anything.

If you think you might be entitled to a portion of your spouse's pension plan, profit-sharing plan, or 401(k) or 403(b) retirement savings plan, look into getting a Qualified Domestic Relations Order (QDRO). It would list you as a beneficiary of your spouse's plan even after your divorce. The QDRO itemizes the amount of your spouse's plans that you would be entitled to after the divorce or if your spouse were to die. For the QDRO to have enforcement teeth, the divorce court and your spouse's pension-plan administrators must approve it.

Sherry's Story

Sherry Miller discovered during her divorce proceedings that the "valuable" stamps her husband, Jeff, had supposedly been buying with their savings, were, in fact, almost worthless. So their community assets were a tenth of what he had led her to believe.

But Jeff had another secret. The stamps he showed Sherry were almost worthless because he had been using only a small fraction of their savings to buy those stamps. What had he done with the rest of the money? He had been sending cash to an offshore bank in the Cayman Islands. It was hard for Sherry to trace the cash deposits and virtually impossible for her to retrieve them. "I guess I should have had Jeff's stamp collection appraised sooner," says Sherry. "Then I might have been alerted to our money being siphoned off somewhere, but I took my wedding vows seriously, and trusting each other was supposed to be the basis of our marriage."

STEP 17 GUARD AGAINST SURPRISES.

When you know that a divorce is imminent, take precautions so that your spouse can't sell assets or run up huge debts without your knowledge and approval. Close joint credit card accounts and any other joint credit lines, such as a home equity line. Tell your bank not to allow withdrawals from a joint account without both of your signatures. Notify your stockbroker not to make any trades on your account without your written authorization. Follow up these calls with letters confirming these instructions in writing to your bank and broker.

STEP 18 REASSESS YOUR INVESTMENT PORTFOLIO.

After your divorce, what will your new tax rate be? Will your current investments still be worth owning, given your new situation? For instance, municipal bonds may have yielded a great return when you were in a high tax bracket. But if your tax bracket has dropped, it might make more sense to sell these bonds and invest the proceeds where they would yield a better after-tax return.

If you and your spouse own a business together, hire a business appraiser to determine the real current and projected value of the business. Then decide whether you want your ex-spouse to buy you out, and if so, at what price, or whether you should buy out your spouse's share of the business. You'll need the appraisal to determine a purchase price or a selling price. If your spouse has a business, that you are not involved in, get that appraised as well, so you'll know the value of *all* marital assets.

STEP 19 DISSOLVE DEBTS WISELY.

If you and your spouse had joint credit cards during your marriage, close those accounts and get written verification from the card issuers that your former spouse has paid off all debts that formerly included your name. Otherwise, the creditors can come after you—even if the divorce settlement states that your ex-spouse (and not you) is responsible for paying them.

If you have any doubt that your former spouse will pay off the debt on time, consider assuming the debt as part of your settlement and paying it off yourself. *Note:* Insist on getting, in the divorce settlement, additional assets to cover the cost of paying off your ex-spouse's debt.

STEP 20 INSURE YOUR FAMILY'S FUTURE.

Protect your future spousal support and your kids' child support payments by taking out a life insurance policy on your ex-spouse. If something should happen to him or her, you and your kids won't be left high and dry.

Reassess your own insurance needs. If you don't already have them, consider taking out a good term life insurance policy and a disability insurance policy, to protect your kids and your earnings.

Following your divorce, don't forget to remove your ex-spouse's name as a beneficiary on your life insurance and your pension or retirement savings accounts. Most people don't want their ex-spouse to benefit from their assets, so be sure to draw up a new will.

The Death-of-a-Spouse Milestone:
Gaining Your Own Financial Identity
While Coping with a Major Loss

The biggest mistake many married women make is failing to understand their financial situation—what assets they own or where important documents are kept.

The biggest mistake recent widows and widowers make is doing things hastily—selling their home, moving to another town, immediately investing the proceeds of their spouse's life insurance policy, and buying new investments that they don't understand from strangers who call after reading the spouse's death notice in a newspaper.

Esther's Story

"My telephone never stopped ringing from the day my husband's obituary appeared in the local newspaper," recalls Esther Peterman. "Stockbrokers, insurance agents, and even burglar alarm companies all said they could help me in my time of need, if I would only buy what they had to sell. All of them prodded me to make a quick decision.

"The real estate agents all wanted to quickly sell my house and help me find a more suitable place to live 'now that you are on your own.' Some even had the audacity to tell me, 'Esther, until you make some decisions on your own, you will never be able to take back control of your life.' These people were strangers to me, and I was offended by their phony familiarity and psycho-babble. They were calling day and night; finally, I just let the answering machine pick up their calls. I never called any of them back.

"Then I started getting requests for loans from some long-lost relatives of my late husband. I never heard of half of them and don't even know if they were really related to my husband."

As many recent widows and widowers will tell you, dealing with the onslaught of advice and requests for money can be very taxing to anyone who is in mourning and is emotionally fragile. It's easy to see how someone can get strong-armed into making some quick decisions that are not in his or her best interest.

Does making some decisions—any decisions—on your own seem like a way to take back control of your life? Resist the temptation or you'll regret it—maybe not today or tomorrow, but soon and perhaps for the rest of your life. The bigger the decision (selling your home; moving in with, or near, your family; or making changes in your investments), the more you will regret it later. Any irrevocable change—financial or otherwise—should be put off for at least a year (if possible). Here are the steps to take soon if your spouse dies.

STEP 21 TRACK DOWN IMPORTANT PAPERS.

There are some important papers you need to get your hands on. The first thing you want to find is your spouse's original, executed will. Your spouse's lawyer may be holding the original. Then look for a letter of instructions, which should tell you where other assets can be found, plus any instructions about the funeral or other final wishes.

Next, head to the bank to take an inventory of the contents of your spouse's (or your joint) safe deposit box. Gather any other financial documents that you might need: the deed for your house; bank statements and checkbooks; CDs, stock certificates, or stock options. Don't throw out any papers that you might possibly need later.

STEP 22 TAKE A FINANCIAL INVENTORY.

Tally your income and expenses (review Chapter 2 for tips on doing this) to make sure your income will at least cover all your costs, including income and estate taxes.

If you are no longer working, avoid buying investments, such as a deferred annuity that will pay a fixed sum for the rest of your life. It may sound like a good investment, but it could be a bad one. If you live for several more decades, its yield probably will not keep pace with inflation, let alone taxes.

STEP 23 BEGIN FILING FOR BENEFITS.

After you've tracked down your deceased spouse's life insurance policies—individual and group policies from employers, unions, and/or professional associations—start filing claims with the insurer(s) right away. Also file claims for other benefits you are entitled to, such as Social Security, retirement, and, if applicable, accidental death insurance. Ask the funeral director to supply two or three dozen certified copies of your spouse's death certificate. You will need them when you file for Social Security benefits, make a life insurance claim, or transfer assets into your name.

STEP 24 CONSOLIDATE YOUR CREDIT.

Change any joint credit cards so that they carry only your name. It's vital that you maintain (or establish) a good credit rating, so don't fall behind in paying your bills. During your first few months without your spouse, consider asking a relative or friend for help in getting organized—especially, compiling your bills and making sure that they are paid on time. Do NOT let anyone else write or sign your checks. Only *you* should do that!

STEP 25 ARRANGE TO CONTINUE HEALTH CARE COVERAGE.

If you were on your spouse's health plan, make arrangements to continue your coverage. Contact your spouse's health insurance carrier within sixty days, to transfer your coverage to your name so you can keep the insurance. Under the federal COBRA law, you may be able to keep the group coverage, although you will have to pay the premiums (the amount your spouse previously paid, plus the amount your spouse's employer paid, plus a small administrative fee). If COBRA does not apply, ask your spouse's insurer to convert your spouse's group coverage to an individual policy in your name. (It should cost you less than your "family" policy that covered you and your spouse.)

STEP 26 FORTIFY YOUR SAFETY NET.

Review your own estate plans. Update your will, any trusts you may have established, and your powers of attorney (both durable and medical). Replace your spouse's name with the name of someone else you trust. (See Chapter 11.)

Aging-of-Parents Milestone: Surviving the Demands of Your Parents and Your Kids

It's been dubbed the "sandwich generation." With people living longer, you could end up spending more time caring for aging parents than you spend raising your children.

Sara's Story

At 6:25 one Thursday morning, Sara Thomas was awakened by a phone call. An emergency room nurse was telling her that her mother had been admitted with a broken leg. "Mom tripped on the hallway carpet the night before, but fortunately she was able to reach the phone to call 911 for help," says Sara. "Since Dad passed away two years ago, Mom has been living alone in the house I grew up in. I always worried about something happening to her while she was alone, but she would always assure me that she could take care of herself."

After dropping her kids off at school, Sara drove the 97 miles to her hometown. "On the way, I began crying and worried, 'How could I care for her from such a distance?'" she recalls. "I was relieved when I entered her hospital room. She looked drowsy and a bit bruised, but was in remarkably good spirits." The doctor said that she would be in traction for five weeks and then could go home, but she would need round-the-clock help for at least six more weeks until her cast came off.

The sandwich generation refers to Baby Boomers and Generation X'ers, who are caring for their aging parents while simultaneously raising their own children. Whether it's as a result of an accident or a sudden illness, with little notice you could be notified to come to the aid of your parents, financially or medically.

If you're taking care of your aging parents at the same time you are struggling to raise your children and keep your marriage vital, you're doing a juggling act that can be financially and emotionally draining. Even the most organized Baby Boomer or Generation X'er can become tired and overwhelmed by these multiple responsibilities.

You may also be plagued by doubts: Are you making the best choices for your parents? If you wait until your parents are ill or in financial trouble, it may be too late to discover and/or carry out their wishes. Many adults get their first indications that their parents may be headed for trouble when they:

- Find a stack of unpaid bills.
- Uncover "turn off" notices from utility companies.
- Notice that their parents look disheveled when they previously took pride in their appearance, or their parents' home has been neglected for basic cleaning and upkeep.

It's important to start discussing the future with your parents as soon as possible—before illness or other problems set in, and while there's still time to follow your parents' wishes. These steps will help you to know that your parents are well cared for.

STEP 27 MAKE SURE BILLS ARE PAID.

If you've been notified that one or more utilities are about to be turned off because bills haven't been paid, you'll need to step in. If your parents haven't already done so, ask each of them to draw up a durable power of attorney. If they become unable to pay bills or make financial decisions, you (or another trustworthy person named in the document) can then take care of your parents' finances. Otherwise, if your parent is unable to take care of his or her bills due to illness or mental impairment, you will have to go to court to get the legal authority to manage your parent's finances. This court proceeding is costly, time-consuming, and very public. Make sure that a *durable* power of attorney is drawn up. Any other kind of power of attorney would become invalid if your parent became seriously ill or mentally impaired—just when you need it most.

STEP 28 LOCATE IMPORTANT DOCUMENTS.

If you suspect that, at some future time, you will help your parents out, it's a good idea to know their financial situation—their assets, sources of income, and locations of life, health, and long-term care insurance policies. Where are their financial documents (bank accounts, checkbooks, wills, and trusts) kept? If your parents won't open up to you about this information, consider asking their clergyman, attorney, or physician; a family friend; or another relative, to intervene or at least to turn the conversation to this topic. If your parents don't have wills, insist that each parent draw up a will with the assistance of an attorney who specializes in estate planning. (See Chapter 11 for details on choosing an attorney.)

STEP 29 DISCUSS MEDICAL WISHES.

Many people find it hard to broach the subject, but you need to ask how much medical care your parents do or do not want, and make sure they have enough medical coverage to pay for any needed treatment. Specifically:

- Do your parents have a comprehensive health care plan—traditional health insurance or an HMO? If they are eligible for Medicare, supplement it with a comprehensive Medigap policy, which you buy through an insurer. Contact the AARP at www.aarp.org, for help in assessing the many types of Medigap policies available.
- Consider buying a long-term care insurance policy, if your parent doesn't already own one. Nursing home care can cost from $30,000 to $100,000 per year. If your parent has assets that he or she wants to leave to you, look into this policy. There are new tax breaks for some long-term policies, so take tax deductibility into consideration when you're comparison-shopping. (See Chapter 15 for more information on buying a long-term care policy.)

- Encourage each parent to draw up a health care proxy (also called a medical proxy) naming you (or some other responsible person) to make medical decisions for your parent if he or she becomes unable to do so. Ask how much (if any) artificial life support your parent would want. Then get your parent's wishes in writing by drafting a living will. (See Chapter 12 for more on this topic.)

STEP 30 ENLIST A NEIGHBOR FOR HELP.

If you live in a distant town, you'll need to be creative. Enlist one of your parents' neighbors to visit or phone them daily to make sure they are okay. Arrange to have someone do chores that your parents can no longer safely do, such as shoveling snow or mowing the lawn. Many seniors aren't able to shop for food or cook as much as they used to. Is there a neighbor or a community organization that could provide a meal daily or a few times a week?

STEP 31 DETERMINE WHETHER ADDITIONAL ASSISTANCE IS NEEDED.

If your parents need more help, you may have to hire a part-time in-home caregiver. In-home care can be costly; compare it with an assisted-living arrangement—a seniors' residence that offers some basic medical assistance. If those arrangements are not enough, it may be time to consider bringing your parents to your home to live, or applying to a nursing home.

Don't rush your parents into life-altering changes. Let them have some time to think about alternate situations and to talk with friends and other seniors that are coping with similar issues of aging.

STEP 32 CONDUCT A SAFETY CHECK OF YOUR PARENTS' HOME.

Do a walk-through at your parents' home so you can find and eliminate tripping hazards (loose stairs, throw rugs), insufficient lighting, and electrical hazards (frayed electrical wires, overloaded electrical outlets). Consider hiring someone to add safety features in the bathroom, such as a sturdy bar affixed to the wall behind the tub to make it easier to get in and out of the tub, and no-skid treads in the bathtub or on the shower floor.

STEP 33 MAKE THE MOST OF YOUR OWN EMPLOYEE BENEFITS.

If you have a flexible spending account at work, you may be able to pay for your parent's eldercare with pretax dollars. And if your employer has fifty or more employees, you may be eligible to take time off to care for your ill or disabled parent by utilizing the same law (Family and Medical Leave Act) that lets new parents care for a new baby or an ill child.

Tip: If you provide all or some of your parent's financial support, you may be entitled to a dependency exemption on your tax return. Ask your tax adviser for details.

Chapter 11

Raise a Money Savvy, Self-Reliant Child

How you handle money, and even how you feel about money, sends a strong, nonverbal message to your children. Yet, *money is the topic many parents say they are least comfortable discussing with their kids*. "I'd rather talk to my kids about almost anything else, including drugs or sex," admits Paul, the father of three. "And believe me, I don't feel comfortable talking to them about those topics either, but money really baffles me."

So how old should your kids be when you start discussing money, and what should you say? And what do your kids need to know about money so that they can become financially independent and won't be returning to your doorstep again in their 20s, 30s, or 40s, continually looking for a handout from you?

Susan's Story

"When I was five years old, my parents gave me a piggybank and four quarters to put in it. The bank was shaped like a cash register and as I put the coins in, it rang up like a sale. It even made a *'ca-ching'* noise like the real thing. I loved that piggybank. Every time I got any money, I would run to my piggybank and push the coins through the slot. It was amazing. The bank somehow kept a running total, and one day I reached the magic number—$10. Lights flashed and a jingle played. I was so excited. I ran to show my parents.

"My mom said, 'Congratulations.' Then my dad took the bank from me and I never saw it again. I didn't get to spend one cent of my money, and I still feel cheated. What kind of money lesson was this? Save and save, and then you get nothing. To this day, I have trouble delaying gratification—putting off a purchase. I think that maybe the money won't be there when I need it. When I have kids, I'm doing it differently. I'll let them spend some of their money."

Many parents readily admit they don't know what to tell their children about day-to-day money management, investing, or credit cards. Some parents fear that their kids will find out that they're not handling their own finances well (two-thirds of adult credit cardholders don't pay off their credit balances each month). Others worry about saying the wrong thing, so they choose silence instead.

If you think schools are picking up the slack, think again. Like driver's education and other vital topics that are sadly called "electives," classes on personal finance are being taught in relatively few schools. If you want your children to learn about money, you are going to have to teach them yourself.

Andrew's Story

"My father worked for an aeropsace company while I was growing up. In some years, business was good and we lived very well. But other years we could barely make ends meet, but instead of tightening our belts, my dad would go on a spending spree. 'Boys, you must never let anyone smell failure on you,' he would tell my little brother, Steve, and me. 'If you want to be successful in life, you must always give the appearance of success.'

"Here's how he practiced what he preached: If he missed his sales quota, he'd buy a brand new Cadillac for himself and expensive jewelry or another fur coat for my mother. To continue this charade, when his boss or coworkers would come to dinner, they'd be wined and dined on prime rib and champagne. My brother and I were fed much more cheaply; hamburger helper (not the brand name one, but the cheaper store version) and macaroni and cheese.

"To help make ends meet I got a newspaper route and would do yard work for neighbors. My brother would walk the neighbors' dogs. Then early on Monday mornings my father would wake us up at 5:30 A.M. and take us to a country club in another town. Our job was to retrieve lost golf balls, even those that had landed in the lake, from whatever golf course we were trespassing on that day. When we got home, our dad instructed us to 'scrub the golf balls with soap and water until they sparkled.' The following weekend my dad would drive us to another country club so that we could sell the cleaned golf balls back to the golf pro at that club."

Whether you say anything to your children or not, you can bet that your kids pick up money habits from you, starting at a very early age. So it's important to be honest with them about your financial situation. Your children don't need to know your net worth or how much your earn, but if you're going through a rough financial patch, you need to acknowledge it.

If you might be laid off, for instance, tell your kids about some of the money decisions you may be facing. They are going to sense that *something* is wrong, and they are likely to imagine a situation that is far worse than what's really happening. Not knowing the real problem can make kids sad and very insecure. At a minimum, their schoolwork will be affected. Later in life, they may develop financial problems themselves.

So use your money problems as a teachable moment. Your kids' response and generosity may even surprise you. They may offer to chip in some of their savings to help you out, or at least to forgo some expensive toy or vacation they were expecting. It's important to keep the lines of communication open so that if your child is having a financial problem now, or develops one in the future (see Chapter 32 about teens and credit), he or she knows that you care and want to help.

What should you be telling—and showing—your children about money? And when should you start? Interwoven with the recommended steps in this chapter are some of the questions I am asked most frequently about kids and money—and my answers which are based on strategies that have worked for many families.

Step 1   PLAY OFF YOUR CHILD'S INNATE CURIOSITY.

Children become fascinated by money at an early age—typically, by the age of three, if they have an older sibling. But little kids don't understand delayed gratification. To get your child into the habit of saving, allow periodic raids on the savings, and modest spending of *some* of the money.

You can use your child's curiosity to teach life lessons about money—what he or she will need to know to become an independent, self-reliant adult. Here are some concerns voiced by parents.

Q: How can I start teaching my three-year old about money?

A: You can start teaching a preschooler the value of a dollar when you're shopping at the supermarket. In the produce aisle, point out what to look for when selecting fruits and vegetables, and how to weigh them. In the cereal or cookie aisle, teach how to use the unit-price tags on the front of the shelf to comparison-shop. At that age, they obviously can't do the math, but they can start learning what to work for.

Let your youngster make a few choices independently—for instance, picking out a couple of apples or pears from the display. If the selected fruit is not up to your standards, don't criticize. Instead, show what to look for among the other choices (stems intact, no visible holes, shiny skin). Keep the task manageable for your child's age. Offer a choice between two options—say, the macaroni box in your right hand or the corkscrew pasta box in your left hand. Choosing between two options will make your child feel grown up. Asking for a choice of a box of pasta from an aisle-long display is likely to make your child feel overwhelmed by too many choices.

Your paying for groceries with a credit card can be very confusing to a young child. Because no money was handed over, there may be a mistaken impression that it's okay to leave the store without paying. From time to time, consider paying for your groceries with cash. Better yet, as you stand by, give your child a $5 bill to pay for a couple of items and to receive the change. Count it aloud, so that bills and coins eventually become recognized. Later, you can introduce their relative values and buying power.

Tip: Bring along some coupons that you have cut out from the newspaper. Explain their purpose. Your child will feel very mature when handing the coupons to the cashier and getting some coins in return.

STEP 2 UNDERSTAND THE ABCs OF ALLOWANCES.

Q: Why should I give my kids an allowance?

A: Because it teaches children how to manage money in a safe environment.

The sums are small, and mistakes aren't fatal. Children don't have to worry that if they make a bad decision they won't be able to make their rent or car payment, something an increasing number of college students are facing (more on this in Chapter 32).

Q: When should I start the allowance?

A: By the time your child turns five or six, he or she should be responsible enough to handle this new task.

Warning: Don't give a child an allowance, or any kind of money, until you are sure he or she will *not* put it in his or her mouth.

Before starting an allowance, begin discussing with your child what he or she would do with the money. Start drawing up a budget. Write down what he or she would like to buy with the money, and best estimates of how much these items would cost. Then go to the store or surf to an online store together to find out the real prices.

Get input from parents of your child's friends and classmates. How much do they give their children, and what do they expect their children to pay for with the money?

Q: Should I tie the allowance to chores around the house?

A: It works well for some families, but not for others. When parents give an allowance in exchange for work, some children mutiny. At some point, you may hear: "For that amount of money, I'm not going to do that work."

Many families compromise by paying a base allowance to the child free and clear, and then giving extra money to compensate them for specific *additional* chores (painting the lawn furniture, cleaning the garage, and so on). When a child performs a job around the house, be realistic about the quality of the work. A ten-year-old isn't going to paint the lawn furniture as deftly as a professional would, but you're probably paying your child much less.

Q: What, if anything, should my child be required to pay for with an allowance?

A: If you expect your child to pay for necessities, such as school clothes, sports gear, or other things you would normally pay for, the allowance will have to be fairly large. These items should be reflected in the budget you draw up together.

Q: A couple of times a year, one of my kids will tell me they haven't gotten their allowance in weeks and would like the back pay now. I can't remember whether I paid them or not. Do you have any suggestions?

A: In a busy household, keeping track of cash disbursements isn't always easy, so why not formalize the procedure a bit? At the beginning of the year, give each of your kids a notebook or calendar containing fifty-two IOUs, one for each week. Then pick a day (Friday and Sunday are popular) to give each child an allowance in exchange for one IOU. In that way, you know your children are not double dipping, and it will be easier for you (and your kids) to keep track of the money coming in and going out.

Tip: You can take this system one step further and teach your children how to write checks. Draw up the IOUs to look like bank checks (the Bank of Mom and Dad?). To get the allowance, each child must write a check to him- or herself, fill in the amount, and sign it. You then act as the bank and "cash the check."

STEP 3 MAKE SAVVY INVESTING AND SPENDING DECISIONS WITH YOUR KIDS.

Q: How much of their savings should I let my kids spend at any one time?

A: Kids who learn the most about money typically have some restrictions on the timing and use of their allowance. A portion can be spent right away, another portion must be saved, and a third portion is to be used to help others via established charities or helping individuals they know who are in need of assistance. You can get three piggybanks, or create a simpler system by labeling three plastic jars, boxes, or envelopes (glass jars are dangerous because they can shatter).

Institute a Family 401(k). Set up your own version of a 401(k) savings plan at home by matching some of your children's savings. To encourage savings (or not buying items you disapprove of), match some of the money they saved by *not* purchasing items they didn't need or that you disapproved of.

Q: My kids' piggybanks are full (about $25 and $35 each), so I would like to open up savings accounts for them. But I can't find a bank that will let them open an account without charging fees that more than offset the interest they would earn.

A: Many grammar schools have arrangements with a local bank so that students can make deposits every week or two. If your children's school doesn't offer this arrangement, propose it at the next PTA meeting. Meanwhile, start calling local banks, especially ones where you do business, and ask if you can negotiate a "no frills" kid's account with no fees.

Q: My son wants to buy a battery-operated vehicle that is overpriced and, I'm sure, won't do half the things the ads make it look like it does. How can I stop him from throwing out his money?

A: Sometimes, kids will only learn the value of a dollar by spending their money on a toy or other item that is clearly (in your eyes) a rip-off. If you can't reason with him, and if he has enough money and the toy won't harm him, let him buy it.

If the toy turns out to be a big disappointment, use the situation as a learning experience. Ask him what he thought the toy was going to do, and why it didn't live up to his expectations. Then, if possible, view the advertisement together and point out where special effects or other tricks were used to lure unsuspecting kids.

Q: What other ground rules should I set for my son?

A: It's a good idea to discuss, and settle ahead of time, any other restrictions on how he uses his money. For instance:

- Can he buy anything at all with this money? Or are there certain toys or other items that you will not permit in the house? Spell them out, to avoid disagreements later.
- Is there a maximum amount (or percentage) of his saved money that he can spend at one time?
- Can he use his allowance to upgrade gifts you would be buying for him (a pricier tennis racquet, or better seats at the ball game)?

Q: Several times a year, my middle child will come to me begging for more money because he has used up his allowance before the week was up. My husband thinks there's nothing wrong with giving our son a little extra money to tide him over until his next allowance, but I worry that this is starting a bad precedent.

A: Your first task is to find out why he's coming up short several times a year. For most kids, the problem comes about for one of two reasons:

1. Your son may be spending his allowance on things he doesn't need and simply can't afford. In this case, you and your husband should talk with your son about how he is spending his money. If, like many adults, he can't recall where the money went, ask him to start keeping a *spending journal* (see Chapter 2) for one month, and review the entries with him.

Tip: Unless you want your son to continue to ask you for extra money when he becomes an adult, running short of money can be an important life lesson for him. It will bring home the point that there are limits to the amount of money he will have at any time in his life, and he can't always buy things whenever he wants them. Remind him that, for certain purchases, he may have to save for weeks or months, and he may have to forgo some of them altogether.

2. Your son's budget may no longer be realistic. In this case, ask your son to draw up a new, more accurate budget and present it to you and your husband. Then, the three of you can decide whether a

raise is due and—based on your son's presentation—how much it should be. By the way, this is a good rehearsal for your son's later work life, when he tries to persuade a boss (presumably, a nonrelative) that he deserves a raise in pay.

STEP 4 START YOUR CHILD ON STOCKS.

Q: What's a good way to introduce my kids to the stock market?

A: The ups and downs of the stock market can give your children another important money lesson. Consider buying your children a few shares of stock in a company they recognize, such as Toys 'R' Us, Disney, or McDonald's. Once they own some shares, show them how to read the daily stock market results, and how to chart the ups (or downs) of their company.

STEP 5 GET THE SKINNY ON YOUR CHILD'S FIRST JOB.

Q: Should I let my 15-year-old daughter take an after-school job?

A: A part-time job can be a great way for a child to learn both time-management and money-management skills. Some work experience can also pep up a college application. But sit down with your daughter and set some ground rules ahead of time. For instance:

- Limit the number of hours she works each week to 16 (or less). More than 16 hours will eat into her spare time, when she could be taking part in after-school activities, spending time with friends, or doing homework.
- Make sure that the job is suitable work for a teenager. Check with the Department of Labor to make sure that your teenager is not expected to use dangerous machinery (a teenager may be barred by law from using some kinds of machinery) and will not be exposed to dangerous chemicals.
- Explain that if her grades drop, she will have to quit the job.

STEP 6 GUARD YOUR GIFTS FROM GREED.

Q: If I give my grandchild money, what control would I have over how he uses it?

A: If you're hoping that your grandchild will use the money you give him for college tuition, understand that, once you give him money, you lose control over how he spends it. It could be spent on tuition or on a motor-cycle or something else you might not like.

To increase the chances that your gift won't be squandered before your grandson becomes an adult, you can open a bank account or mutual fund account using the Uniform Gift to Minors Act (UGMA). Banks and mutual fund companies have the forms to do this. This way you (or any adult you name—maybe his parent) can then manage the money and use it only for his benefit, such as for school tuition, a computer, or summer camp. But be aware that the UGMA protects the use of the money just so long. When the child turns 21 (18, in some states), this money uncon-ditionally passes to the child.

If you're giving a large sum, consider setting up a trust (see Chap-ter 12) so that you can keep the child from getting access to it until he or she is older—and, hopefully, more responsible. (Be aware that putting money in a child's name can keep him or her from getting needed college financial aid. See Chapter 31 for more information.)

STEP 7 TEACH YOUR CHILD THE FINANCIAL ROPES.

Q: Are there any good magazines that I could subscribe to that would help my daughters learn the financial ropes?

A: For an older child, a subscription to a financial advice magazine, such as *Kiplinger's Personal Finance* magazine, *Money,* or *Smart Money* is a good choice. For the younger set, check out *Zillions* magazine, published by Consumer Reports. It can teach your child ways to manage money and become a savvier consumer in general.

STEP 8 GET YOUR CHILD OFF TO A GOOD START BEFORE COLLEGE.

Q: My son will be heading off to college next year. What do I need to be teaching him about daily money life?

A: He needs to know:

- How to pay bills. Most parents say their kids watch them pay bills, but most kids tell me that they "never paid attention." For the next few months, sit down with your son while you pay bills. Have him fill out your check (you sign it), and let him put it in the envelope and put a stamp on it.

- How to balance a checkbook. Most banks have simple instruction booklets or will give one-on-one lessons, if you aren't comfortable explaining it.
- How to budget his money. At least have him track his expenses for one or two months. Trust me, he, and probably you, will be surprised to see where his money goes.

Q: My son just graduated from college and is starting his first job in the fall. How can I help to get him off to a good financial start?

A: As a supplement to what you have been teaching him as he grew up, consider giving a gift of one or two hours with a *certified* financial planner. Since many so-called financial planners are really insurance salespeople or stockbrokers who make commissions and bonuses from financial products they sell, find a fee-only financial planner. (For advice on choosing a planner, see Chapter 3.)

The best things in life may be free, but you can make the rest more affordable by teaching your children about money. And the sooner you start these lessons, the faster their money will grow. (In Chapter 32, I discuss what every parent must know, and tell children, about teen credit cards.)

A final thought on allowances: Many parents say they can't recall whether they paid the allowance this week or several weeks back for that matter. So, once your kids have learned the financial ropes to your satisfaction, you and your kids may decide to end the allowance. That's okay. Just work out a mutually agreeable financial system with your kids.

Chapter 12

Look Out for Loved Ones
with Trusts and More

Trish's Story

Kevin Wood always told his wife, Trish, that if something were to happen to him, she and their infant daughter, Amy, "would be well taken care of." But when Kevin unexpectedly died last year of a massive heart attack, Trish, 32, was shocked to discover that she was not the beneficiary of his life insurance policy or pension. Instead, his money was to go to his brother, Amy's uncle.

"Kevin took out the life insurance policy before we were married, and the insurance company said only relatives, not girlfriends, could be named as beneficiaries," explains Trish. After they married, Trish began paying the premiums each month from her own checking account, and says, "I just assumed the beneficiary had been changed and that the money would be there for our daughter's living expenses and education."

Trish and her husband also overlooked another vital document: a will. "We talked about it, but never got around to writing a will," she admits. "We never even designated a guardian for Amy in case something happened to both of us. I guess it was more comforting to think we both would always be there for her."

To be sure that your loved ones have a strong safety net if something happened to you, there are four important steps you should take as soon as possible:

1. Use estate planning as the way to help your family now and in the future.
2. Make it easy for your wishes to be known and followed.
3. Make the most of the unified estate tax credit.
4. Understand which types of trusts might help your heirs.

STEP 1 USE ESTATE PLANNING AS THE WAY TO HELP YOUR FAMILY NOW AND IN THE FUTURE.

Many people mistakenly believe that estate planning is only for the really, *really* rich. But don't dismiss the idea of planning your estate just yet. First, you probably have more assets than you realize (Step 3 shows a quick way to calculate your net worth) in which case, now is the time to consider taking some steps to reduce the amount of estate tax your heirs would have to pay after you died. Done right, these steps can also get your assets to your heirs sooner. That's not all. Second, estate planning isn't only about money. If you have kids, especially young ones, or even if you just worry about what would happen to you (financially or medically) if you were to become seriously ill, a little estate planning now could be just what you need. Estate planning can accomplish the following for you:

- It can allow you to name someone in writing whom you want to get which of your assets (real property, investments, and anything else you own) after you die.
- It can allow your loved ones to get your assets as quickly as possible and without public scrutiny.
- It lets you name a guardian to raise your minor children if you *and* your spouse were to die.
- It lets you name someone, even a different person than the person you name to raise your minor children, to be your children's financial guardian to look out for their money and see to it that they are properly housed, fed, clothed, and educated.
- It can keep the tax collector and the probate court from getting one cent more than necessary.
- It increases the chances that your financial decisions and medical wishes will be followed while you are alive. And after you die it's a way to inform loved ones of your financial wishes (not only who gets your assets, but also how or when they can use them) and nonfinancial concerns (such as your organ donation or your wishes for burial).

The amount of estate planning you need depends on your personal situation (including the number of marriages, children, stepchildren, and grandchildren) and the size and complexity of your assets.

MAKE IT EASY FOR YOUR WISHES TO BE
KNOWN AND FOLLOWED.

Here are six things I suggest you consider doing in order to protect yourself and your family:

Draft a Will

By writing a will, you tell the world who is to get your assets after you die.
If you die without a will, your property will be divided according to the
laws of your state, regardless of your wishes. For instance, in most states,
your kids would share equally one-half to two-thirds of your assets, and
the balance of your property would go to your spouse. If, at the time of
your death, you have no spouse or children (and no will), your other relatives would share your estate. No money or property could go to friends,
charities, or your alma mater. As you can quickly see, getting your final
financial wishes down on a legal, binding document is vital.

Whatever the value of your assets, if you have minor children, you
need a will in order to name a guardian for them. If you don't specify
a guardian in your will, the court will appoint one after your death. Not a
good strategy.

Guardian hearings are time-consuming, and they waste money,
which would be better used to help your kids. Even worse, there's a
chance the court might choose a guardian who would be your last choice
to carry out this very important responsibility. For instance, you might
prefer to have a friend raise your kids, but the courts tend to favor giving
children to relatives. Why leave that outcome to chance? Put your life-
altering wishes on paper in your will.

Before naming a guardian, be sure to ask the person (or couple) if
they want this responsibility and agree to take on this task. Then name
a backup guardian (with their prior approval, as well), just in case. Next,
consider whom you want to name as the *financial* guardian for your
children. Choose someone who has a good head for money and shares
values similar to yours. (The financial guardian can be someone other
than the legal guardian because you want the best person for each of
these responsibilities.)

Update your will whenever a major life change occurs: you move to
another state; your marital status changes; you have new children or
stepchildren in your family. Updating a will should cost much less than
drafting the original will.

Don't leave money directly to your minor-age children. By law, they are too young to manage it for themselves, so their financial guardian would be required to regularly report expenditures and investments to a judge who may know nothing about your kids or your wishes about how the money is to be spent. When minor children reach age 18 (21, in some states), they get full control of assets left to them. They can choose to do anything with them at that time, and paying for college may not be their choice.

A better option is to set up a trust that can manage the money on your children's behalf for as many years as you choose (to age 25, 30, 45—whatever you specify). The money in the trust can be used for your children's living expenses and education (or anything else you stipulate), but it will not be turned over to your children until they reach the age you have specified in the trust. (More information on trusts is given later in this step.)

Hire an attorney to write the will. Look for someone who specializes in estate planning and who practices law in your state. You can buy fill-in-the-blank will forms or computer software, but I don't recommend either choice. If you make a mistake in drawing up your will, or you overlook some important contingencies, it may not be discovered until you have died and it's too late to fix it.

A lawyer will charge $150–$400 for a simple will, and it's money well spent. Ask friends, coworkers, relatives, your employer, and the local bar association for referrals. Then go to the local library, check out the credentials for each candidate (use the Martindale-Hubbell Law Directory). Contact your state bar association to see if there are outstanding complaints or if the lawyer has ever been disciplined for improper conduct. When you meet with the lawyer, here are some questions to ask:

- Where did you go to school, and what degrees do you hold?
- How long have you practiced law?
- What bar associations are you a member of?
- How do you charge (by the hour, or a flat fee)? How much will it cost to draw up my will? What, if anything, could cause it to cost more, and how much more?
- Can you give me three references of satisfied clients?

After you've chosen the lawyer, ask him or her to send you a letter spelling out what services will be performed and how much they will cost.

Don't store your original will in a safe deposit box under any circumstances; some states still seal boxes when one owner dies. Instead, let your attorney hold the original. Keep a copy at home, and tell your family where the original is.

An executor (sometimes referred to as a personal representative) is the person who tracks down your property, deals with your heirs, creditors, and life insurers, and takes care of other odds and ends, such as paying your final bills. You can name a trustworthy friend or relative, and that person may agree to do this time-intensive job for free. (If so, stipulate in writing that they will refuse the payment that is allowed by law.) Or, you can name an attorney or a bank as the executor of your estate, but their fees can eat up a good part of your estate.

To cut costs, some couples (spouses or significant others) make out a single will, leaving all their assets to the other person. After they both die, the remainder is often left to the couple's children. Don't do it. It's a penny-wise and pound-foolish mistake. Among other problems, the surviving partner may be precluded from drawing up a new will after the death of the other. Instead, each person should draw up his or her own will.

Videotaped wills are becoming popular; unfortunately, they have no legal standing. A will must be in writing, signed, dated, and witnessed by at least two people, depending on state law.

Draft a "Letter of Instructions"

This do-it-yourself letter will tell your loved ones everything they need to know after you die: where important documents can be found (such as any life insurance policies, the location of a prepaid burial plot, the location of the original will), as well as instructions for your funeral (burial or cremation) and whom to notify of your death. Be sure to tell your family where this letter is kept.

Draw Up a Durable Power of Attorney

With this document, you authorize someone to manage your money and pay your bills if you become mentally impaired from an accident or a disease like Alzheimer's. Be sure that it's a *durable* power of attorney; other types of powers of attorney become void if you become mentally impaired. Have an attorney who specializes in estate planning draw up the document. Update it every five years.

Draw Up a Health Care Proxy

This document, sometimes referred to as a Health Power of Attorney, allows you to name someone to make medical decisions for you (how much medical intervention you want if you can't speak for yourself). Whether you choose a spouse, relative, or close friend, he or she needs to be someone whom you can trust to be a strong advocate for you. The person who is best qualified to manage your money may not be the best person to serve as an advocate for your health care, and vice versa. Consider choosing two different people: one to manage your money and one to direct your health care.

Discuss your wishes ahead of time with your advocate, doctors, and family. To increase the chances that your wishes will be followed, be sure to give executed copies of your Health Care Proxy to relatives, or anyone else who might try to override your choices, as well as anyone who could stand up for your wishes. Choice in Dying is an organization that can provide the forms used in your state and answer relevant questions. They can be reached at (800) 989-WILL or www.choices.org.

Draw Up a Living Will

This document varies from state to state, but a living will generally comes into play if you are near death (due to a terminal illness, or as the result of a coma). It tells how much life support you do or do not want, but it may not address every contingency, so have your lawyer help you fill it out in as much detail as possible. Choose very carefully the person who will act as your advocate if you are near death. (Consider appointing the same person you selected as the advocate for your Health Care Proxy; but perhaps not someone with a conflict of interest who would benefit financially from your premature demise.)

Consider Setting Up a Living Trust

You can establish a living trust to state how you want your assets managed if you become mentally or physically disabled. A living trust can also be used to pass your property to others after your death, without going through probate (a court procedure required by state laws to validate a will before a deceased person's property can be distributed).

Living trusts became household names in the 1960s and were sold for all sorts of reasons—some good, others not. Their popularity grew as living-trust salespeople starting combing the countryside telling naïve consumers that these trusts could do a wide range of things—getting assets to heirs more quickly, avoiding probate (a court process that verifies your will), and even avoiding estate taxes.

For some people, a living trust can be an important part of a well-thought-out estate plan. That's the good news. The bad news is that many unscrupulous salespeople discovered that hawking living trusts (or books about trusts, do-it-yourself trust workbooks, and software packages to grow your own living trust at home) could be a gold mine for the sellers. Contrary to what consumers have had hammered into them for years, living trusts are not for everyone.

Let's look at some of the pluses of a living trust:

- Your estate can avoid the public scrutiny, delays, and cost of going through probate court.
- Your estate can be settled months or years sooner than if it had to go through probate court.
- By avoiding probate court, your estate won't owe pricey probate fees; more of your assets will go to your heirs.
- Without the spotlight of probate court on your estate, it will be settled privately. Did you know that the contents of a will become public record?
- A living trust is considered "revocable"; you can change it or cancel it outright before you die.
- You can be your own trustee while you are alive.
- You can appoint a cotrustee who has financial expertise (a bank, a trust company, or a financial planner) to help you manage large or complex assets.
- You can name a successor trustee to take over for you if, in a future time, your doctor certifies that you are no longer able to handle your affairs. Your family won't have to go to court to get a conservator named to handle your property. That court appearance is costly, time-consuming, and part of the public record. Conservators don't come cheap; they can charge about one percent of your assets each year, and their qualifications are sometimes questionable.
- When you die, the trust can become "irrevocable" so that your wishes can be carried out after you are gone. Or, you can stipulate that the contents of your living trust are to be distributed to your heirs at the time of your death.
- Successfully contesting a trust is much harder than contesting a will. After your death, your wishes listed in a trust are more apt to be followed than those in a will.

A living trust has these important minuses:

- It's a hassle to rename all your assets to your trust's name. Any assets (mutual funds, stocks, bonds, bank accounts, deeds to property, and so on) that are not renamed precisely will not be covered by the trust and will then be subject to probate.

- The contents of your living trust are fully subject to estate taxes. That's a big difference compared with some of the other trusts discussed later in this chapter.

Do most people need a living trust? No. The fees you pay to set up a trust (and the hassle of renaming your property from your name to the trust's name) may exceed any benefits you will ever realize. Not only would you be wasting your money, but you could be living with a false sense of security and not making more appropriate estate plans for yourself and your heirs.

Would a living trust benefit you? Here are three circumstances where setting up a trust is at least worth considering:

1. If you have minor children, you could use a living trust to state how you want the money in the trust used (for their education, or to buy a bigger home) and at what age your children will ultimately gain control of what's left of your estate.

2. If you have a mentally or physically handicapped child, you could set up a living trust to provide for his or her food, shelter, and care.

3. If you have been married before, a living trust can be used as a way to minimize conflict and to keep your current spouse from financially shutting out your kids from the prior marriage.

If you meet any of those criteria and might benefit from a trust, should you set up the trust yourself? Absolutely not! You need the advice and counsel of *two* types of professionals: an experienced attorney who practices in your state, and who specializes in estate planning, as well as a reliable, fee-only financial planner.

Drawing up a trust—or even deciding whether you need a trust—is not a do-it-yourself job. A trust is a complicated legal document. Steer clear of do-it-yourself workbooks, kits, or computer software. You could unwittingly make a mistake that would invalidate your wishes. Count on spending $1,000 or more to have a trust drawn up.

Tip: The more contingencies you have discussed and resolved before meeting with your attorney, the less time you'll need for legal consultation, so the less it may cost you to execute your wishes.

Have your attorney also draw up a "pour-over will" to pick up any assets you may have missed during the process of renaming your assets to the trust's name. The pour-over will is also a good place to name the persons to whom family heirlooms and other sentimental possessions are to go.

Dealing with the Details of Living Trusts

Living trusts are originally drawn up as "revocable" (you can change them or cancel them while you are alive), but they become "irrevocable" when you die. By itself, a living trust will not allow you to avoid taxes. To cut taxes, a living trust must be used in conjunction with one or more other trusts (itemized in Step 4, below).

Assets held in a trust do not go through probate (a court process that verifies your will), so your assets may be disbursed to your heirs sooner. *But you still need a will* to cover any assets that were not specifically listed in the trust.

Living trusts by themselves do not lower your estate taxes. As explained in Step 4, there are other types of trusts that can cut your tax bill. But first, read Step 3 to learn what all the tax-evading moves are about.

STEP 3 MAKE THE MOST OF THE UNIFIED ESTATE TAX CREDIT.

The federal government lets you give away a certain amount of your assets (currently $675,000, but rising to $1,000,000 by 2006; see the maximum unified credit chart below) during your life or after your death without owing any federal estate tax.

Maximum Unified Credit, by Year(s)

Federal taxes can eat up 37 percent to 55 percent of your estate, and some states also will claim a portion of any assets that exceed the following (maximum unified credit) amounts:

Year(s)	Exemption
1999	$ 650,000
2000–2001	675,000
2002–2003	700,000
2004	850,000
2005	950,000
2006	1,000,000

Do these amounts seem like more assets than you have? Not so fast; you need to do the math. Add up your retirement accounts [IRAs, 401(k) plans]; the value of your home; your mutual funds, bank accounts, and life insurance (the policies you bought, as well as your employer's offered coverage). (Review Chapter 2 for more specifics on calculating your net worth.)

Are you shocked to discover that you own that much? Have you included property that you own jointly with someone else, such as your home, car, or investment accounts? While jointly owned property is exempt from probate, it is NOT exempt from estate tax. Do you see why some estate tax planning may be in order? Tax avoidance is often cited as the reason people choose a trust.

If your sole goal for creating a living trust is to cut the estate taxes after you die, here are two simpler strategies to consider first. They may be enough to get you below the estate tax threshold.

"Gift Away" Assets During Your Lifetime

You can give up to $10,000 every year, tax-free, to anyone you choose. Larger gifts come out of your exemption (see the maximum unified credit chart) and could trigger taxes, possibly after you die.

Aside from tax savings, by giving away assets while you are alive you can reap two additional benefits: (1) recipients can show their gratitude to you, and (2) recipients may be in more need and able to make better use of the money earlier in their lives. For instance, they may be paying for college or saving to buy a home. A money gift given at this stage could improve their lives or their family's lives more than it could later on.

Tax Tip: You can give away up to $10,000 each year to any person you choose, without triggering any gift tax. Or, you and your spouse jointly can give a total of $20,000 per year per recipient.

"Name Away" Life Insurance
While You Are Alive

To take the insurance proceeds out of your estate, consider giving your life insurance policy to your spouse, your kids, or an irrevocable trust. But beware. The recipient of your life insurance policy can *cancel* the policy or take out the cash value while you are still alive. If someone you care about is going to need the life insurance benefits after you die, naming away your policy may not be a good move. Also if you give the policy to your spouse, make sure your spouse names someone other than you as the beneficiary. Otherwise, the policy could come right back to you if your spouse dies before you.

STEP 4 UNDERSTAND WHICH TYPES OF TRUSTS MIGHT HELP YOUR HEIRS.

A well-chosen and executed trust can not only reduce your estate taxes but can also ensure that your loved ones are taken care of in the way you wish. The most popular types of trusts are outlined below, along with their possible benefits to you. Remember that establishing and maintaining a trust is a complicated financial and legal matter. It is NOT a do-it-yourself task. You should only create one with the guidance of an experienced estate attorney and a professional financial planner.

Credit Shelter Trust (also called a Bypass Trust or a Family Trust)

When you die, the income from this trust goes to your spouse. When your spouse dies, the principal goes to your heirs. This type of trust is becoming increasingly popular, due in part to the planned increases in the estate-tax exemption (the maximum unified credit, discussed above).

Here's how it works. When one spouse dies, he or she can leave all assets to the other without triggering the estate tax. But when the surviving spouse dies, the heirs will owe tax on any amount of these assets that exceeds the maximum unified credit ($675,000 in 2000, rising to $1,000,000 in 2006).

To make the most of the maximum unified credit, arrange your finances so that when the first spouse dies, he or she passes the maximum amount of the unified credit along to this trust—instead of to the surviving spouse. The surviving spouse can get the benefit of this money in the form of income from the trust. When the second spouse dies, the assets in the trust are then distributed to the heirs. Avoid a common mistake: The assets forwarded to this trust must have been owned solely by the deceased spouse—not jointly owned by the couple.

Marital-Deduction Trust

If you worry that your surviving spouse might remarry and a new spouse or family would get access to your money, consider setting up a Marital-Deduction Trust. You could fund this trust with any money that does not go into a Credit-Shelter Trust. You can maintain even more control from the grave by naming someone with financial experience (other than your spouse) as the trustee. This could keep your surviving spouse from making financial mistakes because he or she didn't know the intricacies of money management or came under the influence of someone whose motives are different from yours.

Disclaimer Trust

This trust is for a couple who have not amassed enough assets to trigger an estate tax, but who expect their income to soar soon. (They may own stock options that could soon be worth substantial sums, or they are in line for a huge inheritance.) When one spouse dies, the other inherits everything but has the option to disclaim some of the estate—which then goes into a Credit Shelter Trust (see above).

Generation-Skipping Trust

This trust allows a couple to pass along up to $2 million in assets to grandchildren, tax-free. (If you are single, up to $1 million can be passed.) The assets must be transferred to beneficiaries who are at least two generations younger, although your children can receive the trust income and use the principal for benefit of the grandchildren (such as for education, housing, health care costs). If you exceed the $2 million or $1 million limits, the excess is taxed at a high rate, typically 55 percent.

Qualified Terminal Interest Trust
(Q-TIP Trust)

With this trust, the surviving spouse can collect income every year and may also have use of the principal (under terms that you can stipulate when drafting the document, such as for medical or housing needs). When the surviving spouse dies, the remaining assets go to the person(s) you chose (typically, your kids) when you set this up. For tax purposes, assets are taxed as though they belong to the surviving spouse (after his or her death). This is popular with couples who have kids from prior marriages. This may not be a good type of trust if your new spouse is close in age to your kids. They will have to wait until the new spouse dies before they may see a dime of this money.

Charitable Remainder Trust

With this trust, you can give away assets, get a tax write-off, and continue to get income for the rest of your life. This trust can be good for people who need income and whose assets (such as land or stock) have gone up a lot in value on paper but would generate hefty capital gains taxes if sold. After you give the property to the charity, they can sell it and owe no taxes.

Assets you give to the charity won't go to your heirs. Do you want to make up for these assets? You can take some income from the trust, give it to your kids, and let them buy a life insurance policy on your life. When you die, the proceeds of this policy will substitute for assets you gave to charity.

Charitable Lead Trust

If you have substantial assets, this trust allows you to keep these assets in the family but reduce the cost before passing them on to beneficiaries. You donate an asset to the trust for a fixed number of years, and, during that time, the trust pays income to a charity.

Life Insurance Trust

This irrevocable trust allows you to put in an existing life insurance policy (or pay to buy a new life insurance policy) and shelter the death benefit from estate taxes. Several restrictions apply, including the inability to change the beneficiary. A savvy estate planner, however, may be able to get around many of the restrictions.

Qualified Personal Residence Trust (QPRT)

With this trust, you remove your home or vacation home from your estate, fix it at today's price, and continue living in it for up to a specified number of years. (If you die before the term expires, your home will be considered part of your estate and taxed as such.) This trust is especially useful for people who own a costly vacation home that they wish to pass on to their heirs, but with a minimum of taxes.

Regardless of which type of trust you establish, choose your trustee (the person who will administer it) with great care. A trustee can be a friend, a relative, or a bank. He or she needs to be money-savvy, honest, and gifted with the wisdom of Solomon (to resolve any disputes that may arise). If you set up a trust, don't forget to rename your assets in the name of the trust. It's a common error that defeats the whole purpose of the trust.

Strengthen Your Safety Net

In earlier chapters, we discussed how you can make the most of any life insurance, disability insurance, or health insurance benefit offered by your employer. We also reviewed the importance of looking out for your loved ones by having a properly written and executed will and doing some careful, customized estate planning. Here, I'll show you ways to patch any holes and buy additional insurance that you didn't—or couldn't—get through work. I'll also take you through, step by step, to make sure you've got all the other types of insurance you and your family need now (such as homeowner's insurance and auto insurance) as well as in the near or distant future (the long-term care insurance that you, your spouse, or your parents might need).

This solution wouldn't be complete without my showing you ways to make sure you're not paying more than you have to for any of this needed coverage. Money freed up here could be better spent making well-chosen investments, paying down your debt, or increasing your retirement savings.

Chapter 13

Shop Smart for Life Insurance

How can you make up to three times current bank interest rates and get an instant inheritance for your family, for just a small initial investment? According to many insurance agents, the answer is with cash-value insurance, such as a whole-life or a universal-life policy.

But, according to many consumers who have bought one or more of these policies, cash-value insurance is often a better deal for the person selling the policy than for the person buying it.

Michael's Story

"When I bought a $300,000 cash-value life insurance policy ten years ago, my insurance agent told me I would owe only eight annual payments of $4,523," explains Michael. "So when I got a bill for a ninth annual payment I called my agent immediately to tell him that I had gotten a bill by mistake. Much to my surprise, my agent said it wasn't a mistake and I would owe another $4,523 payment this year and probably for three more years. I told him that was outrageous and I wanted my money back. My agent chuckled and said, 'That's not the way it works.' He said that interest rates had tumbled, so my policy's value hadn't grown as projected. He then gave me three choices: (1) make four additional annual payments of $,4523 each (50 percent more than I had originally been told); (2) convert to a policy that would be much smaller than $300,000; or (3) cancel the policy and get only a fraction of my money back. Some investment! I feel like a chump. If I'd known what my agent knew—namely, that I could end up owing so much more on this policy a few years later—I never would have bought it."

Despite the potential pitfalls, life insurance is an important part of a family's financial plan. If you're a working parent with children or others to support, or a homemaker whose contribution to the family would be expensive to replace, a life insurance policy can provide your family with money to pay the mortgage, finance your children's education, or hire someone to run your home if you die.

If you or your spouse died and the survivor could not afford to maintain the lifestyle you have (or pay the balance of the mortgage), a life insurance policy could be an important part of your safety net and could also make sense for estate-planning purposes.

Buying life insurance can be a confusing process. About half of all policyholders cancel their insurance within ten years. You'll get more for your money—and face fewer surprises—if you know the risks and the reasons many agents push policies that are better for them than for you. Here's what you need to know before you buy a new or replacement policy.

STEP 1 CHOOSE BETWEEN TERM AND CASH-VALUE INSURANCE.

There are two kinds of life insurance: *term insurance* and *cash-value insurance. Term insurance* is purchased for a specified time, usually between one and twenty years. If you die during that time, your beneficiaries collect the "death benefit." If not, the policy ends. Although premiums (the payments you make) rise as you age, your need for insurance is likely to taper off as your children grow up, other assets accumulate, and Social Security kicks in. If you decide to purchase term insurance, buy a "guaranteed renewable" policy. You'll pay a bit more, but it will enable you to continue your insurance to age 65 or 70—without undergoing a new physical exam—even if your health deteriorates.

Many insurance agents recommend the costlier *cash-value insurance* policies, which earn them higher commissions. "In their sales pitch, these agents call cash-value policies 'permanent insurance' and like to say, 'Why would you rent a house when you could buy one?'" says Robert Hunter, a former Texas Insurance Commissioner and a consumer advocate. "But what they don't tell you is that often you can 'rent' life insurance, for the years you need it, at a fraction of the cost to 'buy' it. Don't forget most people only need insurance protection when they start a family and until kids graduate from college—and maybe to retirement." With term insurance, your entire premium (less a small commission and administrative fee) goes toward the "mortality charge," which is the company's yearly cost for paying the death benefits of other policyholders your age.

With cash-value insurance, if you're under age 40, you'll pay a much higher premium (up to ten times more) than you would for term insurance with the same death benefit. After the insurer's expenses, hefty commissions, and mortality charge are deducted, the remainder is placed in a "reserve," also called your investment, savings, or cash value. The reserve grows, tax-deferred, and some policies let you borrow against it at below-market rates.

Whole-life insurance is the least risky type of cash-value insurance. You pay a fixed annual premium to keep the policy "in force" (active). If you die, your beneficiaries get the death benefit less any outstanding loan(s) and unpaid interest on the loan(s).

Introduced more than two decades ago, *universal-life insurance* is another type of cash-value insurance. It's similar to whole-life but riskier because you choose your annual premium payment. You can even skip some payments. The insurer will recommend yearly "target" premiums, but you can pay less. However, pay too little and the insurer—often without notification (as authorized in the policy)—will make up for the shortfall by reducing your cash value. During the "no-lapse period" (up to five years), your policy stays "in force" even if you pay less than the target premiums. But at the end of that period, you'll have to either make up for the shortfall or lose the policy.

The fastest-growing and riskiest type of cash-value insurance is *variable-life insurance*. You decide (from a list of insurer-selected stocks, bonds, and mutual funds) how your cash value is to be invested. Your cash value *and your death benefit* then rise and fall with the financial markets.

LLOYD'S LAW

If any financial adviser or tax adviser recommends that you buy a cash-value policy, make sure, before taking the advice, that he or she isn't getting a commission from the sale of the policy.

STEP 2 | BE SURE YOU UNDERSTAND HOW POLICIES WORK AND ARE SOLD.

Whether you're buying your first life insurance policy, purchasing supplemental coverage, or trading in an existing policy, it's important that you understand what you're getting, giving up, and paying for. Read this Step's advice carefully, and before you buy, terminate, or swap a policy, read it again.

- *You can't believe the sales illustrations.* When an agent is trying to sell a cash-value policy, his or her chief tool is a "sales illustration," a computer-generated projection of your policy's expected death benefit, premiums, and cash value. In addition to being difficult to decipher, the projection is often based on an undisclosed set of assumptions about interest rates, insurance company expenses, and so on.

Insurers may add a "dividend" or interest to your cash value. But because interest rates are often lower and/or company expenses are higher than projected, cash values are frequently less than the amounts shown in the sales illustrations.

LLOYD'S LAW

Get two more illustrations: one figured at two points below the insurer's current interest rate, and a "guaranteed" illustration—what the insurer is obligated to pay you (the worst case, figured at a low interest rate and high expenses). If the illustrations you get are missing pages, numbers, or footnotes, don't buy from this salesperson.

- *Your premium payments never really "vanish."* Some illustrations make it look as if you can stop paying premiums after a few years. This is referred to as the "vanishing premium," but it's a misnomer. Your premiums never vanish. The truth is, they're still due, but they are projected as deductions from your cash value. Lower interest rates and higher insurer costs will likely require you to pay additional premiums now—or years from now—to keep your policy active.

LLOYD'S LAW

Don't be seduced by vanishing-premium promises. Ask for an "in force" (or "ledger") illustration every few years and whenever interest rates drop, to determine whether you need to increase your premiums or cancel the policy. Request an illustration that projects your policy to at least age 85, so that you won't start owing premiums again, unexpectedly late in life.

Get everything in writing, including projected interest rates, company expenses, conversion options, and vanishing-premium promises. If your agent refuses to give a written record, don't buy.

Examine any new insurance policies immediately. You typically have only ten days to cancel and get a refund.

- *Surrender fees can gobble up your cash value.* For the first few years, the most you can borrow (or get back if you cancel the policy is the "cash-surrender value"—the cash value less any surrender fees (such as a policy cancellation penalty). For example, if the policy's cash value is $5,000 and surrender fees are $3,000, the cash surrender value is $2,000 ($5,000 minus $3,000).

LLOYD'S LAW

Plan to hold a policy at least until the surrender fees end (up to twenty years).

- *Your beneficiaries typically can't claim your cash value.* When you die, most policies allow your beneficiaries to *get only the death benefit.* Some insurers offer policies that pay the death benefit plus the cash value, but you will pay more—possibly a lot more—for this feature.
- *Your insurance company may be financially shaky.* Insurance companies sometimes fail, and although state guaranty funds will eventually pay most death benefits, the process can take years. If the insurer caves in while you're living, you may have a long wait to get your hands on your cash value.

    At your local library, check your insurance company's financial stability in at least three of these ratings books: A.M. Best Insurance Reports, Standard & Poor's (or at www.standardandpoors.com), Moody's (or at www.moodys.com), Weiss, and Duff and Phelps.
- *Other investments can outperform cash-value insurance.* Due to its high costs and the relatively low interest and dividends (which are paid on only a fraction of your money) paid on cash-value insurance, you'll likely get a better return and more flexibility by buying a term life insurance policy and investing the difference. Choose tax-deferred retirement savings plans [401(k)s and IRAs], low- to medium-risk no-load mutual funds, and possibly tax-free municipal bond funds for investing this money.
- *Replacing your policy can mean big bucks for your agent and may be a better deal for your agent than for you.* After discovering that the policy they've been paying into for several years has a low cash

> **LLOYD'S LAW**
>
> *Don't buy a policy with the intention of borrowing against it. Unlike home equity loans, the interest isn't tax-deductible, and you may be hit with fees and penalties. Before you borrow, get all fees in writing.*

value, many policyholders—at the urging of an insurance agent—trade in the policy for a new one.

With commissions and bonuses, agents get 50 to 125 percent of the first year's premium on cash-value policies. These trades are very profitable for insurance agents, but this money is coming out of your pocket.

> **LLOYD'S LAW**
>
> *Don't just dump your existing policy without analyzing it carefully. Once you've paid the up-front fees (including a hefty commission to the policy salesperson), it often makes more financial sense to keep an existing policy*—even if it wasn't a good deal in the first place.

- *You don't need an agent to buy insurance.* Check out insurance offered by your employer or union. If you know your insurance needs, consider buying directly from a "low-load" (low-commission) company. For details, contact: Ameritas, Houston, TX, (800) 552-3553 or www.ameritasdirect.com.

STEP 3 — MAKE THE MOST OF YOUR INSURANCE DOLLARS.

Some salespeople make a bundle on unnecessary extras, such as:

- *Accidental death benefit rider*—pays more if you die in an accident. But your beneficiaries will need the same coverage, no matter how you die.
- *Waiver of premiums rider*—pays your premium if you become disabled. Most of these riders go into effect only if you cannot work at *any* job. Before buying this feature, ask the insurer to itemize the conditions under which it would kick in. For most consumers, instead of paying a higher premium for this rider, a better choice is to

buy (or increase) long-term disability insurance. The disability benefits are more flexible. You can spend them in any way you choose.
(See Chapter 14 for more information on disability insurance.)

- *Kids' life insurance*—not needed unless kids contribute to the family's income.

 KNOW WHERE TO TURN FOR HELP.

If you have a problem with an insurance agent or company, contact your
state's insurance commissioner for help or to file a complaint. To find your
state insurance department, consult the blue pages of your phone book, or
visit www.naic.org, the Web site for the National Association of Insurance
Commissioners, which has links to state insurance commissions.

Chapter 14

Protect Your Earnings with Good Disability Insurance

Whether you're married or single, with or without children, chances are you need disability insurance.

Think you don't? Consider this: During your working years, you're more likely to become disabled than to die. Whether you're single with no dependents (and so don't need life insurance), or you're the only breadwinner in the family, disability coverage is an especially vital part of your financial plan. Unless you're independently wealthy, how else would you be able to pay out-of-pocket medical costs and living expenses?

Warren's Story

"Skewering two of my fingers with a wayward fishing hook could only be described as a fluke accident," recalls Warren. "The nearest hospital was more than 60 miles away and it was getting dark, so my brother, Joe, pulled out the hook and bandaged my fingers. When I got back home on Monday, my fingers were very swollen and throbbing, so I saw my doctor. It turns out I had damaged the nerves in both fingers and severed a tendon. I had to undergo two operations to try to straighten out one of my fingers. I'm a computer programmer, so I spend a lot of time at the keyboard, typing; but even after six months of physical therapy, I still can't get my fingers to move properly. My boss said that they could reassign me to a job that didn't require typing, but it pays $17,000 less than I'm making now, and I don't know how I'd get by on that much less."

The bad news: Despite its importance, disability insurance can be tough to get if you're self-employed, and it's rarely portable if you change jobs.

The good news: Unlike other types of insurance (such as homeowner, auto, or life insurance), you needn't worry that you'll be sold too much disability insurance. If anything, some insurers may want to sell you too little coverage. Why? Because they want you to have an incentive to go back to work. And if more money is paid for *not* working than for working, they fear that some policyholders might malinger.

As a result, it's hard to find a policy that would pay benefits of more than 60 percent to 70 percent of your gross income if you become disabled. That could still exceed your take-home pay from work because any disability insurance benefits you collect *from a policy you paid for* are tax-free. Benefits from an employer-paid policy are taxed just like income.

Tip: It's best to buy a policy when you are young and healthy. If you wait until you are older or have a preexisting condition, you will pay much higher premiums—if you can get a policy at all.

If you are offered some group coverage through work, but it's not enough (not at least 60 percent to 70 percent of your gross earnings), you can buy more. But before you search for an individual policy through an insurance agent or directly from an insurance company, ask your employer whether you are eligible for less costly and less restrictive group coverage. If you currently have disability coverage through your employer but need more, you might be able to save 15 percent to 25 percent on premiums by buying *supplemental* coverage through your employer rather than an individual policy on your own. Check with your union and with any professional organizations to which you belong. They may offer disability policies. Before you sign on the dotted line, compare the coverage and costs for at least three companies.

LLOYD'S LAW

Don't replace an existing policy with a new one unless someone who does not stand to make a commission or other money from your change *recommends it. Chances are you have better coverage (often at a lower price) than you can get today. If you need more coverage than your old policy offers, buy a second policy to supplement it.*

Take these five steps before you buy disability insurance.

STEP 1 — UNDERSTAND HOW THE INSURER DEFINES A DISABILITY.

When you're shopping for a disability policy, the first thing you need to find out is how the company defines "disability." Imagine paying premiums for years, becoming disabled from an accident or illness, being unable to work, and hearing your insurer say: "Sorry, that's not covered." Covered conditions vary greatly from company to company. Insist on seeing, in writing, the disability clause in a prospective policy.

STEP 2 FIND THE BEST TYPE OF POLICY FOR YOUR NEEDS.

One type of disability policy is called an "own occupation" policy. Say you're a musician and you permanently damage one of your hands. This policy would pay even if you took a job in another profession. This is a desirable but expensive policy, and it's getting hard to find.

An "any occupation" policy says that if you can't work in your own field but can work in another, you will not be considered disabled. The insurer decides whether you qualify to collect anything. This type of policy has serious drawbacks.

A third type—the one you will likely be offered—is a "loss of income" policy or "income replacement" policy. It's usually the best buy because the premiums are much lower than for an "own occupation" policy. If you must take a lower-paying job (in the same field or a different one), this policy would make up the difference in your income.

STEP 3 DETAIL YOUR DUTIES.

Be very specific when describing what you do. It's a good idea to have your insurance agent ask the underwriting department for a written explanation of the circumstances under which you would be considered disabled, based on the description you wrote.

STEP 4 SHOP FOR THE FEATURES YOU NEED.

When you're shopping for a disability policy, look for:

- *Benefits and coverage at least to age 65.* It's cheaper to get one to two years' coverage, but it won't be enough if you can't return to work that soon—or ever.
- *"Guaranteed renewable."* As long as you pay the premiums, you can keep the policy without having another physical exam. But don't skip a payment, even if you don't receive a bill. The issuer can cancel your policy.
- *Waiver of premiums.* You stop paying premiums if you become disabled, even if they rise sharply afterward. Be sure a waiver of premiums is included in your policy.

- *Cost of living rider.* If inflation picks up again before you reach retirement age, your benefits will keep pace.

You may cut costs and get better coverage by looking for:

- A long "elimination" period—a waiting period of at least 90 or up to 180 days before benefits begin. How long could you afford to live without the benefits money? Add up your unused sick leave, accumulated vacation days, and any short-term disability insurance from your employer. You would need payments to start when those have expired. If you can afford it, go to a longer elimination period. Then apply the money you save with the lower premiums toward extending the benefit period. You want a policy that covers you to age 65 (or older, in the twenty-first century), when you can start collecting Social Security.
- A nonsmoker's discount.
- Group coverage through a professional or trade association, but before signing up, make sure the price is competitive.
- A unisex policy if you're a woman. Some companies charge women more because, statistically, more women than men file disability insurance claims.

LLOYD'S LAW

Pass up disability coverage offered by your credit card, even if it sounds like it will pay off your credit card balance if you become disabled. It will only pay the minimum monthly amount, and it's typically overpriced relative to the benefits. There are long waiting periods and other restrictions before you can collect.

STEP 5 BE CANDID.

Do you have a chronic illness or preexisting condition? Disclose it. Disclose everything. Coverage for a preexisting conditions may be excluded for two years. But if a preexisting condition is later uncovered by the insurer, it could void your policy. To be on the safe side, consider listing all doctors you've seen, and have the insurer contact them in case you forgot anything.

If you become disabled and need to file a claim, involve the agent who sold you the policy. He or she should know the policy's loopholes or hidden "gotchas." Also, consult with a lawyer before filing a claim. The insurance company knows all the fine print in the policy, and you don't.

Some insurance companies sell disability insurance policies that turn into long-term care policies when you retire.

Chapter 15

Look into Long-Term Care Insurance

A growing number of seniors who have managed to build up a nest egg still harbor fear that a serious illness or disability will eat up their life's savings. Specifically, they worry that they will use up all of their money on nursing home care for themselves or their spouse, or that they won't have enough money to be considered for admission to a decent, private nursing home.

Lila's Story

"My father was diagnosed with arthritis when I was in college about two decades ago," says Lila. "He's been on a slew of medicines ever since, but he says he's constantly in pain and finding it hard to even do simple things like getting out of a chair. My mother is small and frail, but that didn't stop her from trying to help my dad get into the car. It was too much for her. She broke her arm when he tripped getting in.

"Mother spent two nights in the hospital as a result of the accident, and will be getting some physical therapy which will be mostly paid for by Medicare. The problem is: My dad also needs some in-home help so that he can get around and make some meals while my mom recuperates, but Medicare won't pay one cent for that. My parents are pretty tapped out after my mom's accident, so my husband and I are going to have to foot the bill for my dad's in-home help. Have you priced in-home care lately? It's costly, so my husband and I are going to have to dip into our kids' college fund to pay for it. If either of my parents had to go into a nursing home I don't know how they would be able to pay for it."

Nursing home fees of $125–$200 per day are not uncommon. In-home care, which is preferred by many people who need some medical assistance but who like living in their own home, can cost even more. Do you think your health insurance or Medicare will pick up the tab? Think again. In most cases, neither will.

It's no wonder that a growing number of financial planners are advising seniors to consider buying long-term care policies for themselves or their relatives. Many younger people are even buying the policies for their parents, partly because they worry about their parents, but also to protect their own inheritance.

STEP 1 DETERMINE WHETHER YOU OR YOUR PARENTS NEED LONG-TERM CARE COVERAGE.

Who needs long-term care coverage? Several studies indicate that women over age 65 have up to a one-in-two chance of being confined to a nursing home for some period of time. Men have a slightly lower chance—about one-in-three—of being in a nursing home. A long-term care policy could ease the financial burden and worry for many families.

But good policies don't come cheap. There are tax considerations that make some policies more desirable than others. Some consumer advocates worry that many of the new policies are being offered too inexpensively. They fear that, years down the road, when the policyholders may need to collect, the insurer's reserves won't be big enough. Premiums might then skyrocket to cover unanticipated costs.

Should you be in the market for a policy? If so, what should you be looking for?

One group of people doesn't need the policy: those who have enough assets to "self-insure" and pay for extended care out of their own pocket.

Another group literally can't afford to pay the premiums, which can run several thousand dollars a year. The good news for the latter group is that Medicaid (a state-run welfare program) will pick up nursing home fees for most of them.

In fact, Medicaid foots the bill for the majority of nursing home patients (rules and coverage vary from state to state). Many of the people who are being cared for under this program did not start out poor. Instead, they spent down their assets by paying for the first months or years of care out of their own pocket, but when their assets were depleted, Medicaid took over the payments. Some people have even illegally depleted their assets (through gifts to relatives, or other financial moves) so that they could present themselves as poor enough to qualify for Medicaid but still take care of their relatives financially.

If you try to enter the nursing home system initially through the Medicaid route, your name will be added to a lengthy waiting list. But that's not the worst part. By going the Medicaid route, you will likely be shuttled through lower-quality nursing homes than if you first entered as a private, paying patient. Even if you expect Medicaid to eventually pick up your nursing home costs, you may get into a better-quality facility if you can pay for six months of care out of your own pocket.

A third group has trouble getting long-term care insurance. Their health is so poor (due to preexisting conditions or disabilities) that they are considered too risky to insure at a reasonable price.

A growing number of adult children are giving long-term care insurance policies as gifts to their parents. It's one more way to make sure their parents can afford to get the help they need, and it keeps the children's inheritance from being eaten up by medical costs.

STEP 2 GET THE RIGHT FEATURES FOR YOUR FAMILY'S NEEDS.

Whether you are buying the policy for yourself or for a parent, here are some questions to consider when you're shopping for a long-term care policy:

- What is the maximum daily benefit? Call nursing homes in your area to determine what they currently charge per day; then make sure the daily benefit on the plans you are considering covers at least that amount.
- What (if any) inflation protection does it offer? If, fifteen or twenty years down the road, you need to start collecting on your policy, payment at today's rates won't be nearly enough. Look for inflation protection of at least 5 percent per year.
- How many years will the policy pay? (Two years? Five years? For the rest of your life?) Some policies have a dollar cap instead of a time limit.
- How long is the "elimination" period (the number of days before the policy starts paying, following a qualified illness or disability). If you can afford the premiums, look for a policy with an elimination period of no more than 20 or 30 days. With a 60- or 90-day elimination period, you could deplete the assets you were trying to preserve.
- Under what conditions will benefits begin? Many older policies would only kick in if the person was entering a nursing home following a covered hospital stay. Nowadays, many policies start paying benefits when the policyholder needs assistance for two or more of the essential "activities of daily living" (bathing, dressing, eating, toileting, and transferring from bed to chair) or develops a cognitive disability (including Alzheimer's disease).

Tip: Some lower-grade policies exclude bathing from the activities list, yet bathing is often the first activity to go, so coverage for it is important.

- Will it pay anything for in-home care? Some policies offer payment for in-home health care as a rider to a long-term care policy. Look for a policy that pays in-home benefits that are equal to at least 50 percent of nursing home benefits.

  If you can afford only one option, go with the nursing home coverage instead of in-home care coverage. Even though in-home care may seem more desirable, chances are that the in-home benefit will be too low to cover the in-home care indefinitely. You would then be entering a nursing home without the needed long-term coverage.
- Will the premiums stay level? The biggest potential problem with some policies is that the premiums rise so high that policyholders are unable to keep up the payments. Level premiums are a good idea, but a guaranteed premium may be less of a guarantee than it seems. Why? Because insurers who are not earning hefty enough profits for any group of policies can (with state approval) raise premiums.
- Is there a waiver of premium? With this waiver, you could stop owing premiums once you've started collecting benefits.
- Is there policy lapse protection? Mental illness or memory loss is often the reason a policyholder starts collecting. When such a condition takes over, remembering to pay the long-term care bills may be too much to expect. Ask the insurer to notify a relative and/or friend if you miss payments and are about to lose your coverage. Provided that you—or your relative or friend who is contacted—pay all the back premiums, your insurer should let you reinstate the policy within five months of missing the first payment.

STEP 3 BUY A POLICY AT THE RIGHT TIME FOR YOU.

You'll pay much lower yearly premiums if you start the policy in your early fifties instead of your late sixties. But realize that if you buy the policy when you're relatively young, but then can no longer afford to continue paying the premiums, the premiums you have already paid will have been a waste of money. At the other extreme, if you wait until you are older to buy the policy, you may have developed a serious illness and may only be offered a very costly policy.

Tip: Check whether your employer offers long-term care coverage for you, your spouse, and your parents. You'll often get a better deal through an employer than on the open market.

STEP 4 UNDERSTAND THE TAX CONSEQUENCES OF VARIOUS POLICIES YOU ARE CONSIDERING.

Don't automatically swap an older policy for a newer one. Some policies purchased before 1990 have many restrictions (for instance, no coverage for Alzheimer's disease or if you didn't have a covered hospital stay immediately before) and may be worth dropping, but others could offer some good coverage, which could be made very good by supplementing specific areas. Before you replace an existing policy with a new one, ask your current insurer to give you a cost estimate for upgrading your existing policy or replacing it with a newer one. Then comparison-shop with at least three different insurers.

Tax Tip: If you itemize deductions, you may be able to deduct part of your premium payments. (An older policyholder can deduct more than a younger one.) To get any deduction, your health care expenses must exceed 7.5 percent of your adjusted gross income.

Chapter 16

S-t-r-e-t-c-h Your
Health Care Dollar

Question: What do you call the person who finishes last in a medical school class?

Answer: "Doctor."

Yes, it's a bad joke, but what do you really know about the person whom you entrust with your family's medical care? Misconceptions about health care choices abound, and what you don't know could endanger your family's health and your pocketbook. If you are not satisfied with your health plan, consider switching. In late summer or early fall, when many companies have their "open season," your employer may let you swap your current plan for one that better fits your budget or your family's medical needs.

Until recently, few people gave health insurance a second thought. Many employers provided ample coverage for their workers' families—and generously picked up all or most of the premiums. Unions picked up the slack for millions of other workers. Even if they had to go it alone, most consumers could find several affordable policies from which to choose.

Fee-for-service plans were the norm. With this traditional (indemnity) insurance, you could see any doctor or use any hospital you chose. Once you met a yearly deductible of, say, $150, your insurer would pay the bulk (typically 80 percent) of the doctor's, hospital's, or lab's "usual and customary" fee. You would pay the difference.

To save money, many companies are now cutting back. Workers are forced to pay more, to switch to managed care, or to scramble to find their own medical coverage. Whether your employer offers one or more health plans, or you're going it alone, be sure you're getting the best care you can for your money.

STEP 1 DETERMINE YOUR NEEDS.

When you're shopping for a health plan, one size does not fit all. Your satisfaction and a plan's total cost and ease of use will be affected by your family members' health and age, and by how often you like to or have to see a doctor.

Choices you make now can have unexpected consequences later. Days before her thirtieth birthday, Pam Wright, a wife and the mother of two-year-old twin daughters was diagnosed with lymphoma. She was given a 20 percent chance of survival. "But fighting my illness wasn't the hard part," she says. "Getting insurance to pay for treatment was."

Shortly after her diagnosis, her husband lost his job and the health insurance he got through work. Citing Pam's "preexisting" condition, her recently diagnosed illness, she and her family were now barred from joining her employer's plan. The Wrights had only one viable choice: Under the federal law known as COBRA (the Consolidated Omnibus Budget Reconciliation Act of 1985), Pam and her family were allowed to continue the coverage of her husband's former employer's health plan for an extra 18 months. With no employer to subsidize them, the Wrights' premiums shot up from $42 a month to $228 a month. "When the 18 months are up, I don't know what we're going to do for insurance," said Pam.

STEP 2 PONDER YOUR PRIORITIES.

When they hear the words *managed care*, most people think of an HMO. But, to contain costs, many traditional insurance plans now come with a managed care provision. Before you enter a hospital, you may be required to get a preauthorization. Or when you need to get a prescription filled, you may be limited to certain pharmacies.

What is important to you in a health care plan? Getting the coverage you need without overpaying, so when you're weighing your present options, ask yourself:

- How much can I afford to pay each year? With a fee-for-service plan, you would pay premiums, deductibles, and copayments for doctors' and hospital visits, lab fees, and prescriptions. In an HMO, you would pay a monthly fee plus any copayments required to see a doctor, use a medical service, or fill a prescription. (See the worksheet at the end of this chapter.)

- Do I mind keeping records and filing insurance claims? (HMOs require less paperwork.)
- Is the care convenient, or must I drive a distance and have a long wait?
- Can I continue seeing *my* doctors, or will I have to switch to the personnel in the new plan? Most HMOs limit the number of patients a primary-care doctor can see, so even if your doctor is in the plan you are considering, get a written agreement that you can keep seeing him or her.
- Can I see a specialist when I want? Or must my primary-care doctor make that decision and give me a referral (or else I pay for the consult)?
- Are second opinions allowed or encouraged? Who pays for them? How much, if anything, will the plan pay if I see a physician whose practice is outside the plan?
- Does a family member have a preexisting condition? If so, does the plan have many/any specialists to choose from? Will there be a waiting period before the condition is covered?
- What does the plan exclude? For instance, will I have to switch from a brand-name prescription to a generic one? In an emergency, can I use a nearby hospital or will I have to drive a long distance to a hospital affiliated with the plan?

Next, consider whether your circumstances will be changing in the foreseeable future.

- Do you plan to start a family soon? If so, examine fertility, maternity, and well-baby coverage.
- Are you contemplating staying home with your kids? Or will you be retiring soon? If so, consider signing up for your spouse's policy. Even if it costs more, you could continue using it after you leave the workforce.
- Do family members travel or go to school out of the area? If so, ask whether prior approval is required, and how much you will have to pay to see a doctor or use a health care facility in another town.

STEP 3 **KNOW THE CAPS AND GAPS OF YOUR COVERAGE.**

With a fee-for-service plan (traditional insurance), you pay a monthly premium and can see any doctor (including a specialist) or go to any hospital you choose. After you've met a yearly deductible (typically $150–$250), your insurer pays, say, 80 percent of the covered medical costs (doctors' visits, lab tests, hospital stays). You would owe the difference.

The Stars' Story

As Suzie and Ray Star discovered, limits on benefits can render an otherwise good policy useless. When their son Pete was born two years ago, he was diagnosed with a serious blood disorder. Medical bills during his first year of life topped $300,000. His dad's insurance paid the bulk of his bills, but Pete hit the $1,000,000 *lifetime* cap at age 2½. When the cap is reached, parents or spouses of chronically ill people are often left with little choice but to try to find another job with a good health plan (one that covers preexisting conditions) and a brand new $1,000,000 lifetime cap. "That's almost impossible to do," says Ray.

Million-dollar caps have been in effect since the 1970s. Despite soaring medical costs, some insurers are actually slashing the lifetime limit to $500,000. When shopping for a policy, look for one with a lifetime cap of at least $1,000,000 *per person*. Also, look for a yearly out-of-pocket limit of $1,000 or $2,500, but not more than you can afford.

Tip: If you or someone in your family is a heavy user of medical services, choose a plan with a low yearly deductible.

STEP 4 LEARN THE ABCS OF HMOS, IPAS, AND PPOS.

Because of lifetime caps and rising out-of-pocket costs, many consumers are swapping a fee-for-service plan for a health maintenance organization (HMO). For a fixed monthly fee, members get a smorgasbord of health services. Emphasis on preventive care is often an HMO's big draw, but critics say that long waits to get appointments can stymie care.

HMO doctors and other services often reside in one building. Many HMOs also contract with individual doctors or physicians' groups located in private offices. These groups are known as individual practice associations (IPAs).

A primary-care physician traditionally acts as the "gatekeeper" for HMO services. He or she coordinates your family's care and decides when or if you need referral to a specialist for a test or treatment. Lately, many HMOs have been substituting nurse practitioners or physicians' assistants as gatekeepers. They decide whether you can even see a doctor.

Depending on the terms of the HMO plan, you may pay $5 or $10 (or more) each time you use a service, or you may pay nothing. HMO quality and consumer satisfaction vary greatly from plan to plan. Before joining, talk to prospective doctors. If they have difficulty referring patients for tests or for consultation with specialists, you may not be satisfied. Ask your coworkers about their experience with the HMO.

Scrutinize the plan's details. If a family member has a preexisting condition or a chronic illness, does the plan have a wide selection of specialists? If not, or if you are denied a list of doctors to choose from, how cooperative will this group be in a medical emergency if they can't be helpful during this courtship phase?

Tip: To help you assess a managed care plan, call the National Committee for Quality Assurance (NCQA) at (888) 275-7585, or visit its Web site at www.ncqa.org to see whether NCQA has accredited the plan. NCQA inspects patients' records, complaints, equipment, and plans' staff members. [Note: NCQA collects a fee from, and uses data collected by, each health plan.]

Accusations persist that some HMOs discourage members from getting costly treatment or seeing specialists. If you are unhappy with your care and can't get satisfaction, complain to the head of the plan. Also tell your benefits manager at work; he or she may be able to intervene. Talk to your coworkers. If yours isn't the only complaint, ask to have the current plan replaced with a better and more cooperative one next year.

Tip: Stash some cash, in case you need to go outside the plan for a medical service the plan won't cover.

Many HMOs offer a preferred provider organization (PPO) option. With it, you get a list of health providers who have agreed to take a lower payment in exchange for referrals from within the plan. You will owe a co-payment ($10 or more) to see a doctor within the PPO, but you don't need a physician's referral.

Don't believe the hype; an HMO isn't always less expensive than traditional health insurance. "If you're young, healthy and rarely seek medical care, you may be able to get a traditional indemnity insurance plan for a very low premium and pay much less out of pocket than you would for an HMO," cautions Robert Hunter, Director of Insurance for the Washington-based Consumer Federation of America. HMO fees are based on average use, so if you seldom use it and can qualify for low-cost insurance, you may save money by buying traditional health insurance.

STEP 5 COMPARE PLAN COSTS.

Get out your medical bills and records for the past two years and use the following worksheet to estimate what you might pay with each of the

What It Could Cost You	Plan A	Plan B	Plan C	Plan D
Individual Coverage:				
• Monthly premium	$_____	$_____	$_____	$_____
• Yearly cost (monthly premium × 12)	$_____	$_____	$_____	$_____
Family Coverage:				
• Monthly premium	$_____	$_____	$_____	$_____
• Yearly cost (monthly premium × 12)	$_____	$_____	$_____	$_____
Deductible:				
• Individual	$_____	$_____	$_____	$_____
• Family	$_____	$_____	$_____	$_____
Coinsurance rate or copayment	$_____	$_____	$_____	$_____
Annual limits plan will pay (Is it more than you could afford?	$_____	$_____	$_____	$_____
My yearly out-of-pocket cap (When you reach this amount, typically $1,000 or $2,500, in one year would the plan pick up any additional out-of-pocket costs?)	$_____	$_____	$_____	$_____
Lifetime plan's maximum coverage (Is it at least $1,000,000?)	$_____	$_____	$_____	$_____
Annual estimated cost	$_____	$_____	$_____	$_____

plans you are considering for similar care. Be sure to allow for any recent changes in circumstances, such as a new baby or a newly diagnosed chronic illness.

STEP 6 CHECK UP ON THE PROVIDER'S SERVICE AND SOLVENCY.

Before signing up for any health plan, investigate the provider's record:

- Call your state insurance department (listed in the blue pages of the phone book) to request a copy of the complaint ratios (number of complaints per thousand) for the health plans you are considering.

- Look up the financial records for potential insurers at your local library. "Only consider policies rated 'A' or 'A+' in A.M. Best's Annual Insurance Report," advises Hunter. "Companies in financial trouble are stingier with claims."

STEP 7   SQUEEZE OUT MORE SAVINGS.

Here are more cost-saving ideas:

- If you're married but have no dependent children, a family medical plan may cost you more than if you and your spouse each sign up for an individual plan through your respective employers.
- Make the most of your employer's flexible spending account. The program allows you to use *pretax* dollars to pay for health care deductibles, copays for doctors' visits, prescriptions, and eyeglasses, among other things.

Tip: Most plans cap the benefit at $5,000 a year. You will forfeit money left over at the end of the year, so analyze your qualifying expenses in the prior year to determine more accurately the amount to set aside for the following year.

- Don't pay more than you owe. Many health plans quietly negotiate lower costs with doctors, hospitals, and pharmacies. If you aren't aware of the discount, you could end up paying more than you actually owe.

Pete's Story

When Pete Patrick got injured on the playground and was taken to a hospital emergency room, his parents were billed $400 for the visit. Their health plan stated that they would owe 20 percent of any bill for emergency room visits, but they didn't actually owe $80 (20 percent of $400). They actually owed less.

Why? Because their health plan had negotiated a lower fee with that hospital. "The hospital reduced Pete's fee to $220 instead of $400, so we only owed $44 (20 percent of $220), rather than $80," says Claire Patrick. But that didn't stop the hospital from trying to recover the difference from the Patricks.

"The hospital kept billing us not for $80, but for $224 [the original bill of $400 minus $176 (80 percent of the $220 that the insurer paid)], even though we didn't owe it," she says. "They even threatened to send the bill to collections."

Before you make a copayment for health services, be sure you won't be overpaying. Get a breakdown from your plan; see what amount was allowed (or disallowed) and how much was paid. Then get a corrected bill from the hospital or other service provider itemizing the new, reduced total fee and all monies paid by your plan. When you send your check, be sure to mark it "Paid in full." This could protect you if the service provider tries to collect more after cashing your check.

STEP 8 **UNDERSTAND YOUR PLAN.**

Whether you're in a managed care plan or a fee-for-service plan, you can increase your satisfaction and decrease your out-of-pocket payments if you understand how the plan works.

- Read the booklet, and keep it handy for future reference.
- Understand what qualifies as "an emergency." Broken bones? Bleeding? High fever?
- Know which hospital the plan uses. In an emergency, go to the nearest one and call the plan—typically, within 48 hours—for approval (to avoid running afoul of most plans' rules and having your claim rejected).

If your claim gets rejected, don't cave in. To help you resolve the dispute:

- Ask the doctor who treated you to support your claim by writing a diagnosis and stating why an emergency room visit seemed justified.
- Resubmit the denied claim. "Have them put in writing which provision of the plan they based a denial on," says Hunter. "It keeps them from changing the reason."
- Document your letters and calls. Jot down whom you spoke to, the date and time, and what was discussed.
- Escalate an unresolved complaint by writing to the plan's president. Send a copy of your letter to your state insurance department (or state health department, if you belong to an HMO). As a

last resort, you may want to hire an attorney to help plead your case.

STEP 9   HUNT FOR INDIVIDUAL COVERAGE.

If at all possible, try to hook up with a group. You'll likely pay less and get better coverage. Professional or trade associations, unions, alumni organizations, and support groups are good places to start.

If you're not eligible for group coverage, look for an individual plan that covers all hospitalization and surgery costs, and the bulk of prescriptions and outpatient care. Contact your state insurance department (in the blue pages of your phone book) for a list of companies that sell individual policies. Call Quotesmith (800) 431-1147 for free price quotes.

Here's my advice if you have to buy individual coverage:

- Call several insurance companies or an independent agent to get multiple options.
- Look for a lifetime cap of $1,000,000 or more, and a yearly out-of-pocket cap of $1,000 (or $2,500, if you can afford to pay that much before qualifying for any reimbursement).
- Check the start date, the exclusions, and the waiting periods for preexisting conditions.
- Look for a "noncancelable" (or "guaranteed renewable") policy; you can keep it as long as you pay premiums, regardless of your health. Get a written guarantee that premiums won't rise for at least a year (preferably longer).
- Skip dread disease insurance. This would kick in only if you develop one prespecified illness, such as cancer. You'll get no coverage for any other illness, so buy a good, broad-coverage health care policy instead.
- Examine your new policy immediately. You typically have ten days to cancel it and get a refund if it's not what you thought you bought.

It should go without saying, but I want to emphasize that you should never lie on your application. Even though the plan may cash your premium checks, at a minimum, you may be denied payment when you file a claim.

Tip: If your health is poor and you can't get an individual policy, ask your state insurance department if a high-risk pool is available. If not, consider joining an HMO.

STEP 10 CONSIDER A MEDICAL SAVINGS ACCOUNT (MSA).

If you are self-employed or work for a company that has fewer than fifty employees and does not offer group health coverage, you could be eligible to sign up for a medical savings account (MSA). This relatively new type of account operates quite differently from traditional health plans. For one thing, you pay for medical expenses using tax-free money. And, money in an MSA grows tax-free, and you can *keep* any money left in your account at the end of the year. Proponents of these accounts say MSAs encourage consumers to think twice before spending money on medical services that might not be necessary.

How do you sign up? To start an MSA, you buy a catastrophic health insurance policy with a high deductible: up to $2,250 for an individual policy, or up to $4,500 for a family plan. (The deductible is the amount you would have to pay in medical expenses before the policy begins to pay for additional covered medical costs.) Catastrophic, high-deductible insurance policies typically cost much less than traditional, comprehensive health insurance policies.

Who pays for an MSA, and what does it cost? To set up the savings account part of the MSA, you open an individual savings account and deposit up to 65 percent of the deductible for an individual account, or up to 75 percent of the deductible for a family account. Your contribution qualifies as a deduction when you file your income tax return.

Your employer could set up and contribute to an MSA for you, but if the contribution is less than the maximum, you cannot augment it with your own money.

Under what circumstances can you tap the money? Your MSA money can be used tax-free for a range of medical expenses. But if you use the money for nonmedical purposes, you will owe tax on the amount you spend (you are expected to report this amount as taxable income), plus a penalty of 15 percent if you are under age 65. If you use the money for nonmedical purposes and you are age 65 or older, you will still owe tax on the money, but no penalty.

A bank or insurance company can hold the money, acting as the custodian. Your money can be held in a bank account or invested in a mutual fund. The returns on consumers' bank accounts have been relatively low: 4 to 5 percent.

What's the most you would have to pay out-of-pocket each year, in covered medical costs? If your medical costs exceed your deductible, you may have to foot the bill for a percentage of your additional medical expenses. At this writing, the maximum amount you would have to pay annually, out-of-pocket, for covered medical expenses is $3,000 for an individual plan or $5,500 for a family plan.

You may also use the MSA money to pay for medical costs that are not covered by your insurance, including prescription eyeglasses, any portion of a physician's bill that is deemed "excessive," charges for seeing a physician outside of your managed care plan (if you are in one), or fees for cosmetic surgery. The money used for these purposes is not taxed, but it does not count toward your annual deductible.

Tip: Your insurer should keep a running tab of your covered medical costs that count toward your deductible, but it's a good idea to keep the bills and set up your own running tab of your covered medical costs.

How do you get access to money in your MSA account? Usually, by writing a check, although some plans may allow you to use a debit card.

What happens to money left in the account at the end of the year? Don't confuse your MSA account with a flexible spending account you may have at work (which also lets you use tax-free money to pay for some medical costs). You won't forfeit any unused money in your MSA. Money not used in one year can stay in your account for future use, and it continues to grow, tax-free. An MSA can be a great way for healthy, wealthy people to shelter money from taxes after they've reached their limit on other tax-deferred accounts, such as IRAs and 401(k) plans.

For more information on MSAs, your employer can contact the Employers Council on Flexible Compensation, in Washington, DC (202-659-4300). Or, you can visit the Council for Affordable Health Insurance at www.cahi.org or write to:

The Council for Affordable Health Insurance
112 S. West Street, Suite 400
Alexandria, VA 22314

STEP 11 CHOOSE YOUR DOCTOR WITH CARE.

How much you will pay for health care, as well as the quality of care you and your family receive, is determined in large part by the doctor you choose (or are assigned to by your managed health care plan). Primary care doctors are fast becoming the gatekeepers for many health care plans; they help to decide whether a plan will pick up the cost for needed tests, for brand-name prescriptions, or for a visit to another doctor to get a second opinion. Be aware that the doctor you choose can have a huge impact on your family's current and future health and what it will end up costing you.

Are you in the market for a new doctor? If you're moving to another town or are changing health care plans, you can start your search by asking your former doctor or a coworker for a referral. Many consumers rely on recommendations from their managed care plan. Others are turning to one of the many physician referral services that are springing up almost everywhere via telephone.

Regardless of who refers you, it's a good idea to do a little independent verification of a potential choice's medical education and certifications. The American Medical Association has its own Web site. You can check into a doctor's training and specialty at www.ama-assn.org. To verify that the American Board of Medical Specialties has board-certified a doctor in his or her specialty, surf on over to the Board's Web site at www.certifieddoctor.org. (Many libraries let patrons use their Internet service free of charge.)

Before making your selection, request a face-to-face interview with the doctors. Here are some questions to ask:

- Are you board-certified and in which specialties? (Certification would show at least some training in his or her specialty.)
- Where do you have hospital privileges? (If the answer is "Nowhere" and you must enter a hospital, you will need to start working with a new doctor who has privileges there.)
- How long is a typical wait for an appointment?
- Do you accept my health insurance? Will you file the forms for me?
- Do you require full payment at the time of service? Will you accept my insurer's payment as payment in full?
- What kinds of preventive health regimens would you suggest for someone my age and with my medical history? (Give brief details.)
- What role do you consider a patient should have in decision making?
- What steps do you take to preserve the privacy of patients' records?

Observe the doctor's manner. Does he or she listen patiently or seem to be in a hurry to leave the room? Next, look around the office. Is it clean? Does the equipment appear to be current and in good shape? Is the staff courteous and professional? Or is patient information discussed in a loud voice that could easily be overheard by others?

Because of heavy patient loads, many doctors are under pressure to spend less time with each patient. To make the most of your visit, do some homework and jot down some notes before you get to the doctor's office.

You'll want to explain your condition and ask questions. Arrange your questions in order of priority. If you can't get to all of them, you'll at least address the most important ones:

- Describe your symptoms and what you were doing when they started.
- If you recently began a strenuous exercise program or started taking a new medication (prescription or over-the-counter), ask if that could be causing your symptoms.
- If you're having a recurrence of an old malady, summarize the prior circumstances and how the illness was treated.
- If you have recently traveled to another country, mention where you were. You could be suffering from a rare or exotic virus or bacteria that a doctor wouldn't normally look for.

Consider taking some notes while the doctor is speaking or after he or she leaves the room, while your dialogue is still fresh in your mind.

STEP 12   FILL PRESCRIPTIONS FOR LESS.

Most health plans pay some or most of the cost of a prescription medication. Once you've met a yearly deductible (nowadays, it's often separate from the medical deductible), your plan may pay up to 80 percent of the prescription cost, and you pick up the remaining 20 percent. But in many managed care plans, consumers pay a fixed fee of $5 to $12 for each prescription, regardless of the medication's price.

To keep costs down, health plans often negotiate lower prescription costs with one or more local pharmacies. If you use a different pharmacy, the plan may pay little or nothing. Read your plan to see what is covered, where the participating pharmacies are located, and how long you have to file a claim.

Some plans cut prescription costs by negotiating a deal with a mail-order pharmacy fulfillment center. If you have a recurring or chronic illness that requires medication, this system could be convenient and save you money. You mail in the prescription and receive up to three months' medication for a flat fee of $10 to $20.

If your medications will be sitting for hours in a hot mailbox in the summer or in a freezing mailbox in the winter, mail order may not be the best choice for you. Many medications lose their potency at extreme temperatures or might even become toxic. And unattended medications could be a temptation for tampering.

Here are some other ways to cut prescription costs:

- Try generic instead of brand-name medication. The active ingredients are the same. Medication absorption rates can be different, however, so don't keep alternating between different manufacturers.
- Call at least three pharmacies to get price quotes. Ask the nearest pharmacist to match any lower quoted prices. Many will agree in order to get your business. Some will accept discount coupons offered by competing, local pharmacies. (A few will even add a dollar to the coupons' value.)
- Ask for a discount. If you use a medication on a regular basis, you could save by ordering three to six months' worth at a time. Ask the pharmacist how to store the extra medication. But check with your managed care plan before ordering. Some plans will only pay for one or two months' medication at a time.
- Count your pills when you get home. Pharmacies are busy places. Miscounts are not uncommon. If you are shortchanged, call the pharmacist immediately to get the remaining pills.
- If you've just been prescribed an expensive medication for the first time, ask the pharmacist if you can get a lower-cost partial fill, so you can try it for a few days. If the medicine works and agrees with you, you can then pick up and pay for the remaining prescription.

Tip: Some prescription medications and/or over-the-counter medications can interact, either making the medication ineffective or, in rare cases, causing fatal complications. Tell your pharmacist about all prescription and over-the-counter medications you are taking, and read the insert that comes with your prescriptions. It will tell you when and how to take your medication and any precautions to follow. If your pharmacist refuses to give you this insert, switch pharmacies.

Chapter 17

Coast Your Way to
Car Insurance Savings

Ted's Story

The red sports car was loaded with every feature Ted had dreamed of—
and a few more he didn't even know existed. The test drive was the
clincher. "The engine purred," he recalls, wistfully. "I figured the monthly
payments would be more than I could afford, but it was the end of the
month and the salesman said he was 'in the mood to deal.' The monthly
payments were more than I had planned to spend. But, hey, you only go
around once. Five hours later, the car was prepped, the sales manager
gave me the keys, and I was off. It felt like the happiest day of my life."

But his glee turned to panic the next day, when Ted called his insurance agent to notify him about the new set of wheels. Not only was Ted's
new car a popular model with car buyers, it also was high on the list for
car thieves and lead-footed drivers—and the insurance premiums reflected this. "The premiums were going to be $2,880 a year," explained
Ted. "I could barely afford the monthly loan payment on the car, so there
was no way I could swing an extra $240 for insurance."

The dealer said he had sympathy for Ted's predicament, but he
wouldn't take the car back. So Ted's only choice was to sell the car himself. He placed ads in the newspaper. "Many sightseers stopped by for a
test drive, but they weren't serious about buying," he recalled. "I walked
by that car every day, but I couldn't even drive it because it wasn't insured. I owned that car for ten days and I lost $3,348 on the sale." What
would he do differently next time? "I would call my agent before I even
started looking for a car," he says. "Why get your hopes up about a car if
the insurance bill will put it out of your reach?"

You say this couldn't happen to you? Think again. Choosing a car that
is popular with speeders or car thieves isn't the only reason that sky-high
insurance premiums might put a car out of your financial reach.

If you have a lead accelerator foot, a teenage driver in your house, or
late or overdue payments on your credit card bills, you're probably paying
more in insurance premiums than consumers who play by the rules.

Whether you have a somewhat checkered driving past or your record is squeaky clean, it pays to comparison-shop for auto insurance the same way you would comparison-shop for a car.

You'll pay less for your car insurance if you take the five steps described here.

STEP 1 UNDERSTAND WHAT DRIVES INSURANCE COSTS UP.

Statistically, a high-performance car is more likely to be in a costly accident than a family-type vehicle, and insurance premiums reflect this risk. Some car makes and models are very popular with car thieves, which elevates these cars' insurance premiums. It's essential to get auto insurance price quotes before you buy or lease a new or used car.

If you pay your credit card bills late, you'll likely be charged higher insurance premiums—if you can get insurance at all. Insurance companies base your insurance worthiness on "predictors"—behaviors they believe show your potential future cost to them. In the past, they looked at such predictors as your driving history or where you lived. Nowadays, they believe that the way you handle credit and pay your bills is a better predictor of your future behavior.

Insurers now regularly peruse customers' (and potential customers') credit reports to see how they handle their finances. So before you shop for insurance, take the time to take a look at your credit report. Unfortunately, mistakes on credit reports are still common, although it's a little easier now to get them fixed. (See Chapter 4 for phone numbers for contacting the three big credit bureaus.)

Remember, it will likely cost you $8 or more to get a copy of your report (some states allow residents to get one free credit report each year), so only order *one* credit report and read it carefully. If you find an error, get copies of all three, to be sure the other two companies are accurately reporting your credit history. (See Chapter 4.)

STEP 2 DETERMINE WHAT KIND OF COVERAGE, AND HOW MUCH OF IT, YOU NEED.

Insurance is designed to shield you from hefty losses, so don't pay for more insurance than you actually need. Many insurers will jack up rates after you file a claim—some insurers even cancel policies altogether—so it often makes sense to "self-insure": pay for small damages out of your own pocket and only file a claim for larger damage. And if you're not going to submit the smaller claims, it may make sense to raise your deductible.

But be careful: Don't sign up for a higher deductible than you can afford to pay. Unlike with health insurance, where you must pay the deductible, at most, once a year, with auto insurance—and some bad luck—you could end up paying deductibles out of your pocket several times in one year—each time you had an accident or other loss. If you're contemplating raising your deductible from, say, $250 to 500, ask yourself, "Could I afford to pay a $500 deductible two or three times in one year?" If not, keep the deductible lower.

If you raise your deductible, your premiums will drop—sometimes significantly. Don't squander this savings. Stash some cash in an emergency kitty, so that if you have an accident or other car or property damage, you'll have some money on hand to pay for it.

Here are some of the various types of coverage you can buy, and what I recommend on each:

- *Uninsured and underinsured motorist coverage.* Some financial experts recommend cutting insurance costs by eliminating uninsured motorist coverage. But canceling uninsured motorist coverage is rarely a good idea. This coverage would take care of medical, rehabilitative, and funeral costs caused by a hit-and-run driver or a driver with inadequate insurance or no insurance at all. It would also pay for pain and suffering for the driver and family members in the insured car. This is mandatory in some states— and worth the money in all states. The minimum amount you should buy is $100,000 per person and $300,000 per accident.

Tip: If you have sizable assets (more than $200,000), you may need more liability coverage for property damage and bodily injury. Consider buying an umbrella policy. For about $200 to $350 per year, you could increase your liability protection to $1 million or $2 million (depending on your total assets).

Note: If you carry an "umbrella policy," which is explained in Chapter 18, you may be able to choose lower minimums than these because the umbrella policy should pick up where these amounts end.

- *Bodily injury liability.* Following an accident in which you were at fault, this insurance would pay the medical, rehabilitative, and funeral costs for the victims injured in the accident (the driver of another car involved, passengers in your car or another car that was involved, and pedestrians). It would also cover legal costs and pain and suffering to the extent of your policy's coverage. Get coverage of at least $100,000 per person and $300,000 per accident. Buy a policy for coverage that exceeds two or three times your assets, otherwise a judge could order that you pay the balance (the difference between your insurance limits and your assets) out of your own pocket.

- *Property damage liability.* This would pay for damage to property, or to another vehicle, caused by you or by someone who uses your car and is covered by your automobile insurance policy. This coverage is required by state law. Get coverage of at least $100,000.

- *Collision coverage.* With collision coverage, your insurance would pay the cost to repair or replace your car (up to its market value), whether you or someone else is at fault. Payments are subject to your policy's deductible. By the time your new car reaches its fourth birthday, its market value has plummeted, and some financial experts recommend eliminating collision coverage after that milestone. But as the value of your car drops, the cost for collision coverage also drops, so if you wouldn't have enough money to pay for a replacement car, it may make more sense to keep this coverage.

- *Comprehensive coverage.* Comprehensive coverage would pay to replace or repair your car if it were stolen or were damaged or destroyed by a fire, a storm, an act of vandalism, or a variety of other perils. The benefit you receive is subject to a deductible, and you can slash your premiums by increasing your deductible to $500 or more. But never agree to a higher deductible than you could afford to pay out of pocket. As with collision coverage, to save money on your premiums, you could consider dropping comprehensive coverage when your car gets older, but if you wouldn't have enough money to pay for a replacement car, it may make more sense to keep comprehensive coverage as well.

- *Medical payments.* This optional coverage would pick up the tab for many medical and rehabilitative services and some funeral expenses. Usually, it comes with no deductible. It may overlap with health coverage you already have. But if you have no health coverage or must pay high deductibles or copayments, this is worth buying.

- *Personal injury protection (PIP).* This is a more wide-ranging medical coverage. It also may reimburse some lost wages or pay for in-home assistance needed after an accident. It is required coverage in states with no-fault insurance laws, even though it may duplicate health, life, and disability coverage you already have. Check your policies. If it does overlap, buy only the minimum required by law.

- *Towing coverage.* If your car can no longer be driven as a result of a collision, towing coverage will pick up the tab to take it to a body shop. If your battery goes dead, towing coverage usually pays for a tow truck to come to your car and jump-start the battery. It's inexpensive and would pay for itself with one use. I say this coverage is well worth the money.

Tip: If your car is fairly new, the manufacturer may have thrown in free emergency road service. Check whether that perk overlaps with this coverage.

- *Rental reimbursement.* This policy feature pays for a rental car while your car is being fixed following an accident, or if your car is stolen. It may cost a couple of dollars a month and is a good buy if you have only one car (no backup) in the family.

STEP 3 PRUNE YOUR PREMIUMS PRUDENTLY.

Here are some tried-and-true cost savers:

- *Boost your driving skills.* Driver education isn't just for high school students any more. Completing a state-approved defensive driving course could get you a discount of 5 percent or more on your insurance premiums.
- *Increase your deductible.* Doubling your deductible from $250 to $500 can slash your premium by at least 15 percent.
- *Ditch your duplicate coverage.* Medical payments features is one of the overlaps that is easiest to spot. (Compare your health care policy's protections versus those offered in an auto insurance policy.)
- *When you're shopping for a car, look for features insurers love.* Air bags and antilock brakes are safety features that may qualify you for discounts. A car alarm could also get you a discount. Before buying a particular car, find out what the auto insurance premiums will be. Statistically, high-performance cars are more likely to be in costly accidents, and their insurance premiums reflect this history.

Remember to ask, ask, ask. The squeaky wheel gets the best auto insurance deal. You could be eligible for a discount based on any of these reasons:

- Insuring more than one car with the same insurer.
- Carrying your homeowner's policy with the insurer that has your auto insurance policy.
- Posting low annual mileage.
- Being over age 50 and the sole family driver.
- Carpooling to work.
- Parking your car in a garage, not on the street.
- Moving to a safer neighborhood.
- Having an accident-free driving record.

Any of these discounts could save you 5 percent or more on your premiums, so ask your insurer if you qualify. Also, comparison-shop with at least three insurance companies to get the coverage you need at the best price.

Safety Tip: If your car was in an accident with your child's car seat inside, replace the car seat even if it looks okay. Car seats can suffer structural damage and still look fine to the naked eye. Some insurance companies will pay to replace car seats, but even if yours doesn't, don't risk your child's safety. Throw out the old seat; don't give or sell it to a friend, relative, or charity. Destroy it so that it can't be used by an unsuspecting person.

STEP 4 — TRIM YOUR TEEN'S INSURANCE BILL.

Teens and cars can be a costly combination. Here are some discounts that may keep your teenager's license from making your insurance rate soar:

- Have your teen graduate from a state-approved driver education course.
- Tell your teen to keep his or her grades up, to qualify for a good student discount.
- If you have more than one car, limit your teen's driving to your least expensive car (if your insurer allows this), and never let the teen drive any of your other cars.
- If your teen, or older child, who has been insured on your auto policy heads off to a college that is more than 100 miles from your

home (and will seldom be borrowing the car), ask your insurer to reduce your rate.

STEP 5 READ UP ON CAR RENTAL RULES BEFORE TRAVELING.

No matter how great the car rental rate you were promised, you could squander all the savings, and then some, by signing up for overpriced rental car coverage that duplicates coverage you already have. Before you rent a car, call your insurance company to see what coverage you already have, and what, if any, additional coverage you should buy. Here's what to ask about:

- *Collision.* If you drive an older car at home and you ditched the collision coverage, then say "yes" to the collision damage waiver unless the credit card you are using *currently* offers this coverage. Also ask if the car rental company would charge for "loss of use" if the rented car spent some days in the repair shop and was not producing revenue after a collision.
- *Liability.* Your own auto insurance policy should offer this, but double-check.
- *Personal accident.* Your health insurance and the personal injury protection (PIP) in your own auto insurance policy should offer adequate coverage following an accident, but again, double-check.
- *Personal effects.* Home owner policies usually pay for personal effects that are stolen from a rental car, so ask. (Your deductible would still apply.)

Before you pay for any extra coverage, check whether your corporate travel department at work has negotiated a deal with any rental car companies. Some such arrangements throw in assorted coverage at little or no cost—but you will likely have to ask for the corporate contract terms and may need the corporate-rental car contract numbers, which your employer can give you.

Also call your credit card company. Some premium platinum and gold cards (including some corporate cards) still offer some coverage if you pay for a rental car with their card. But these credit card deals are getting hard to come by and have many restrictions. Ask these questions:

- If you are traveling on business (not vacation), is the credit card coverage valid for your trip?
- Whether you're traveling on vacation or business, does your coverage go beyond 30 days?
- If you are traveling outside the United States, is the same rental coverage available?

Chapter 18

Safeguard Your Home
and Its Contents

Harvey's Story

"It wasn't much of a rainstorm, and in a few minutes it was over," recalls Harvey. "The wind suddenly gusted, and then we heard a crunching noise followed by glass shattering in the kitchen. My wife Marla and I rushed into the kitchen and saw our neighbor's tree had snapped in two and part of it had come through our kitchen window and was now resting on the kitchen table. Fortunately, no one was hurt.

"I called my neighbor to tell him that his half-dead tree, which I had been asking him to remove for years, had come crashing through our house, and to ask about his insurance coverage so I would know where to send the repair bills. He told me, 'Sorry to hear it, but it's not my problem, so take it up with your own insurer.' Then he hung up."

If a fire, theft, or natural disaster were to damage or destroy your home, would your insurance pay you enough, quickly enough, so that you could start over? You don't have to live in an area that might be considered high-risk for fires, hurricanes, or earthquakes, to be at risk for costly property damage.

Don't wait for a disaster to strike. There are things you can do now that could make your life easier following a disaster. First, review your insurance policy. Do you have enough of the right kind of coverage and at the right price? Here are eleven steps to guide you.

STEP 1 ADD UP HOW MUCH HOMEOWNER'S COVERAGE YOU ACTUALLY NEED.

For a variety of reasons, many homeowners carry the wrong amount of homeowner insurance—sometimes too much, other times too little. Are you paying more than necessary and still not carrying adequate coverage? You could be, if you calculated your needed coverage by using any of these incorrect assumptions.

- *An amount equal to your mortgage balance.* Don't rely on the amount your mortgage company suggests; its only goal is to get your mortgage balance repaid if something were to happen to your home. The mortgage balance could be far less than it would cost to replace your home, especially if you've paid down the mortgage over the years.
- *An amount equal to the purchase price of your home.* This amount would include the value of your land—which is not insured by your policy—so if you bought the home recently, you would be overinsured. Even if you bought the home several years ago, and its value has risen, going by the purchase price is still not a good idea. Instead, have your insurance agent reevaluate the amount of coverage you need. Having your agent determine the amount of coverage you need (this includes measuring the structure and noting architectural features and materials used) could also give you a little extra protection if you find later that you are underinsured because your agent recommended a value that was too low. Be sure to keep all correspondence from your insurer in a safe place, in case you have to reconstruct how that value was determined.

LLOYD'S LAW

Insure your home for the amount that it would cost to rebuild it from the ground up with comparable materials.

- *An amount equal to the original construction cost of your home.* Materials and labor costs have surely risen since your home was built, and building codes may also have changed.

Your insurer can help you determine this amount by calculating the total square footage, multiplying it by the construction costs per square foot in your area, and then adding another 10 to 20 percent to cover assorted costs, such as an architect's fees. Double-check the amount by speaking with a construction company in your town.

FIND OUT EXACTLY WHAT'S COVERED.

Ideally, you would like a policy to cover everything except perils specifically excluded—such as flood, earthquake, or war. Less comprehensive policies would cost less but would cover only a limited number of natural hazards, such as fire or wind damage.

STEP 3 — CHECK THAT YOUR POLICY CONTAINS A "GUARANTEED REPLACEMENT COST" CLAUSE.

With this clause, your insurance company would pay to replace or repair your home, even if it costs more than the face value of your policy. If possible, buy a guaranteed replacement cost policy. Less expensive policies only cover you for the depreciated value of your home and contents. Unless you like shopping at garage sales, you probably couldn't collect enough to buy replacement furniture.

Here is a comparison of the different types of homeowners' policies:

- *HO-1.* It offers the most basic coverage, protecting policyholders against, at most, a dozen "perils," which is often not enough. Hold out for something better and more comprehensive.
- *HO-2.* For a small amount more than you might pay for an HO-1 policy, you can upgrade to this type. It protects against, at most, eighteen perils, and it may limit coverage to actual costs at the time of purchase (depreciated loss, not the cost to replace your stolen or destroyed property).
- *HO-3.* This popular coverage offers much more protection and may cost just 10 or 15 percent more than an HO-1 policy. Unlike the first two policies, this one would cover all perils *except those specifically excluded* (such as a backed-up sewer or an earthquake).

  With a standard HO-3 policy, you would automatically be covered for a replacement cost, but only up to the limits on your policy. You would need to buy a supplement to the HO-3 policy to get the "guaranteed replacement costs." It's also a good idea to buy a rider that would reimburse you if you upgrade your home to current building codes.
- *HO-4.* This is often known as a "renter's" or "tenant's" policy. It covers a policyholder's possessions, but not the actual building (the landlord's policy should do that) against more than a dozen listed "perils." You can also buy protection for any built-in improvements you make to the dwelling, as well as liability coverage. Roommates are typically covered under one policy.
- *HO-6.* This is a policy for condominium and co-op owners. It offers liability and personal property coverage similar to the HO-4 coverage for renters. The dwelling itself is insured by the co-op or

condo association. This policy basically provides coverage from the walls in. You would need to purchase an endorsement to cover any additions to the building, such as a deck.

Tip: Consider buying "loss assessment" coverage to fill any insurance gap your co-op or condo may have. For example, if your co-op or condo loses a lawsuit or is subject to other damages, for which it is underinsured, you would not have to pay your share out of your own pocket.

- *HO-7.* Vintage or unique home coverage. If you own an old house that would be prohibitively expensive to replace, you might not be allowed to purchase an HO-3 replacement cost policy. Instead, you may only be offered this less-comprehensive policy (comparable to an HO-1), which would pay to restore damaged property, but not necessarily with comparable materials.

STEP 4 — INSIST ON BEING INSURED FOR AT LEAST 80 PERCENT OF THE ESTIMATED COST TO REBUILD YOUR HOME.

If you don't have the 80 percent provision, the insurance company will prorate any settlement and you won't collect enough to repair or rebuild. (If you had $6,000 damage when a falling tree crashed through your kitchen window, but were only insured for 70 percent of your property ($140,000 on a $200,000 home), your reimbursement would be reduced. You could only receive 70 percent of $6,000, less the policy's deductible.

STEP 5 — CHOOSE AMPLE LIMITS TO PROTECT YOUR POSSESSIONS.

Most homeowners' policies cover your possessions for up to 50 percent (sometimes 75 percent) of the value of your home. So, if your home is covered for $150,000, your furniture, clothing, and most other possessions would be covered for $75,000. There are usually lower limits for items such as electronic equipment, silver, jewelry, and home-office equipment. Make sure those items are adequately protected with a "rider" (endorsement) to cover the items you have listed.

If you run a home-based business, you may need additional coverage to pay for loss of (or damage to) office equipment, on or off your property. Depending on the size of your business and whether you employ workers outside your family, you may be able to get by with a supplementary "endorsement" to your policy. An alternative is a separate business policy. Also look into a liability policy for professionals.

STEP 6 KNOW YOUR LIABILITY IF SOMEONE TRIPS AND FALLS ON YOUR PROPERTY.

In another scenario, your dog bites a visitor or a stranger or unintentionally damages a neighbor's property. These are times when your policy's liability coverage would kick in. Some consumers settle for $100,000, but that's taking a chance. Sign up for at least $300,000 of coverage. If your assets are sizable, even this coverage could be too limited and could put your family's financial future in jeopardy. If you have assets of more than $200,000, look into buying an umbrella policy. For about $200 to $350 per year, you could increase your liability protection to $1 million or $2 million.

If you employ a domestic worker, such as a housekeeper or a babysitter, the basic personal liability protection that comes with your homeowner's policy may not be enough. Consider supplementing it with a standard workers' compensation policy (this protection is required in some instances). It could protect you from a lawsuit brought by an injured worker in your employ; the policy would offer your employee medical benefits and a way to recover lost wages. You don't need to cover independent contractors (such as lawn mowing services or similar contractors), provided you've double-checked that they have coverage—and that it is still in force.

STEP 7 ASSESS YOUR RISKS FROM RISING WATER.

Contrary to popular belief, flooding is not limited to damage caused by an overflowing body of water, such as an ocean, river, or creek. Insurers define flooding as water entering your home—often through the floor— and that can occur even when no body of water is located near you. Depending on the way your home was constructed and the land was graded, even if you live on the top of a mountain, you could still suffer flood damage.

If you live in what the government has declared a high-risk area, but choose not to buy a flood insurance policy, nowadays, following a flood, the federal government is apt to turn down your request for *any* assistance—including a low interest loan. Only very low-income people are given outright grants, and, at most, they'll receive only a few thousand dollars. That's not enough to rebuild a house.

Currently, you can insure your home for up to $250,000 and the contents for up to $100,000. Even renters should consider buying a flood insurance policy to protect personal possession (clothes, computers, and so on) that could be destroyed in a flood. You'll pay the same amount for the same coverage no matter which insurance agent sells you a policy. If your insurance agent doesn't sell them, to get names of agents that do, you can call the Federal Emergency Management Agency (FEMA) at (800) 427-4661. There is usually a 30-day waiting period for this coverage to kick in, so don't wait for a severe storm warning to sign up.

STEP 8 INVESTIGATE WHETHER YOU NEED EARTHQUAKE OR HIGH-RISK INSURANCE.

You don't have to live in California to worry about whether an earthquake will destroy or seriously damage your property. Despite costly limitations on payouts—such as deductibles of up to 20 percent of your home's insured value, and coverage on your contents that is capped at a few thousand dollars—earthquake policies aren't cheap. You may be able to add earthquake coverage to your basic homeowner's policy; otherwise, you'll have to buy it separately.

There are many circumstances that can make buying homeowner's insurance tough. Even strong winds or living on a coastline can make it difficult for you to get coverage on your home, sweet home. If you, or your property, are denied coverage, ask your state insurance department for information on high-risk pools.

STEP 9 CRUNCH THE NUMBERS TO SEE WHETHER YOU ARE OVERPAYING.

With so many natural and other disasters in the past few years, insurance rates are rising in many parts of the country. Here are some ways to avoid overpaying and still buy adequate coverage:

- *Read your policy closely.* Are the facts about your home and possessions accurate? Here are some common errors to look out for: overstating the square footage of your home; describing your brick home as "wood construction"; overstating the distance from your home to the nearest fire hydrant. Any of these can raise your rates.
- *Comparison-shop.* Call at least three different insurers. To avoid comparing apples to oranges, provide each agent with a copy of

your current policy. When you're given the price quotes, you'll know they are for the same coverage.

- *Boost your deductible.* Going from a $250 to a $500 deductible may shave about 10 percent off your insurance bill each year.

Tip: Don't choose a deductible that's higher than an amount you could afford to pay several times a year. That's right; with some bad luck, you could end up paying a homeowner's insurance deductible more than once in a year. Unlike health insurance, for which you pay the deductible (at most) once a year, homeowner's insurance keeps you subject to a deductible each time you have a covered loss (fire, theft, whatever). If you're contemplating raising your deductible from, say, $250 to $500, ask yourself: "Could I afford to pay a $500 deductible two or three times in one year?" If not, keep the lower deductible.

- *Demand discounts.* Have you installed deadbolt locks? Do you own a working fire extinguisher? Do you have a centrally monitored security system? These could be worth discounts of 5 percent to 12 percent off your premiums. Could you offer this insurance agent your auto insurance policy, or other policies, and then ask for a multipolicy discount? Are you a long-term customer (three years or more)? Ask for a loyalty discount.
- *Read up on ratings.* There's nothing worse than filing a claim after paying premiums for years and finding out that your insurer is insolvent and can't pay. Check prospective insurers in the local library. Look up their ratings in A.M. Best and Standard & Poor's listings or on the Web at www.standardandpoors.com.

STEP 10 DOCUMENT YOUR RECORDS SO YOU COULD SUBSTANTIATE A FUTURE CLAIM.

If you're satisfied that you have enough insurance, what can you do now to maximize your repayment in case of a future loss? For reimbursement, you'll need proof. Good records can expedite a claim later. Snapshots and receipts are a good start, but a room-by-room video inventory is better. But don't make the mistake of keeping this inventory in your home. In a fire or other disaster, it could be destroyed along with your possessions. Keep it in your safe deposit box.

Tip: If you have a claim, bolster it by asking friends and relatives for photos of your home, possibly taken over the holidays or other celebrations.

STEP
11 GET YOUR DUE WHEN YOU FILE A CLAIM.

Here is what to do if your home is damaged or demolished or if your personal property is stolen or destroyed:

- File a police report immediately following a fire, a theft, or an accident that might be covered by your policy. Keep a copy, to help substantiate your claim.
- If someone is injured on your property, *don't* admit liability.
- Contact your insurance agent or the insurance company immediately, to start the claims process. Schedule a visit by the insurer, to assess the damage. If the damage is extensive and repairs need to be made immediately, ask for an advance payment. (This money will be deducted from your claim later.)

Tip: Before the adjuster arrives, get a ballpark estimate of the damage by having a contractor of your own choice estimate the cost of repairs.

- Start a separate file for all paperwork related to the claim. Eventually, the file will contain: receipts for repairs and for purchase of replacement items; "before" and "after" photos of damaged areas or items; appraisals of the damage; medical bills; canceled checks; and correspondence with the insurance company.
- Document the damage. Go through your home room by room, and write down a detailed description of the damage. Take photographs or make a videotape as you go.
- Make only emergency repairs. Get prior approval for all other work. Only make emergency repairs until the insurance company has seen the damage and given written approval for specific repair work. Unless your insurer has preapproved the expense involved, you could end up footing the bill. But do any temporary fixing that's needed to keep the problems from getting worse. For instance, if your home's security has been compromised, hire someone to board up windows or other entryways, to keep out vandals, kids, wildlife, and the elements. Get a receipt for this or any other emergency work you must get done immediately. Also keep bills for temporary living expenses you incurred when your home was uninhabitable.
- Track down contractors that have good records. Get a list of approved repair contractors from your insurer. If these contractors

have worked with your insurer before, they may bill your insurer directly. Get an idea of which repairs will be handled this way; the reimbursement you receive will be lowered accordingly.

- Don't jump at a low-ball settlement offer, which is what the first offer from the insurance company might be. By endorsing and cashing a check sent by the insurer, you will likely be accepting "settlement in full," even though the amount of the payment is less than you should receive.

Tip: Additional damage sometimes shows up weeks or months after a settlement has been reached. If a contractor documents the additional problem—and why it wasn't obvious earlier—most insurers will pay for the additional work.

- Consult your own experts if you can't come to terms with the insurer. Consider hiring a lawyer if the damage was extensive or if you are considering filing an appeal.
- Escalate your claim. If you still can't resolve your claim to your satisfaction, contact your state insurance department (listed in the blue pages of your phone book) or visit www.naic.org, the Web site for the National Association of Insurance Commissioners, which has links to state insurance commissions. Give a brief chronology of the incident, the actions you've taken, and the additional action you are seeking from your insurer. Include copies of receipts, letters, and so on, but keep the originals in your file. Send a copy of your letter to your insurer; this alone may spur your insurer into cooperating.
- Consider court action. As a last resort, you can file a lawsuit against an insurer, but it could take a long time and cost you a small fortune. See whether your case qualifies for small claims court. You can represent yourself there, but I would consult a lawyer for advice before telling your case to the judge.

Sharpen Your Shopping Skills

The rules of shopping used to be so simple: The one thing you didn't pay the full asking price for was a car. These days, some car dealers advertise "no-dicker stickers," but, advertised or not, the price of merchandise you buy almost everywhere else—from the supermarket to the shopping mall, and every place in between—can be negotiated. In this solution, I will show you the best ways to ask for everything from lower prices to extras you may never have considered. The skills and negotiating strategies you learn and master on small purchases can save you even more on big-ticket items, such as a car or a home.

If you've never purchased anything over the Internet or from a cata-log because you couldn't see or touch the item first, at least take a look at both resources. Each is a fount of data on products specifications and pricing information, and they enable you to do crucial comparison-shopping from the comfort of your home. Thanks in part to the Internet, prices on a vast array of merchandise (from automobiles to computers) and services (from long distance calls to travel arrangements) can change at the speed of light. Sometimes these rapid price changes can work to your advantage, and save you big money, but other times these price changes can leave your wallet unnecessarily thin. To be a savvy con-sumer, you need to be armed with the latest available prices, as well as printouts of earlier offers, which you may be able to use as a bargain-ing chip.

Chapter 19

Buy or Lease a New Car
Without Overpaying

Some people believe you are what you drive. Whether you choose to drive a brand-new luxury car or a slightly used fuel-efficient one, it's easy to spend more than you planned. And choosing between a car lease and a car loan can add up to a difference of thousands of dollars over the years when you have the car.

Scott's Story

When Scott decided that he "deserved" a new car the first thing he did was his homework. He surfed the Internet, and then spent time at his local library. He researched which safety features are available on which models, how specific models performed on their crash tests, and which makes and models had the best records for maintaining their value. He also checked into auto insurance rates. Armed with this information, he headed to a dealership to buy a new car. "I struck a hard bargain and got the car for 1½ percent over dealer invoice," he boasted.

But what Scott didn't know—and the dealer didn't tell him—was that the manufacturer was giving an extra $500 to any dealer who sold that model car during that month. "If I'd known about the manufacturer's program, *I* could have pocketed the money, instead of the dealer," he says.

How can you keep from leaving money on the table at the car dealership? Nowadays, there's an abundance of car information on the Internet—including what the dealer paid for the car, and details about specific rebate and incentive programs currently being offered by car manufacturers. But suppose surfing the Net is more work than you have time to do, for a small fee, some nonprofit car-buying services will provide you with this information; and for a little more money, they can also get you competitive bids from several local dealers. Later in this chapter, I will show you where you can find specific cost information. But, first things first.

Before you can strike a good deal on a car, you need to make some personal choices. Here are seven steps that will help you to narrow those choices and to make the best decisions for *you*, based on your financial situation, the way you use a car, and your personal preferences.

STEP 1 DECIDE WHAT YOU WANT VS. WHAT YOU NEED IN A CAR.

Everyone has a different idea about how a car should look and handle, and what it should cost. But unless you have a big bank account, your list is probably divided into three parts: what you want, what you must have, and what you can afford. Before you start closing in on specific makes and models of cars, here are some questions to consider:

- How many people will typically be in the car? Just you? Your whole family, including kids and pets?
- Will you be driving the car to work every day? If so, how far? Or will this be only a second car—used for local errands, or driven to and left at the nearby train station on work days?
- Will you be parking it in a safe place? Inside a temperature-controlled garage, or outdoors where it will be buffeted by the elements? In an assigned space in a secured lot, or taking its chances with on-street parking?
- Will you let your teen drivers take their turns behind the wheel?
- What are creature comforts worth to you? Will cloth or vinyl seats do, or will you only be happy with fine leather? Bucket seats or a bench seat?
- Automatic or manual transmission? Power steering, heated seats, a video player in the rear for the kids, and so on, or can you get by with the basics?
- How concerned are you about safety features? Does "looking cool" count for more? Front air bags only, or side bags, too? Is a satellite communication system a must?
- Will you be driving mostly on the paved roads or on rougher terrain? Is two-wheel drive sufficient or is all-wheel drive a necessity?
- How much trunk space or other cargo area do you need?
- Any other must-have features?

Next, arrange your list so that what you must have is on top, and the rest is ranked down to what would be nice to have but may not be affordable. Be sure that the car you choose today will be able to meet your anticipated lifestyle changes, such as upcoming nuptials, pending births, planned adoption of pets, or a move to the country or the city.

Now that you have a better idea of what you want and need in a car, it's time to start selecting specific makes and models that could fill the bill. Head out to the library, or surf the Internet, to get a consensus of cars that have been rated well for price, performance, and safety features. Some sources to consult are:

- *Consumer Reports* magazine or www.consumerreports.com
- *Edmund's* or www.edmunds.com
- *Kiplinger's Personal Finance* magazine or www.kiplinger.com
- *Money* magazine or www.money.com
- *The Car Book,* by Jack Gillis.

STEP 2 — DETERMINE WHETHER LEASING OR BUYING A CAR MAKES MORE SENSE FOR YOU.

The ads make leasing sound irresistible: For a small monthly payment, you can drive away in a brand-new luxury car. Should you lease or buy?

Some car manufacturers seem very fond of car leases and will give a variety of subsidies to consumers who will lease one of their new models. It's not until their lease expires—or their car is stolen, or totaled in an accident—that many consumers find out that the car lease was a better deal for the leasing company than for them.

To help you decide whether to buy or lease, the key thing you need to know is that you can't compare monthly lease and loan costs. The monthly lease cost is often much lower than the loan payment for the same car, but the two amounts should not be compared. At the end of the lease, you own nothing—you have to give the car back. But when you make your final loan payment, you own the car and can either continue to drive it or you can sell it.

LLOYD'S LAW

It's the <u>total</u> lease cost that matters.

Car leases often come with the following array of costs, which can make them much more expensive than many consumers realize:

- *Some "deposits" are nonrefundable.* When any money you hand over is called a deposit, you might assume that you will get the money back at the end of the lease. But with car leases, some so-called deposits are nothing more than additional down payments; it's an easy way for some car leasing companies to get and keep more of your hard-earned money.
- *"Excess wear and tear" charges are subjective.* The leasing company determines the exact amount. Before you sign the lease, have the leasing company *put in writing* exactly what constitutes "excess." For instance: Would a penalty be charged for a small scuff on the dashboard? How about a tiny wear spot on the carpet? Or will it only apply to serious damage, such as crumpled fenders or burned upholstery?
- *Excess mileage can quickly add up.* Most car leases cover you for driving 12,000 or 15,000 miles per year. Extra miles are billed at a rate of 15 cents or more per mile. And there's no carry-over provision. If you run up more than your allotment in one year but you drove less than the max in earlier years, or in later years to balance higher mileage in early years, you'll still get charged for the excess. Most leasing companies look at service records to see where the mileage stands during each year. If you expect to drive more than the allotment, negotiate a higher cap or a lower extra mileage rate before you sign the lease.
- *Early termination charges can be prohibitive.* If you want out before the lease is up, even if you find someone to assume your lease, you'll probably be hit with early termination charges. Many leasing companies won't allow you to transfer your lease to anyone, so comb the fine print before you sign.
- *Insurance shortfalls can mean money out of your pocket.* If the car is stolen or "totaled," you could owe more on the lease than the car is worth, and you'll be on the hook for the difference. Buy "gap protection" from an insurance company; it would pay for an insurance shortfall.
- *Disposition fees can get you at the end.* These are the costs some leasing companies assess to unload a car when the lease expires. Look for a leasing company that doesn't charge this fee.
- *Upgrades can be very costly.* If you're in the market for some upgrades—say, a premium sound system or a sunroof—many leasing companies will charge you the *full retail price* of that option when you sign the lease. Never mind that you'll only have the car for two

or three years; you'll still be billed the full amount—the same amount you would pay if you had bought the car new.

- *You may be charged more than you anticipated at the end of the lease.* For many consumers, the final "gotcha" snags them at the end of the lease. They mistakenly believed that they could buy the car for the "residual price" stated in the lease. Not true. The higher "option price" is the amount the leasing company will quote you if you express interest in buying the car at the end of the lease. So try to negotiate the purchase price with the leasing company again. You may be able to purchase the car for less than the option price, but you'll rarely get it for the residual price.

To compare car leases, you need to know each of these three numbers:

1. The capitalized cost. It's comparable to the purchase price of the car.
2. The residual value. This is the dollar amount the leasing company says the car will be worth at the end of the lease. (Note: The difference between the "capitalization cost" and the "residual value" equals the depreciation. That's the amount of the car's value that you will use—and pay for.)
3. The money factor. It's comparable to the interest rate that you would pay on a car loan, but finding out this number isn't always easy. The leasing company is not required to disclose it, and without it, it's hard to compare bids from different leasing companies.

When Might Leasing a Car Make Sense for You?

Despite its potentially costly pitfalls, here are five circumstances under which a lease may be worth considering:

1. You want a new car every two or three years.
2. You don't want to deal with selling your car two or three years from now.
3. The manufacturer is subsidizing the lease, which offers you a great leasing deal. These arrangements, called "sub-vented" leases, are getting hard to come by.
4. You typically don't drive enough miles annually to exceed the yearly mileage cap on a lease.

5. You're taking a tax deduction for all or part of a luxury car lease. (Tax laws allow a more generous write-off of luxury car leases than of luxury car purchases.)

Unless the manufacturer is offering a special leasing deal, a car dealer is rarely the best place to get a car lease. Credit unions will often give the best terms. Small banks usually come in second, then larger banks.

Negotiating Tip: If you are planning to lease from a car dealer, don't reveal your plan until *after* you have negotiated the *purchase price* of the car.

LLOYD'S LAW

All lease terms are negotiable. Don't let a preprinted form sway you to agree to lease terms you don't want.

To keep out-of-pocket costs down, don't sign a car lease that runs longer than the manufacturer's warranty or you'll have to pay for car repairs out of your own pocket.

 ## STEP 3 WEIGH THE PROS AND CONS OF BUYING A NEW OR USED CAR.

You can get a lot more for your money by buying a slightly used car. But only you know what will make you happy and what you can—and cannot—afford.

If you've set your sights on a new car, or if you haven't yet decided, read on. If you would consider buying a used car ("preowned vehicle" or "previously new" at some dealerships), the next chapter will show you how to cruise your way to used-car savings.

STEP 4 CHOOSE THE FATE OF YOUR CURRENT CAR.

When it's time to dispose of your old set of wheels, you basically have three choices: (1) trade it in at a dealer, (2) sell it yourself, or (3) give it to charity and take a tax write-off. If you're counting on using the equity in your old set of wheels as a down payment on your replacement wheels, then you can't afford to leave money on the table. In the next chapter, I will show you how to take the hassle out of unloading the old wheels, and pocket maximum after-tax dollars.

MAKE THE MOST OF A DAY AT THE DEALERSHIP.

Now that you've taken your personal inventory and have a better idea of what you're looking for and what you can afford, it's time to let the rubber meet the road and head off to the new-car showroom. In addition to seeing what's available on the lot for immediate purchase, you also want to pick up some new-car brochures.

While you're there, why not ask the salesperson about taking a few cars for a spin around the block? Whether it's a blind spot near the rear window or a seat that won't contour to fit your contours, there's nothing like a test drive to discover the downside to some cars you thought you wanted to own. By eliminating the models that don't pan out, you will be able to focus your research and negotiating energies on the models that could work for you.

Stay focused when you're putting the pedal to the metal. A chatterbox salesperson can be very distracting while you are test-driving a car, and may keep you from hearing or noticing car problems (perhaps that's why he or she keeps talking). After you test the sound quality of the radio, turn it off. It can drown out car noises and street noises that you should be aware of.

Carry a spiral notebook, that has a pocket so you won't misplace your notes. You can then jot down features and prices *and* store the brochures that you pick up along the way. If the salesperson sees you taking notes, he or she is less apt to say later, "You remembered wrong; I never offered this price or made that concession."

Bring along a valid driver's license for the test drive, and keep a calculator handy to crunch the numbers—and show the salesperson that you are a serious shopper.

Are You Sticker-Savvy?

With this field research under your belt, it's time to gather more pricing information on the specific models that you like. You're looking for sticker prices, dealer costs, and discounts or other rebates that could shave hundreds or thousands off the cost of your new car.

You can surf the Internet for much of this information. One good site is www.edmunds.com. Or, for $12, Consumer Reports' New Car Price

Service will fax you the invoice prices for a specific make and model. Shortages of specific models, or dealers who refuse to deal, can stymie your best-laid plans, so Consumer Reports also includes information on alternate makes and models that are similar to your first choice. For details, call Consumer Reports (800) 395-4400.

When you start reading the stickers, here are some things you should know:

- The ADM (additional dealer markup) listed on the sticker price is a trick. As its name implies, it's designed to jack up the sticker price. Don't fall for it. You don't have to pay it.
- An "advertising fee" is listed on the sticker when local dealers handling the same make of car agree to pool their money for joint advertising. Each dealer for, say, a Ford Taurus in your area will add the same number of dollars to the price of that car. It's hard to negotiate this number down. But realize that the advertising fee added on for the Taurus's twin, the Mercury Sable, by the Mercury dealer, may differ by several hundred dollars from the amount the Ford dealers add. This same strategy applies for other "twins," for instance, Pontiacs and Chevrolets, Buicks and Cadillacs. Want to know what car is a twin of the car you're interested in? Look it up in magazines, such as *Consumer Reports* and *Kiplinger's Personal Finance,* or in Jack Gillis's *Car Book.*
- The invoice price is rarely the dealer's bottom line. If you're able to negotiate a price that is just barely above the invoice price—or even $1,000 or more below the invoice price, late in the model year—don't start passing the hat for the salesperson. For each car sold, the dealer typically gets a dealer's "holdback"—a percentage of the sticker price. Dealers also make money on other aspects of car sales, including financing, insurance, service, and trade-ins.

Do You Know How to Strike the Best Deal?

When you start negotiating, keep your emotions in check. You can strike a better deal if you don't seem too anxious (translation: desperate). Don't let the salesperson rush you. Despite what he or she may tell you, whatever deal is offered to you today will still be honored tomorrow. If the end of the month is approaching, he or she may even sweeten the deal further in order to reach a monthly quota.

Does it seem that the longer you negotiate, the better the terms get? Here's how you might be able to speed up the process. Tell the dealer, up front, that you are buying then and there, and that he or she has one shot to give you a good deal. Be sure to have enough pricing information at your fingertips so the dealer knows you're serious.

Three more negotiating tips:

1. *Don't* go in with your best offer first. Start at one to two percent below what you would be willing to pay.
2. *Don't* raise your offer until the salesperson gives you a legitimate counteroffer; otherwise, you might as well be handing over a blank check.
3. *Do* walk out if the seller won't come down enough in price. It may take two or three return visits to get the car at the price you want.

If you don't have the time or temperament to conduct a prolonged search yourself, consider hiring a company to do it for you. One such service is called Car Bargains. You tell them the make and model you want, and they will get guaranteed bids from five dealers in your area. With the bids in hand, the other dealers will often match the lowest bid from a competitor. Car Bargains charges $185 to get bids to buy a car. For $295, the service will also get car lease bids. For details, call (800) 475-7283.

One of the best times to shop for a new car is a few days before Christmas. Demand is low that week because few people give cars as gifts. With the end of the month and the year just days away, salespeople may be feeling some heat from unmet month-end and year-end sales quotas.

Late summer and early fall are also good times to buy a new car. Manufacturers will be shipping the next year's models soon, so dealers will be anxious to get this year's cars off their lots.

But weigh this choice carefully. Would it make more sense for you to wait for the new year's models rather than buy the current year's car? From a financial point of view, if you plan to hold on to the car for a number of years, there will be very little difference. But if you plan to trade it in within a couple of years, it will have dropped in value by two years' depreciation versus only one year's if you wait for the new year's models. Also, if the new models will have certain features that you want, it's better to wait.

STEP 6 AVOID COSTLY CAR-BUYING BLUNDERS.

Here are seven common, costly blunders that new car buyers often make—and ways you can avoid them.

- *Blunder 1. Agreeing to a monthly payment instead of a separate purchase price and interest rate.* Many dealers quote a price and an interest rate, but when they draw up the contract, they put in only the monthly charge, which is often figured at a higher interest rate. Don't get taken by this game. Only negotiate the purchase price and the interest rate. And don't say how much you are prepared to pay; you could end up paying more than necessary. Instead, let the dealer propose a price and an interest rate, then you can make a counteroffer.
- *Blunder 2. Paying the "no-dicker sticker" price.* Consider that price to be a starting point, and try to haggle down from there. If the dealer won't budge on the price, ask to have some extras thrown in: a free "loaner" when you take the car in for service, or free feature upgrades.
- *Blunder 3. Succumbing to "extra dollar-a-day" features.* An extra $30 a month on a five-year loan will end up costing you $1,800 more.
- *Blunder 4. Buying extended warranties, rust-proofing, a dealer-installed security system, or fabric protection.* Undercoating and rust-proofing can actually damage your car. Rust-proofing can invalidate your car's warranty, and it adds weight so it will lessen the car's fuel efficiency. Most new cars now come with at least three-year, 36,000-mile warranties, so extra coverage is usually a waste of money. A dealer-installed security system can damage the car's wiring. But if the dealer has already installed the system, leave it there. Removing the system can also damage the wiring.
- *Blunder 5. Buying credit life insurance offered by the lender.* If you were to die, this insurance would pay off the balance on your car loan, but it limits the options for your survivors, who might have more need for cash. If you need more insurance, a term life insurance policy (purchased from an insurance agent) is a better choice. It will cost less, and your survivors can use the money either to pay off your car loan or for more important needs. (See Chapter 13 for information on buying life insurance.)
- *Blunder 6. Not comparison-shopping for financing.* For a car loan, as with a car lease, car dealers can be the most expensive lenders. Banks will often give you better terms, and credit unions frequently offer the lowest price. Comparison-shop in at least three places. Compare the annual percentage rates (APRs). Negotiate—try to delete prepayment penalties and late-payment fees from your loan contract.

When, if ever, does it pay to finance a new car at the dealer? Only if some special, below-market interest rates are being offered. Those rates usually apply only to slow-moving models.

Take out as short a loan as you can afford (preferably for two or three years), because new cars depreciate rapidly. With a five-year loan, at the beginning, you'll owe more than your car is worth—and you'll have to make up the shortfall if you want to trade in the car early or if it's stolen or totaled in an accident.

Tip: If you get a loan or lease elsewhere, you can then qualify for rebates and other incentives offered by new car dealers only to customers who pay cash.

Tip: Ask your bank or credit union to prequalify you for a car loan so you'll know how much you can afford for a car, and you'll resist overpriced extras.

- *Blunder 7. Discussing the trade-in before you've finalized the deal.* Keep these transactions separate. See the next chapter for advice on getting top dollar for your current set of wheels.

STEP 7 KEEP YOUR CAR PURRRR-ING.

It always amazes me how many consumers will drive a hard bargain when buying or leasing a car, but think nothing of driving their car into the ground because they haven't gotten around to doing routine, inexpensive maintenance, such as changing the oil or keeping the tires inflated.

Read your owner's manual to see what service your car requires, and when. It may be okay to have oil changes and other routine maintenance done by a local mechanic (or you can do it yourself), but to keep your warranty in force, you may be required to have work covered by your warranty performed at an authorized dealership. As proof that required warranty work was done on schedule and at an authorized shop, you may need to show service records. Keep this paperwork where you can easily find it.

Did you know that your car might also be covered by a warranty that the manufacturer wants to keep secret? If your car has a defect, your car dealer may or may not tell you about the problem and/or offer to fix it free of charge. If you don't hear about the secret warranty, you could end up footing the bill for repairs.

To see whether your car has a potentially serious defect and a secret warranty that would pay for repairing it, contact:

- National Highway Traffic Safety Administration, at (800) 424-9393 or visit www.nhtsa.dot.gov.
- Center for Auto Safety (a consumer watchdog organization), 2001 S Street N.W., Suite 410, Washington, DC 20009), or visit www.autosafety.org.

Chapter 20

Buy or Sell a Used Car Quickly and at a Good Price

Brad's Story

"I needed a replacement car in a hurry when mine suddenly stopped working, and the three repair estimates I got exceeded the value of the car. One newspaper ad caught my eye. It read: 'Low mileage, cream puff. Must sell for family reasons. Will accept reasonable offer.' I called the number, and Billy, the man who placed the ad, explained that the car belonged to his mother, who recently had a stroke, and they needed to sell it to pay for her physical therapy. He told me to meet him at a nearby shopping mall because his mother didn't like strangers coming to their home.

"So I met him there on Saturday morning. The car looked good, and I was impressed with how well it drove. I looked over the car carefully, but when I asked to see the inside of the trunk, Billy said that his mother had misplaced the key but that I could get another one from the dealer. That should have been a tip-off, but it sounded reasonable at the time.

"Anyhow, before meeting with him, I had checked out the value of the car, but I didn't feel that I was quite ready to make an offer. Billy started telling me how much his mother's treatments were costing, and how desperate they were for some cash to pay her medical bills. He said, 'Look, just make an offer and I'm sure we can work something out.' So I bid $1,000 less than the $12,600 Blue Book value. Much to my surprise, he said, 'Okay,' and shook my hand.

"He walked to my bank with me so I could get a cashier's check. When I handed him the check, he handed me the keys and signed the registration over to me. We went outside, and he removed his license plates and replaced them with the tags I had brought with me from my old car. Billy said, 'Congratulations, you bought a great car!' Then he headed off to the bank to cash my check. I drove off happy in my new car and a little bit proud of the good deal I had struck and that I had helped out his family.

"But my elation soon turned to apprehension and then to disgust. The car started making weird noises and began smoking. I took it to my

213

mechanic, who told me, 'I hope you got a good deal on this car, because it needs some costly work.' My mechanic's estimate was so high, I decided to take the car to the dealer to see if any of the work was covered by a warranty. There, the head of the service department ran a history on the car and found that it had been 'salvaged' after a serious accident and was not supposed to be on the road any more.

"I then took the service records and title information from the dealer to my local consumer affairs office, and, within a couple of weeks, they uncovered the rest of the car's history. It had been 'totaled' in an accident eight months earlier, but then it was sold at a dealer auction for $500. The buyer got the title altered; the mileage was lowered from 76,000 to 43,000, and the word 'salvage' was removed.

"And what about Billy? Despite his Oscar-worthy performance, he wasn't the caring son of an ill woman. Actually, he was what they call a 'curbstoner.' He works for a used-car lot that buys clunkers and sells them off to unsuspecting car buyers like me."

Curbstoning is a growing scam. Later in this chapter, some red flags will alert you to how you could be getting drawn into a curbstoner's web of lies. Still, despite the potential pitfalls, a slightly used car may get you the most car for your money. The depreciation has already been taken, and three- to five-year-old cars shouldn't need costly repairs. The good news is that with the surge in car leasing in the past few years, dealers' lots are packed with used cars. The bad news is that you could get stuck with someone else's lemon or with an overpriced financing or leasing deal that could make a used car costlier than a new one.

Let's face it, kicking the tires won't tell you much. So what should you be looking for—and looking out for, and how can you strike a good price on a previously owned set of wheels? Here are eight steps to get you where you want to go.

STEP 1 CHECK THE PERFORMANCE AND PRICE STATS ON USED CARS.

By choosing a used car over a new one (which would lose a good chunk of its value the moment you drive it off the dealer's lot), you've shown that you're interested in getting the most for your car-buying dollar. But to really optimize this purchase, before you even set foot on a car lot, you should pay a visit to your local library reference department, or surf the Internet, to find out which cars have good service records and have maintained their value.

The National Highway Transportation Safety Administration (NHTSA) Web site, www.nhtsa.com, lists crash test results. Some other good sources for safety and price information are:

- *Consumer Reports* magazine or www.consumerreports.com
- *Edmund's Used Cars Prices and Ratings* or www.edmunds.com
- *Kelly Blue Book* or www.kbb.com
- *Kiplinger's Personal Finance* magazine or www.kiplinger.com
- *Money* magazine or www.money.com
- National Automobile Dealers Association's *NADA Official Used Car Guide* or www.nada.com
- *The Used Car Book,* by Jack Gillis.

Newspaper want ads can help you determine the going prices in your area.

STEP 2 GO WHERE THE BEST CARS ARE.

Flexibility is key when you're searching for a used set of wheels. Believe it or not, you may find some of the best used cars not on a nearby used-car lot or through newspaper want ads, but at a new-car dealership.

That's because new car dealers often get the best pick of late-model used cars because they get trade-ins from new-car buyers, and relatively young cars coming off lease. A new-car dealer is also apt to have its own service department stand behind the cars it sells, and a new-car dealer can also sell you a "certified" used car. These are the pick of the litter—typically, they're late-model cars with a good track record. They pose less risk to a consumer because they've been checked out and they come with an extended warranty.

Another increasingly popular place to shop is a used-car superstore. Quality varies, but most superstores offer a wide range of cars to choose from, and many offer buyers an extended manufacturer's warranty. You will pay a premium of $200 to $1,000 for this extended warranty and, as some consumers have discovered, when a problem arises, what they think the warranty covers can differ greatly from the dealer's interpretation. So to avoid misunderstandings later, have the used-car dealer put all warranty promises in writing before you agree to buy a car.

Beware of little, local used-car dealers, with the possible exception of those who have been in the same location (and owned by the same person) for more than a decade. Small used-car dealers won't be authorized to do warranty work on your car, and persuading another dealer to do work on a car that wasn't purchased there might be a hassle. Some small used-car dealers are fly-by-nights. If you later uncover an undisclosed preexisting problem with a car sold to you by a fly-by-night, you may find the former used-car lot empty and the owners gone. Before buying a car, check the dealer's history of complaints with the local consumer affairs office in your town and the Better Business Bureau.

Banks or credit unions can also be good places to shop for used cars. They need to unload cars that they repossessed when a prior lease or loan went bad. Ask the branch manager at the bank or credit union for specific offerings. Before agreeing to buy a particular car, hire a mechanic to give it a bumper-to-bumper inspection. Then negotiate the price and loan terms separately. Ask the bank to throw in an extended manufacturer's warranty.

As far as answering ads is concerned, there might be a good deal out there, but finding it can take precious time. And, as Brad discovered, not all private sales are what they appear to be. He ran into an increasingly common problem—a "curbstoner"—someone posing as a relative of a used-car owner.

How can you spot a curbstoner? You see an ad in a newspaper, and when you call to get more information, the person offers to show you the car not at a home, but typically at a shopping center parking lot. If you're looking at a car being sold by an individual (not a dealer), here are some red flags that you may not really be dealing with a private owner:

◁ **Sob story.**   The absent owner must sell in a hurry due to a sudden death, serious illness, or other calamity.

◁ **Multiple names.**   You may be dealing with a shill who is working for a shady car dealer.

◁ **Document discrepancies.**   Facts on the title don't match other things you see (such as insurance information or a driver's license) or information you are shown.

◁ **Missing keys.**   The seller doesn't have the trunk key, gas tank key, or other things you would expect a real owner and driver to have.

◁ **Overeager seller.**   The seller seems a little too willing to come down in the price or to make other concessions for a quick sale.

STEP 3 **INSPECT FROM TOP TO BOTTOM.**

Once you've found some cars worth considering, inspect them carefully. You are looking for these problems:

- Body damage. Walk around the car and look for incongruities or things that are askew: side panels or doors that cave in or bow out or just don't match the other side; mismatched trim or paint colors, or other asymmetries. (For older cars, carry a magnet. If it doesn't stick to any place that should be metal, the car may have had extensive repairs with body filler.)
- Sloppy paint on or around the door or trim. It has obviously been repainted—badly.
- Uneven tire wear. Often, this indicates an alignment or suspension problem.
- Fluid leaks. Puddles of oil or other fluids under the car, or a smell of chemicals, could indicate a costly problem.

Next, carefully examine the car inside. A worn-out brake pedal or heavy wear and tear on the steering wheel could signal that this isn't the low-mileage dreamboat that the dealer claims.

STEP 4 PUT THE PEDAL TO THE METAL.

It's time for a test drive. Start up the car, let it run a bit in "PARK," with the emergency brake on, and before you leave the lot, look under the hood while the engine is running. Do you smell anything odd, such as chemicals or exhaust fumes? Then, as you're driving it, do you hear weird sounds, such as ticking or hissing when you accelerate or hit the brakes?

Do the seats and steering wheel easily adjust to your touch? Test the car on the open road by getting up to about 50 miles an hour and hitting the brakes sharply with your hands lightly touching, but not steering, the wheel. Does the car pull to one side? If so, there might be a suspension problem.

If the car passes those tests, you'll still want to make sure that it doesn't have a questionable past. For instance, is it a rebuilt wreck (that was totaled in an accident or flood), or a car that was declared a "lemon" and repurchased by the manufacturer? Has its odometer been turned back to make it look like it has logged fewer miles?

In addition to visual clues (such as the numbers on the odometer not lining up properly) or a dank, musty smell, you may be able to pick up some less visible problems by running a computer check on the car's VIN (vehicle identification number). If you're buying the car from a dealer, you can get a good estimate of the true mileage by asking the dealer to run a check on the car's VIN free of charge.

Also, Carfax offers a telephone and Internet service that delivers the history of a car. The service will check to see if:

- The car was totaled in an accident, flood, or other catastrophe.
- The odometer was turned back.
- The car was a "lemon" and was bought back by the manufacturer.

Go to Carfax's Web site at www.carfax.com, or call (800) FINDVIN. Carfax's Internet search costs less than its telephone search.

SEE THE SERVICE RECORDS AND HIRE A MECHANIC TO GIVE IT A ONCE-OVER.

You're almost to the home stretch, so next ask to see the car's service records. Reputable car dealers should eagerly show them. Some car dealers will even let you contact the car's previous owner.

Hire a professional mechanic to check out the car from top to bottom. If the dealer (or car's owner) says, "No," walk away. Chances are there is something about the car that they don't want you to find out about until they've unloaded it.

Plan to pay a mechanic about $100 for a thorough examination and written analysis of the car. Even a mechanic's report detailing problems can help you get a better deal. With the report in hand, you can negotiate with the salesperson either to get the problems fixed or to knock off the cost of repairs, so you can have them done yourself.

STEP 6 DON'T OVERBID ON A USED CAR.

Avoid a common, costly used-car-buying mistake. Many used-car shoppers follow the wrong number (the retail number) in the *Kelly Blue Book* or the *NADA Official Used Car Guide*. That amount is too much to pay if you're buying from an individual, because you're not getting any warranty or other after-market service that you would expect to get from a dealer. Start by offering the wholesale price (the lowest value in the book), less any options, and let the seller bid you up.

STEP 7 KNOW THE MEANING OF "AS IS."

You can often get a lower price on a car labeled "As is," but that label means there is no warranty. Consider an "As is" car only if you have the skills and the time to make repairs or if you have a bottomless bank account.

If you do buy a car without a warranty, insist that the dealer disclose, in writing, all known problems. In that way, you may have some recourse against the seller if you later uncover a preexisting problem that was not obvious when you bought the car. (For more information on checking the title history, contact Carfax at www.carfax.com or (800) FINDVIN.)

STEP 8 DON'T FALL FOR FALSE FINANCING PROMISES.

After they've negotiated a good deal on a used car, some consumers give up the savings by making poor financing choices. First, leasing a used car is rarely wise. Depreciation has already been taken, so the price should be low enough that you can afford to buy the car with a short-term loan. When the loan is paid off, you will own the car and can continue driving it, or you can sell it and use the cash as a down payment on a newer car.

Second, whether you take out a car loan or lease a used car, keep the term to no more than three years; two years is even better and should be affordable because a used car has already experienced its biggest, first-year depreciation. If you finance for a longer term, you could owe more on the car than the car is worth, and if it's stolen or "totaled" in an accident, you can't just walk away. You would have to make up for the shortfall out of your own pocket. (*Note:* "Gap" policies are available to make up for the insurance shortfall, but your instincts should tell you that a shorter financing arrangement is a better deal.)

Car dealers rarely offer the best financing rates or other terms. For better deals, first contact a credit union and then some banks. Compare terms from at least three financing sources before signing on the dotted line.

Get Top Dollar for Your Old Car

Have you put off buying a car because you didn't want to go through the hassle of trading in (or selling off) your old one? I've known people who have. Between worries that they'll sell it for less than it's worth, and fears of having to invite to their home a stranger whose only connection is through a want ad in the local newspaper, their concerns are all too real.

LLOYD'S LAW

The more you get for your old car, the more financial flexibility you will have. You'll have more money for a bigger down payment on your next car, or you may be able to buy or lease a nicer car. Or, you could consider this found money and use it for other things, such as paying down your credit card bills, increasing your investment portfolio, or adding more to a tax-sheltered retirement savings plan. The choices are limitless.

Challenge number one is to figure out how much your present car is worth. With the Internet and some reasonably priced consumer services, it's easy to hone in on your car's true value. *Edmund's Used Cars Prices and Ratings* is the book most consumers turn to, but if you have access to the Internet, check out the *Edmund's* Web site: www.edmunds.com. The figures on the Web site are updated more frequently than those in the book. Be sure to add costs for optional features, above-average condition, and low mileage. Conversely, dents, dings, rust, or high mileage will all adversely affect the value of your trade-in. For any serious damage, get a couple of repair estimates before trying to sell the car, so you'll have a good idea how much a savvy buyer (a dealer or a private individual) will want to knock off the asking price.

Whether you're planning to trade in your old car or sell it yourself, a little field research at this point can help you pin down the market value of your car. Take your car to a few new-car and used-car dealers, and ask them straight out, "How much will you pay me today to buy my car?"

Tip: To get top dollar for your old wheels, get the car washed and detailed before you take it around for bids. And bring your maintenance records to show that you recently changed the oil and oil filter and have followed the maintenance plan prescribed by the manufacturer.

Challenge number two is to figure out the best place for you to sell your car. You can place an ad in the local newspaper, but that approach is time-consuming and raises serious safety concerns: What do you really know about the stranger who stops by and takes your car for a test drive? Whether you ride along or hand your keys to this person, you could be putting yourself, or at least your property, at risk.

Even a trade-in is not without peril—in this case, a financial risk, because when the price of a new car and the allowance for a trade-in are all figured on one piece of paper, consumers often end up paying more than they were led to believe. If you do decide to trade-in your old car when you buy a new one, keep the two transactions separate. Work out all the details for your new car purchase (price, financing) before you even discuss a trade-in. Then, if you think the dealer is not offering you enough, take it to another dealer. The next one may be more anxious to get hold of a car like yours.

If you just don't want to go through the hassle of selling your old car, consider giving it to charity. In many cases, you can write off the car's fair value on your income tax return.

Chapter 21

Become a Savvier Shopper, Whether Through Catalogs, Online, or in Person

The increasing popularity of online and catalog shopping can be summed up by one word: convenience. But aside from the obvious, that you can't see, touch, or smell a long-distance purchase until after you make it, that may be the least of your concerns. Here are some others to consider: How do you really know whom you are dealing with, and whether the company is reliable and will deliver your merchandise as promised? Will the merchant sell personal information about you, such as your shopping habits, your address, or your phone number? Will a merchant's loose security procedures allow others to get their hands on your credit card number? What happens if you need to return the merchandise? Will the sender accept it back, and will you ever see your money again? In the next few pages, I'll show you ways to protect yourself. The money you save on day-to-day shopping will go a long way toward meeting your other financial goals.

If you're like most people, your purchases, by themselves, are not big enough to seriously affect your wealth, but they can quickly add up. And the negotiating skills and strategies you learn and master for everyday purchases can then be successfully applied when you're negotiating a bigger amount, such as the price of your next car or home, or a stockbroker's commission, or financial aid for your kids' college education. So read on.

Dee Dee's Story

"I put off my holiday shopping until the last minute, so I whipped out some catalogs, found a few things in a hurry that I could give with a clear conscience and placed the call to the catalog merchant," recalls Dee Dee. "I waited on the phone for over twenty-five minutes before a live person, named Catherine, picked up. I ordered my first couple of items uneventfully, but the rest of the things I had chosen were sold out. Catherine made several suggestions that weren't bad, but when she got

221

to the ties for my father-in-law, I told her she'd gone too far. She picked out the ugliest tie I had ever seen, and I told her so. She laughed and tried to reassure me by saying, 'The photo does not do it justice. I promise you'll love it when you see it and if not, call me, and you can send it back and I'll pick up the shipping charges both ways.'

"I was running out of time, so I relented. Two days later, the packages arrived and I have to admit Catherine was right: The photo did not do it justice. The tie was great. It's very attractive in person, which is more than I can say for some of the other things I ordered. A couple of them are so awful in person that I'm sending them back because I can't give them as gifts. It's ironic sometimes: The items that look great in the catalog I would never buy if I'd seen them in person. But some of the items that look the most hideous in their photos turn out to be the greatest in person. Who would have guessed?"

High prices and crowded shopping malls are forcing many cost-conscious or time-constrained consumers to flee traditional retail stores in search of something better. Big beneficiaries of this mass exodus are catalog merchants, outlet stores, and online retailers.

Whether you choose to flip through stacks of catalogs, surf the Internet or scour outlet malls in search of quality merchandise at reasonable prices, do you know how to tell the good deals from the also-rans? Even how you pay for your purchases can affect your bottom line. Some of the most popular payment methods come with a variety of hidden costs and other penalties. And how you and the merchant handle the inevitable returns can affect your bank balance and your psyche—two things that are especially important during the heavy holiday shopping season.

Realize That Reading Isn't Always Believing When You're Catalog Shopping

Catalog shopping is convenient—you can do it from the comfort of your home, twenty-four hours a day. And, from dozens of discounts to waived shipping and handling fees, catalog bargains abound. But many of the best offers are not advertised, so if you don't know what to ask for, catalog shopping can cost you dearly.

Before you place your order, there are some things to ask the customer rep. Start with: "Is the item on sale?" One of the best ways to find out if an item is on sale is by calling first, saying that you're *returning* that item, and asking how much credit you will get. Merchants may not like this approach, but if the item is on sale, you should be allowed to buy it at the lowest sale price.

Then ask: "Do you guarantee prices?" It irks me when I buy a gift at full price and it goes on sale before I've even paid the bill. So, I now ask merchants, "Will you refund the difference if the item goes on sale within thirty days?" If they refuse, I take my business elsewhere. Be sure to get price guarantees in writing.

Always ask about "unadvertised" discounts, such as for a new or returning customer. And get out the magnifying glass to read the fine print about shipping charges and return policies. Are refunds given for any reason, including general dissatisfaction, or only if the item is defective? Does an item have to be returned within thirty days, or is the time unlimited?

Must returns be in their original packing material? Will the seller arrange to pick up the item, or does the customer have to mail it back? Which shipping costs (if any) will the cataloger assume? Will the customer get cash back, or only a credit? If it's a credit, does it have an expiration date? Can the credit be used in the store (if the seller has one), or is it only good for catalog shopping?

Shipping fees can vary from catalog to catalog. Some merchants charge a sliding scale based on weight or the dollar amount of the purchase. Others charge a flat fee or offer a discount for big orders. If that's the case, you'll save money by ordering everything you've selected at one time.

Ask for extras. For instance, does the seller gift wrap free of charge? Some merchants will ship an order via an overnight carrier at no cost to the customer. They might even waive the shipping fees just to get your business. But you have to ask.

Always pay for your catalog order with a credit card, so if the items never arrive or arrive damaged, or if there are other problems, your card issuer can help resolve any ensuing dispute.

Many catalogs—and stores, for that matter—offer discounts to customers who open a charge account with them. These offers are rarely good deals. First, most merchants charge very high interest rates (over 20 percent). Second, to qualify, you'll have to disclose personal information, including your Social Security number, your annual income, and more. Third, if there's a problem with the merchandise, it will be you versus the merchant—no intermediary, such as your bank, can help you resolve it. Even if you are offered a 10 percent discount on your initial purchases when you open a charge account, the disadvantages will probably still outweigh the savings.

Always ask if the merchant has the item in stock. Catalogs must notify you if the item won't be available for thirty days or more. If you then decide to cancel your order, you'll be entitled to a full refund, but you may lose valuable shopping time.

Tip: If last-minute holiday shopping enticed you to that pile of catalogs, consider giving catalog gift certificates in lieu of merchandise. You'll avoid having to return an item that went on sale after it was bought, and the recipient can use the certificate after the holidays, when most things are on sale.

When you're ordering from a catalog, be sure to write down the name of the person you spoke to, the date and time of your call, and what you agreed to. Always get a written receipt. If you're ordering a gift, ask the seller to omit sending a price-annotated catalog along with the gift, unless you don't mind the recipient's knowing how much you paid.

Surf the Internet for Cyber-Bargains

You say the stacks of catalogs don't offer you enough choice? Then, how about booting up the computer and shopping online. It's convenient, fast (except during holiday shopping times when heavy Web traffic can make surfing some unprepared sites seem like *slow* slow motion), but many people worry whether it's safe and whether their information will be kept private. Will a thief grab your credit card information and go on a shopping spree, with you footing the bill? Will merchants sell your name, phone number, and a list of everything you bought—and even everything you looked at?

Let's put these concerns in perspective. If you choose your Web sites carefully—sticking with brand names you know, and merchants who take steps to protect your privacy—you're probably fairly safe. Here are nine steps that you can take to increase your privacy and security:

 BE SURE YOUR BROWSER IS SECURE.

Does it encrypt or scramble your buying information?

 KNOW THE VENDOR YOU'RE VISITING.

Are you familiar with the name of the vendor whose site you are visiting? Is it an established merchant with stores and a real address and phone number? If you're not sure, call the phone number to confirm the vendor's name, and then check the vendor out with the Better Business Bureau (www.bbb.org), the Federal Trade Commission (www.ftc.gov), and your local consumer affairs office. (*Note:* Just because there is no negative information, you cannot assume that a vendor is all right. It may have just begun to do business, or just switched to its present name, and earlier negative consumer complaints may not have caught up yet.)

DOUBLE-CHECK THAT YOUR VENDOR HAS PRIVACY AND SECURITY POLICIES.

Many vendors either post these policies or will provide them if you ask. Search the site for a familiar-looking security seal of protection before you seriously consider buying anything—and definitely before you key in your credit card number. Some security seals to look for include:

- Better Business Bureau.
- TRUSTe (www.etrust.org), a nonprofit organization.
- CPA WebTrust, from the American Institute of Certified Public Accountants.

Warning: Cyber-merchants can—and many do—keep track of everything: not only what you buy, but everything you look at. So you're giving up more privacy with this type of shopping than with catalog or in-person shopping.

 LOOK FOR AN ENCRYPTION ICON THAT SHOWS YOUR CREDIT CARD NUMBER HAS A LITTLE EXTRA PROTECTION.

An icon (such as an intact padlock or an unbroken key) should appear in the lower right-hand corner when you are about to enter your credit card information. If it's not there, consider placing your order by using the vendor's 800 phone number or fax number. (*Note:* Your credit card number is also at risk when you order by catalog or by phone, or even when you hand your card to a waiter at a restaurant.)

STEP 5 ASK ABOUT RETURN AND REFUND POLICIES.

Just as with catalog shopping, there are several questions to get answered before you buy merchandise from an Internet vendor:

- What are the return policies?
- Does the vendor give refunds for *any* reason, or only if the item is defective or the order was filled incorrectly?
- How soon do you have to return an item—within 30 days, or is the return period unlimited?
- Must returns be in the original packing material?

- Will the vendor arrange to pick up the item, or do you have to drop it off?
- Which shipping costs (if any) will the vendor pick up?
- Will you get cash back, or only a credit? If it's a credit, when will it expire? Can you use the credit in the vendor's brick-and-mortar store (if it has one) or is it only good for online shopping?

STEP 6 MUM'S THE WORD.

Even if you're asked, don't give out more personal information about yourself than necessary. *Don't* give your Social Security number, bank account information, birth date, mother's maiden name, or anything else you believe the vendor doesn't need to know. These data are not necessary to make a purchase.

Warning: Never, NEVER give out your Internet password. A vendor could use it to get access to your private information. Anyone who would ask you to disclose your password is up to no good. If the vendor asks you to select a password for a new customer account that is being created for you, always make up a new one that's different from your Internet password (and different from the other passwords you use at the ATM, other Web sites, and so on). Be sure to write it down so you can find it again later to check up on your order and to save time when placing additional orders.

STEP 7 ALWAYS PAY WITH A CREDIT CARD.

In that way, if there are problems with the merchandise—or it never arrives—your credit card company can intervene on your behalf.

Warning: Steer clear of any site that refuses credit cards and insists on checks or money orders. You lose many consumer rights and recourse if there is a problem with the merchandise or it never shows up. Reputable merchants will take credit cards.

STEP 8 DOCUMENT YOUR ORDER.

Jot down the date, time, and exactly what you ordered (merchandise numbers, colors, and quantities). Then print out a copy of your order.

STEP 9 KNOW YOUR RIGHTS.

By law, the merchant should send your order within thirty days unless a different delivery schedule is referred to when you place your order. If, after ordering, you are notified that the deadline cannot be met, you are entitled to cancel the order and get a full refund.

Remember, don't settle for less. If you don't find what you want, surf on over to another site.

If you like to touch or see the merchandise before you buy, cyber shopping may not be for you. But it can be a great place to do some research, especially on high-priced items such as electronics, cars, and home office equipment.

Will you save time by shopping online? Maybe. You won't have to travel, park, or trudge through a crowded mall, but be aware that some sites move at a snail's pace, make you linger on their merchandise, or force you to wade through screen after screen. If the site you're perusing seems too slow, vote with your mouse and click on over to another, more user-friendly site.

Will you save money by shopping online? Occasionally, yes. But realize that merchants that also have stores don't like competing with their store fronts, so you're more apt to find the same price at their Web sites. And once you add in shipping and handling costs, you may be paying more than it appears for this convenience.

Tip: Shipping fees can add up. Some merchants offer low-cost "ground" shipping, but their Web site may be set up to default to a costlier two-day or overnight delivery method.

Warning: Click on ads with caution. At many sites, ads pop up as you are examining merchandise. But realize that if you click on them, you will probably be *moving to a site owned by someone else*—perhaps a company you never heard of. Before you order from this stranger, go back to step 1 above.

Outwit the Outlets

Outlet stores are springing up everywhere, but so are the accusations that some of the merchandise may be several seasons old or not the same quality as items sold at retail stores.

You can increase your chances of getting current, good-quality merchandise if you stick with "factory" outlets—stores that are owned and operated by the manufacturer, and stock only that manufacturer's brand items. Call ahead to find out whether they accept credit cards and checks, what their return policies are, and whether they have dressing rooms for trying on clothing.

When you are at the store, learn to spot the warning flags that indicate you may not be getting a bargain. Does a sign say "For Sale" instead of "On Sale"? Does another promise "Savings up to 80%"? Most items may be only 10 to 25 percent off. Red price tags, bulging bins of merchandise, or the word "discount" as part of the store's name may only give the illusion of low prices. Passé styles, or other items for which you would never consider paying full price, may be a waste of money at any price.

If you're not willing or able to do extensive comparison-shopping, retail stores, which have a bigger selection and often more liberal return policies, may be better places for you to do your shopping.

Remember: Before you travel to an outlet mall or discount store, call ahead, ask for customer service, and find out:

- Are credit cards and checks accepted?
- What are the return policies?
- Is the number of days for returns limited?
- Are return items accepted for any reason or only if merchandise is defective?
- If you return an item, will you get cash or only a restricted store credit?
- Are there dressing rooms for clothing try-ons?

Take It Back, Please!

After the shopping, the wrapping, the shipping, the gift-giving, and the "thank you" notes, comes another holiday tradition—the returning. But if a sign says "No returns, no exchanges," is the merchant bluffing or telling the truth? Here are six savvy secrets you need to know.

- *Secret 1: Stores are not obliged to take back merchandise.* In most states, merchants are only required to take items back if they are defective. If the merchandise is defective and the store won't cooperate, contact your local consumer affairs office for help. If you still can't resolve it, contact your state attorney general's office.
- *Secret 2: Stores can have different return policies for different items.* Even stores with liberal return policies may have stricter ones for products that can be duplicated, such as CDs, videotapes, and computer software, or for electronic items that can be used over the holidays, such as computers and video equipment. Check signs near the cash register, or ask for a printout of the store's return policies. Don't open sealed boxes or wrappers if you think you may have to return the items that are inside.

- *Secret 3: Stores don't have to refund cash.* Whether or not you have a receipt, many stores won't hand you cash. You'll only get a store credit, which may expire in 30, 60, or 90 days. Read the fine print. Get an extension in writing if you won't be able to use the credit before it expires.

Tip: Out of earshot of other customers, try to negotiate with the store's manager for cash, especially if there is nothing else in the store that you want.

- *Secret 4: When you return a gift, you may have to settle for less than the full purchase price.* Without a receipt, most stores will only give you the lowest sale price. But try to negotiate for more. Although I didn't have the receipt, I recently exchanged a toy that was not on sale that week, but had been reduced by 20 percent earlier in the month. The store would only give me credit for the discounted price, but agreed to take off 20 percent on another item, even though it was not on sale that week.
- *Secret 5: If you send back a catalog gift, the giver may find out.* Many catalog merchants will notify the gift giver that you have returned a gift. Some catalogs won't accept returns unless you follow their instructions on time limits and wrapping requirements.
- *Secret 6: If an item goes on sale, even after you give it as a gift, ask for a refund of the difference.* Some stores will give you the "Benefit of Sale" and refund the difference if the price of an item is reduced within a specified time (usually, ten days). Receipts are now very detailed, and most merchants no longer require the item itself—just the receipt. So, putting off your holiday shopping until a few days before Christmas, because many items go on sale after Christmas, can put extra cash back in your pocket just in time to pay upcoming holiday bills.

Shop Safe

Shopping malls have been likened to jungles. When shoppers separate from the pack (to go to their car, or to a remote pay phone or rest room), predators pounce. Here are some safety tips to keep you and your family from becoming victims of crime:

- *Keep your guard up.* If you get jostled by one person, an accomplice may be preparing to lift your wallet. Leave your purse and valuables at home. Instead, use a fanny pack with just the necessities: some cash; one or two credit cards; keys; driver's license, and car registration.

- *Check out on-site child care before you leave your children.* Do they verify that children are handed only to parents, and not to strangers? Are the toys safe? Is the center clean? Better yet, leave the kids at home with a sitter. You'll complete your shopping faster, and they'll be happier in familiar surroundings.

- *Avoid shopping late at night.* Morning is safer, and you'll get through the lines faster.

- *Bury your purse when you're in the dressing room or ladies' room.* Thieves reach over the partition and steal purses while you're fussing, partially clothed. They know you can't run after them.

- *Park close to stores.* Look for shopping centers that offer free valet parking, or ask the mall security unit for an escort to walk you to your car.

Privacy Tip: To activate a product warranty, you don't have to answer every question on the warranty card. Only your name, address, and product information are needed. You can leave personal questions blank, such as your income, age, occupation, number of children, and so on. It's none of their business. But they will probably sell your information if you supply it.

Chapter 22

Get Fit, Not Fleeced, at the Health Club

Many people who succeed at taking charge of their finances say that they get both an energy boost and a motivational boost by doing something, several times a week, that isn't money-related: They work out. Working out may even save you money; it can improve your health (lower your blood pressure or reduce your weight), so you can get lower-priced health insurance and life insurance policies.

Terry's Story

"My money motivation was weaning and I just felt blah. Even my daily walks were boring me, so I had decided to stop walking," recalls Terry. "A few days later, I ran into my neighbor, Vicki. She said I looked like I could use a pick-me-up, so she invited me to be her guest at her health club. I'm anything but a fitness fanatic; in fact, except for my walks, I get very little exercise. That's why I was so surprised by how great I felt physically and emotionally after twenty minutes at the health club. I felt energized. Yet I also felt calmer. So much so, that I convinced Vicki to take me with her twice more. I bit the bullet and joined the club myself.

"The best part about working out is that it makes me feel like I can do anything—including taking charge of my finances. I now try to schedule my money matters (paying bills, balancing my checkbook, choosing investments) on the afternoons after I've exercised. I'm sold on this exercise thing because it works for me. In fact, if I go more than a couple of days without working out, I can feel the difference. I feel logy and blah, and I just don't feel like moving."

Let's face it, huffing and puffing alone isn't much fun. And the encouragement of a fitness trainer and a variety of good-quality equipment to choose from can yield better results and keep your interest and enthusiasm from waning. As with other pricey purchases you make or service contracts you enter into, at a health club you can usually get a better deal than the one you are first offered. Here are six steps for getting in shape without overpaying.

STEP 1   COMPARISON-SHOP.

Many health clubs will give you a free trial membership just for the asking. Most will match offers from nearby clubs by lowering the initiation fee or waiving it altogether. If you join off-season (during spring or summer), you can often write your own terms. But, regardless of when you join, before you shell out hundreds, or thousands, of dollars for a health club that you may use only a few times, you should know:

- *The "nonbinding application" many clubs have you fill out on your first visit may actually be a binding contract* that obligates you for years of payments. Don't sign anything until you're ready to become a paying member.
- *The club may have been cited for health code violations but still be open for business.* Check out a prospective club with your local Health Department to see whether it's up to code. And check with your local Consumer Affairs office and the Better Business Bureau to see if there are outstanding complaints by members.
- *If you move away, or if the club cuts back its hours or closes all branches near you, you'll likely still be on the hook for future dues.* Ask the club to add cancellation clauses (to release you from future dues and to refund a prorated amount of your initiation fee, in any of these circumstances) before you sign a long-term contract. Inspect the facilities carefully, at the time of day you plan to use them (for instance, lunchtime or after work). A club that's empty at 10:00 A.M. may be jammed at 5:30 P.M., and there may be long lines for the latest equipment.
- *If you are later diagnosed with a health condition that prevents you from continuing to work out, you probably cannot cancel your membership.* Get a physical *before* you sign the contract. Also, before signing, try to add a clause stating that if you are later diagnosed with a serious health condition, you can discontinue your membership and owe no additional payments.
- *If you get injured on improperly maintained equipment, or because the club's trainer caused your injury, the club may not be liable.* Buried in most health club contracts is a clause that says members give up the right to sue—even if the club is responsible for an injury. To add insult to your injury, many clubs still won't let you out of the contract. Strike undesirable clauses before signing the contract. Many clubs will go along with your changes, to get your business.

- *The trainer may have no training.* Ask the trainer about his or her qualifications: schooling for this job, length of time as a trainer, and certifications—if any.

Tip: While you're inspecting the facilities, check that the equipment is in good condition. Talk to club members. If they're pleased, it will come through. If they're dissatisfied but can't get out of their contract, they may tell all, to keep the club from getting new members.

- *Restrictions may be unreasonable.* Some clubs close their doors to members while boosting their revenues by offering the use of their facilities to outside, paying groups.
- *Your baby may be at risk if left with the club baby-sitter.* Are the facilities clean and well appointed? What's the ratio of children to child care providers? Some health clubs have lax security. Find out what steps this club takes to ensure that your child won't be given to a stranger.

STEP 2   AVOID CLUBS THAT ARE UNDER CONSTRUCTION, NO MATTER HOW BIG THE DISCOUNT.

Grand openings are often delayed for months, and sometimes for years. You will not be able to join another club in the interim because you'll still be on the hook for the first one.

STEP 3   PAY AS LITTLE UP FRONT AS POSSIBLE.

Don't authorize an automatic debit from your bank account. (Why let a stranger have access to your account?) Even if the club offers you a substantial discount for paying this way, don't do it. Many health clubs have gone bankrupt with no notice, and before closing their doors, the owners have withdrawn an extra two or three months' dues from the account of every member who had authorized an automatic transfer.

STEP 4   HAVE AN ATTORNEY REVIEW THE CONTRACT BEFORE YOU SIGN.

If the club refuses to let you take an unsigned copy of the contract off the premises, that could be a warning flag.

There are other ways to pay less and still get in shape. If joining a chichi health club isn't for you because it doesn't fit your lifestyle or your pocketbook, look into some alternatives.

STEP 5 CONSIDER JOINING A GENERIC GYM INSTEAD.

Joining an expensive club may not be the best choice for you. So before signing on the dotted line, check out the local YMCA or YWCA. Many "Y"s now have top-quality workout equipment and a trained staff, and membership typically costs much less than private clubs. If you must cancel your membership early, "Y"s are often more accommodating than private clubs.

STEP 6 SEARCH FOR SECOND-HAND SAVINGS.

Maybe sweating with strangers isn't your cup of tea. Did you know that, for about the same money you'd spend on club dues, you can buy your own equipment—an exercise bike, a stepper, or a treadmill? You won't have to battle after-work traffic to get to a club. And a few years down the road, you'll have exercise equipment that you can sell or continue to use.

Even if you'd never consider *wearing* someone else's castoffs, second-hand sporting equipment can be a bargain, and much of this recycled gear is still safely nestled in its factory wrapping because the previous owner never got around to setting it up, let alone using it.

How much can you save by buying used equipment? At secondhand sporting goods stores, discounts typically range from 20 percent to 60 percent. The bulk of the items are in a 20 percent to 30 percent discount range.

You can get a bigger discount via the want ads, but when you buy equipment from a private party, don't count on getting a refund if you later discover that the equipment was damaged.

Whether you buy new or used equipment, test it out thoroughly in the store. Shop in comfortable clothes, and wear workout shoes. And don't let the salesperson rush you. Stay on the treadmill, stepper, or exercise bicycle at least fifteen minutes. Does it feel comfortable? If it isn't a good fit in the store, how much will you use it at home?

Next, you can talk money with the salesperson. Consider the price tag to be a starting point; you often can negotiate down. After you've settled the final price of the equipment, ask about the store's returns policy. Most secondhand stores will take back equipment and refund cash, for any reason, within thirty days.

What happens if the equipment breaks or malfunctions? Will the store stand behind the goods, or will you be on the hook for costly repairs? My advice is: Ask the store to throw in a free, one-year warranty. Finally, if you can't fit the equipment into the trunk of your car, ask the store for free delivery. Go get fit, not fleeced!

Chapter 23

Lower Your Phone Bills

Brian's Story

"After I opened my phone bill, I noticed it was for $20 more than I usually owe. It took several passes, but there, buried among the ever-growing list of miscellaneous charges, were two charges for an item called 'consumer options.' I had no idea what those were, so I called my local phone company and was told that these charges were for services from another company—a company I had never even heard of.

"My local phone company told me that they only send out the bill, and if I had questions, I should take them up with the vendor. When I called this mystery company, I had a very long wait to speak to someone. I had to repeat my story three times. Finally, a woman claiming to be a supervisor said they would look into it and get back to me. A week went by, so I called them again, but they told me they had no record of my previous inquiry but if I would explain the problem, they would look into it and get back to me. Another week went by with no response, so I called them again. After being put on hold for over ten minutes, someone got on the line to tell me that I had authorized these services. When I assured them I hadn't, they responded that they had me on tape placing the order, but they refused to let me ever hear the tape, let alone get a copy of it. The tape can't exist because I never placed an order with these people. I'm still not sure who these people are or what service I allegedly ordered but am being charged for.

"What right do these people have to put charges on my phone bill? What galls me even more is why on earth would my phone company take this sleazy company's word for it and never even ask me?"

Anyone who says "Talk is cheap" probably hasn't examined his or her phone bill lately. While per-minute long-distance rates have continued to decline, a variety of new charges (including minimum monthly fees and carrier-line charges) from long-distance companies and local phone companies are offsetting or diminishing the savings for a growing number of consumers. To make matters worse, some unscrupulous companies have discovered that the increasingly dense, and often confusing, phone bill is the perfect place to hide unauthorized charges and still get paid by unsuspecting consumers. (Tens of thousands of consumers have contacted the FCC over the past few years to voice concerns about their phone bills.) Are there hidden charges lurking in your bill?

Here are five steps to lower your phone bills.

STEP 1 CUT OUT "CRAMMING."

Increasing numbers of consumers are getting charged for services such as voice mail, paging, personal 800 numbers, and calling cards that they never ordered, from companies they may never have heard of. The cramming problem stems from the fact that almost any unscrupulous company that can look up your phone number and address in a phone book can start billing you, through your local phone company, for services you never contracted for. The way charges are aggregated on most bills, it's not always easy to spot the phony items.

Why would phone companies agree to put unverified charges on a longtime customer's bill? Local phone companies get paid a fee for processing bills from outside vendors, so they have an inherent conflict of interest. If they double-checked the charges, they would reduce the billing income they get. Phone companies could easily rectify this phony billing by allowing customers to put a freeze on their account (no new services could be added unless the customer personally authorizes them), but most phone companies don't offer this protection.

To curb this problem, the Federal Communications Commission (FCC) has adopted what it calls "Truth in Billing Guidelines" to make phone bills more consumer-friendly. Phone companies are expected to:

- Highlight any changes in service from the previous bill. Not only should this flag any potential cramming charges (for services like voice mail and paging), but it should also point to possible "slamming" (when a long-distance carrier has been changed without the customer's authorization or knowledge; see Step 2, below). Cramming and slamming generate tens of thousands of complaints to the FCC each year.
- Clearly identify the name and contact information for any outside companies posting charges to your bill. Until now, most bills gave contact information for only the local phone company—not for outside vendors.
- Tell when you can withhold payment. When you dispute a questionable charge on your credit card statement, the bill states which payments you can withhold while the dispute is being

resolved. But with phone bills, it has never been clear when, if ever, you could withhold payment and not run the risk of losing your phone service.

Use these defensive strategies to cut the chances of getting crammed:

- Don't sign up for giveaways from companies you don't personally know. Understand that, in many cases, the signatures on these giveaway forms are forged anyway, so you may have had nothing to do with getting these bogus charges.
- Scrutinize your phone bill each month. Report any problem to the local phone company immediately, and refuse to pay fraudulent or questionable charges.
- Report any problems to your local consumer affairs office and the state attorney general's office.
- Consider removing your address from the phone book; without the correct address, it may be harder for a crook to slip a bogus charge onto your phone bill.

STEP 2 SAY "NO" TO "SLAMMING."

Slamming occurs when your long-distance carrier is changed without your knowledge or permission. You may get switched to a fly-by-night company, but even the big long-distance carriers have been accused of this practice and some have voluntarily paid the costs to return customers to their original carriers. You may not find out that you've been slammed until you get your phone bill and spot a different long-distance logo, or notice that your bill is for several times what you normally pay.

How does it happen? Bogus sweepstakes and phone calls from unscrupulous salespeople trigger many cases. For instance, a stranger may call you and ask if you'd be interested in hearing about a way to cut your phone bill. If you say "Yes," the unscrupulous salesperson will record your response and then process the paperwork with your local phone company, claiming that you authorized the change to the stranger's long-distance service.

It could also begin if you fill out a sweepstakes entry at a shopping mall. Buried in the giveaway's fine print, just above your signature, is a statement that you agree to have your phone service switched.

If you get switched, what can you do? Call your former long-distance carrier and explain that you were switched without your knowledge or consent. Tell the carrier that you want to be switched back. Most reputable long-distance carriers will agree to switch you back and not charge you the switching fee (about $5). The good news is that although you will have to pay for that month's phone calls (usually calculated based on your previous carrier's lower rates), you probably won't have to pay any additional charges. And if you paid the bill before you noticed you were slammed, contact your local phone company and ask a customer service representative to arrange for you to get a refund.

Tip: Ask your local phone company to place a "freeze" on your account at no cost to you. With a freeze in place, your phone company should not allow anyone to change your long-distance carrier without your prior approval.

STEP 3 KEEP LONG-DISTANCE CHARGES IN CHECK.

Could you be overpaying for long-distance calls? Here are some recent trends that are nickel-and-diming a lot of consumers but often go unnoticed:

- Directory assistance charges have been rising; fees of just under $1 per call are not uncommon.
- Some long-distance carriers have started—or are about to start—charging monthly minimums (about $3). This punishes consumers who don't make a lot of long-distance calls.
- Daytime calling hours have been extended. The highest-rate phone charges used to apply only from 8:00 A.M. to 5:00 P.M., but daytime rates have been extended by many carriers to 7:00 A.M. to 7:00 P.M., or longer hours, depending upon your carrier.

LLOYD'S LAW

More than ever, if you're not on some kind of calling plan, you are paying too much.

You wouldn't pay sticker price for a new car, but are you paying the full sticker price for your long-distance calls? You are if you're paying the "basic rate" because you are not on a long-distance calling plan.

Consumer Tip: Make sure you are on the right plan for your calling pattern. Otherwise, you could be paying up to twice the necessary amount.

A plan that saves a relative or a neighbor a lot of money could cause your bill to rise unnecessarily. Find the lowest-cost plan for *you:*

- Analyze your phone bills for the past three to six months. See what area codes you call, when (weekday, weeknight, weekend), and the amount of time you stay connected.
- Ask your current long-distance carrier to analyze your phone bills and recommend which of its plans is most economical for you. Even a company you are considering switching to will make recommendations based on the calling information you supply.
- Ask how much you will be charged for operator assistance or directory assistance. Some plans that charge low long-distance rates more than make up for the savings with these services.
- Ask about exclusions, such as for credit card calls or calls made away from home. They are often billed at much higher rates.
- Consider an online billing option. If you are willing to forgo a paper bill, you can find some of the lowest per-minute rates online. But make sure that you understand *all* the charges, because some carriers are adding a fee (about $1, so far) for the convenience of online billing. When the carrier doesn't have to generate a paper bill or pay the postage to mail it, why does it need to charge more for paperless billing?
- Check with your Internet service provider (ISP). It may be offering special long-distance deals to customers. Again, make sure that you understand all the charges.
- Comparison-shop again, every three to six months. Calling plan terms, or your calling pattern, may have changed, so a different plan may offer you a better deal.

Here are two Web sites that can help you compare long-distance plans:

www.trac.org
www.consumer-action.org

Before switching, ask your current long-distance carrier to meet or beat a competitor's offer. Many will, to keep from losing your business.

 STEP 4 DABBLE DELICATELY WHEN DIALING AROUND.

It's hard to miss the ads boasting big savings, and all you have to do is dial 10-10- and three more numbers before you dial the number you're calling. Can you really save money this way?

Maybe. Under certain circumstances, you could save money with these so-called dial-around numbers that let you bypass your chosen long-distance carrier. But here's the rub: Choose the wrong dial-around number—or use it at the wrong time or on the wrong day—and you could end up paying *substantially more* than you would by just dialing the number the traditional way, using your own carrier. But calculating the projected cost for dialing around is not easy, so an increasing number of consumers are using this service without really knowing what they will ultimately pay—or whether it will save them money or cost them more.

Here are some reasons you may not end up saving much, if anything, using a 10-10- number:

- *Hidden fees.* Not until you see the bill do you find out all the costs.
- *Monthly fees.* Use the number once and you could find a hefty fee (about $5) on your phone bill.
- *Redundant "universal service access" charge,* to defray Internet access at schools and libraries, and subsidize rural phone service. You may already be paying this charge to your long-distance carrier.
- *Higher rates.* Some 10-10- numbers charge a low per-minute rate regardless of how long you talk. But others charge a flat fee for the first twenty minutes, so if you talk less (or the call goes to an answering machine), you'll pay a very high per-minute fee. One plan gives you a big retroactive discount if you talk more than twenty minutes, but if you hang up shy of twenty minutes, you pay significantly more than if you hung on the line for even a few more seconds.

The best strategy for some consumers is to sign up for a low-rate weekend plan (say, 5 cents per minute on Sunday), and use that plan during the low-cost hours. Then if you have to make calls during peak weekday business hours, choose a dial-around plan that offers you the best rate for those prime periods.

STEP 5 PREVIEW THE PER-MINUTE PRICE ON PREPAID CARDS.

With a traditional calling card, you place a call and are billed later. With a prepaid card, you pay first and phone later. After you purchase the card, you will likely be given an 800 phone number to call when you want to place a long-distance call. You then enter the card's user number. For college students or travelers who don't want to carry a credit card or a lot of cash, a prepaid phone card can be a relatively inexpensive way to make long-distance calls away from home.

But prepaid cards aren't for everyone. Here are some hidden costs and risks:

- The per-minute charge can be much higher than for traditional calling cards that bill you later (and much more than you would pay for a discount plan that you would use at your home).
- Some cards won't work outside of the United States.
- You may get hit with an activation fee (of 50 cents or significantly more) each time you use the card, which would make your per-minute cost much higher than the advertised rate.
- Some companies selling these cards are fly-by-nights that don't pay their bills, so the card either won't work at all or will only work for a few days until the service is cut off.
- Some cards have hard-to-reach customer service departments, or none at all.
- If the card is lost or stolen, it's like losing cash, and most card issuers will not reimburse you.

If you choose a prepaid card, stick to a well-known company that is financially sound and has a working 800 customer service number (call it before you pay for the card).

Shave Thousands Off the Cost of a Home and a Mortgage

One of the best—and most personally satisfying—investments you may ever make is buying a home. The money that you saved by following my first six Solutions—at the bank, on credit cards, on a car and insurance—can now be put toward something you can use and enjoy day in and day out.

But don't jump into the housing pool too quickly. Innocent home-buying, selling, or remodeling blunders can be costly and will haunt you for years. Overpaying on a home, choosing the wrong type of mortgage, or paying an inflated real estate tax bill can put you behind the money eight ball. Also, home improvements that should be simple and inexpensive can suddenly mushroom into mammoth projects requiring an almost bottomless bank account. How you pay for home improvements can cost you dearly if you settle for the wrong financing choice.

Beginning with this chapter, I'll show you how to avoid these problems. Then we'll come full circle and discuss ways to sell your home quickly and for top dollar, plus how to avoid getting stung if you generously offer to finance part or all of the purchase for the buyer.

Chapter 24

Avoid Costly Home-Buying and Mortgage Mistakes

Carol and Charlie's Story

Carol and Charlie had been looking for a home for only three weeks when they found what they called their "dream house." The kitchen and basement were newly remodeled, and the house was near public transportation. "We liked the house but we hadn't really looked at what else was out there," explains Carol. "But then we got a call from our agent, Maggie. She told Charlie and me that two other buyers were about to make bids on the house, so if we had any interest, we better act fast—and it better be an offer near the asking price, or we would lose it to one of the other families." So they made an offer near the $129,500 asking price. Their $125,000 bid was quickly accepted.

During the first rainstorm after they had moved into their new home, Carol and Charlie discovered that the brand-new basement carpet installed by the prior owner was covering a costly secret—a $7,200 water problem. Had they hired a professional home inspector, they would have been alerted to the problem *before* they closed on the house, and they could have negotiated a lower purchase price or gotten the seller to pay for repairs.

Six months after moving into their home, the Egans have had to borrow an extra $11,792 to make additional needed repairs on an array of undisclosed problems. "We were on a very tight budget when we bought this house, and these extra repairs have really thrown a monkey wrench in our plans," says Charlie. Adds Carol, "Our dream house has quickly become a nightmare."

It's the biggest purchase they ever make, yet most people spend more time researching a new dishwasher than they do a new home. How can you avoid overpaying—or getting stuck with someone else's money pit?

STEP 1 AVOID COSTLY HOME-BUYING BLUNDERS.

Doing your homework takes on new meaning when the sticker price of your contemplated purchase tops $100,000, but the same shopping savvy that you use when you make smaller purchases can stand you in good stead with this big purchase. Here are ten common and costly home-buying blunders that can snag first-time home buyers (as well as more seasoned ones who haven't bought a home in a few years), and ways you can avoid them:

- *Blunder 1. Divulging too much to your real estate agent.* If you're looking for a home, did you know that anything you tell your real estate agent (including how much money you have to spend), even *in confidence,* will be passed on to the seller? That's because traditional real estate agents work for the seller and are paid by the seller. (If you were shown a house by an agent and you eventually buy that house, your agent will split the commission with the listing agent that was hired by the seller.) Don't disclose to your agent anything that could decrease your bargaining ability (such as how much money you're willing to pay, or the fact that you love the house). Your agent is obliged to tell the seller everything you say.
- *Blunder 2. Hiring a buyer's broker who has a conflict of interest.* To get a better deal and avoid showing their hand to a seller, many home buyers now hire—and pay for—their own real estate agent, called a buyer's broker. This could be a good move, but the way some buyers' brokers work (and are paid) can end up costing you money or the loss of a bid on a house. Here are three red flags that could indicate your buyer's broker has a potential conflict of interest that could work against you:

Broker wears two hats. Your buyer's broker also works as a seller's broker. Conceivably, the same agent could be representing you and the seller of a house.

Broker shares quarters. Your buyer's broker shares an office with a seller's broker. Loose lips (or overheard phone conversations) could reveal your bidding strategies or, at least, how much you are willing to pay to the sellers and their agents.

Broker's goals oppose yours. Your buyer's broker gets paid a percentage of a home's *selling* price. The more aggressively your agent tries to get your purchase price down, the less commission he or she will get. This could encourage some buyer's brokers not to negotiate too hard on your behalf.

If you want to hire your own agent, look for one who is *exclusively* a buyer's broker, does not share an office with sellers' brokers, and either charges a flat fee for finding you a home or bills you by the hour. Given the potential conflicts of interest with a broker, you pay for yourself, I think most house hunters could do just as well with a traditional agent, who is paid by the seller. But as a buyer, you must not forget that a traditional agent really works for the seller, and anything you say will be passed on to the seller and could be used against you during negotiations.

- *Blunder 3. Overpaying for the house.* To determine what a home is worth, you need to research the property and the neighborhood. Ask your agent for "comparables" ("comps"—the asking and selling prices for similar homes in that neighborhood). If home prices are falling, be sure to get "comps" for the past six months. Then do some research yourself. Check the real estate tax records, which are part of the public record. (Call the local government for details.) You'll find specifics about the age and dimensions of the house, as well as tax assessments, every price the home previously has sold for, and a record of prior owners. You can also check the tax records for neighboring homes, including the comps you got from your agent.

Tip: If you catch the seller or your agent misrepresenting information and you're not satisfied with the explanation, stop dealing with that person.

- *Blunder 4. Omitting an "out" in the contract for a faulty house.* A contract "out," called a contingency, for a home inspection would allow you to void the contract if costly repairs are needed or if you can't get financing, and still get all your money back. The American Society of Home Inspectors (www.ashi.com) can refer you to inspectors who are members of their nonprofit organization. If you think the home might have structural problems, you might want to hire a civil engineer who is licensed in your state to inspect the property. (Call your local consumer affairs office or your state government for contact information.)

  Accompany the inspector on a tour through your possible new home. He or she may say something significant about the condition of the property that will not appear in the written evaluation.

If the home inspector finds costly flaws in the property and you still want the house, try negotiating with the seller. With the inspection report in hand, ask the seller to pick up the tab for the needed repairs or to lower the price so that you can arrange for repairs after the closing.

Don't rely on the home inspector's estimate if you're considering having the repairs done after the closing. Instead, get written estimates from three independent home repair contractors. And steer clear of any contractors that are recommended by the home inspector. It could be a ploy to get referral business for overpriced or unnecessary work.

- *Blunder 5. Omitting an "out" in the contract if you can't get a suitable mortgage.* Like the contingency for a home inspection, a mortgage-approval contingency would let you out of the contract, with a full refund, if you are unable to get the financing you need. So be specific with the mortgage contingency (for instance: "This offer is contingent on the buyer getting a $125,000, 30-year, fixed-rate mortgage at a rate not to exceed 7 percent and the buyer paying no more than one point"). In that way, if interest rates soar, if you fail to qualify for the mortgage, or if the home's value is too low to get the full mortgage ($125,000 in this case), you can walk away and get back your deposit.

Tip: Keep the deposit to no more than 10 percent of your offer price. Many sellers will accept a lower deposit (2 percent to 5 percent).

- *Blunder 6. Signing a contract before having a lawyer review it.* There is no such thing as a standard contract, so don't sign a preprinted form and assume it's a fair deal for you. You can decrease the chances of having a costly problem down the road by hiring an attorney *before* you sign anything. No lawyer can adequately represent both sides of a contract, yet millions of buyers and sellers try to cut costs by sharing an attorney with the other side. Hire your own attorney so that he or she is only looking out for your interests. Your attorney should specialize in real estate law. (Get referrals from friends, the local bar association, or your banker.) Agree on the fee up front, and get the agreement in writing.
- *Blunder 7. Not itemizing what "conveys."* Can the seller take the light fixtures, the wall-to-wall carpeting, or the appliances? What stays with the home ("conveys") varies by community. If you want it, list it in the sales contract.

Tip: Do a "walk-through" an hour before the closing, to be sure the house is in good condition and that everything the seller agreed to leave there is still there.

- *Blunder 8. Not buying "owner's" title insurance that covers your equity.* Most title insurance covers only the lender's investment in the property, not your equity. It's not uncommon for an ex-spouse of a prior owner, or someone else, to come forward and claim to have a right to the property that you thought was yours. Prices for title insurance can vary a great deal. Contact several insurers, and your lawyer, to find the best deal, but *make sure you have it.* As long as we're talking insurance: *Never* place a bid on a house unless you are sure you'll be able to get adequate, affordable homeowner's insurance.
- *Blunder 9. Letting the sellers stay in the house after the closing.* The sellers could then become tenants with strong legal rights, and you'll have to try to evict them if they refuse to go. Eviction can be costly and time-consuming.
- *Blunder 10. Settling for the best house in a run-down neighborhood.* In terms of resale value, you will usually do better by buying a modest house in a good neighborhood, instead of the best house in a run-down neighborhood or in an area with inferior schools.

STEP 2 MAKE THE MECHANICS OF MORTGAGES WORK FOR YOU.

Mavis's Story

"Finding the house of our dreams (well, almost of our dreams) was the easy part; deciding how to pay for it is hard. Interest rates have been changing almost every day, so my husband, Jim, and I don't know whether to go with a fixed-rate mortgage or an adjustable-rate one.

"But the choice that's really keeping us up at night is whether we should get a large mortgage, which our financial planner keeps suggesting, or a smaller one, to keep the monthly payments down. Dick, our financial planner, says we'd be foolish to take anything but a long mortgage—a 30- or even, he suggested, a 40-year loan—and a small down payment (no more than 3 percent or 5 percent). He keeps saying, 'The less money you put down, the bigger your rate of return will be on the house, and with a lower down payment, you can start an investment portfolio and make your money grow even faster.'

"Jim's father thinks that's crazy. He says, 'Go for a short mortgage and put as much down as possible, so you can pay it off quickly.' I guess I can see both their points, and that's not helping us to make a decision. Also, I would like to stay home after we have children, and lower monthly mortgage payments, I think, would make that a more viable option. So what should we do?"

Overpay on your home and you could be out a few thousand dollars. But choose the wrong mortgage and you could spend tens of thousands of dollars more than you have to, over the life of the loan. Before you apply for a mortgage, or even put a bid on a home, it's a good idea to understand how the mortgage market works—what the pricey pitfalls are, and how you can avoid them. Here are some questions to consider.

How Much House Can You Afford?

As a general rule, your monthly house payments (mortgage payments, taxes, and insurance) should not exceed 28 percent of your gross (pretax) monthly income. Your total monthly debt payments (house, credit card, student loans, and other debts) should not exceed 35 percent. You can ask a bank lending officer to tell you how much you qualify for, or you can visit one of the many Web sites that will run the numbers for you and see what current rates are at many banks. Three sources are:

HSH Associates or (800) 873-2837
www.hsh.com

Bank Rate Monitor
www.bankrate.com

Quicken's Mortgage information
www.quickenmortgage.com

Has Anyone Told You the Downside of Long, Large Mortgages?

Some self-proclaimed financial planners have been advising clients to put down as little as the lender will accept—5 percent or 3 percent of the value of the home, and to take out a long (30-year or 40-year) mortgage. The implied logic is that it's better to invest as much money as possible in things other than a home. For this to work financially, these other investments must be returning more than you are paying on the mortgage. But a lot of people make the mistake of taking out a big mortgage—at a rate of, say, 7 percent—but then leaving the money in a bank account, earning barely 2 percent.

The real reason some financial planners advise very long mortgages and very small downpayments is to make more of your money available for them to invest and manage for you. They stand to earn sales commissions, bonuses, and other management fees for suggesting investments or managing your money.

What's really in your best interest? First, let's talk about the length of the mortgage. I would never recommend a 40-year mortgage. You will save just a few dollars a month, compared to a 30-year mortgage, but for that tiny savings, you will have to make mortgage payments for an additional ten years. You'll pay thousands and thousands of dollars more in interest than with a 30-year mortgage.

An even better idea for many homeowners is to look into a 15- or 20-year mortgage. Compared to a 30-year mortgage, the interest rate on a 15- or 20-year loan should be lower. Your monthly payments may be only a few dollars more than on a 30-year note, but you'll pay off the loan 15 or 10 years sooner, respectively, and save tens of thousands of dollars on interest payments.

Do You Know Why PMI Is Like Gum Stuck to the Bottom of Your Shoe?

They're both hard to get rid of. If you put down less than 20 percent of the value of your home, most lenders will require you to buy private mortgage insurance (PMI) to cover their added risk, and the possibility of their having to foreclose. PMI does not come cheap. It adds about $1,000 or more a year to your mortgage cost.

And many lenders won't let homeowners cancel PMI even when their equity exceeds 20 percent of the home's value. Most lenders go by the value of the house when it was purchased—which doesn't take rising home prices into account. The only way to prove to a lender that your home's value has risen is to get a new appraisal, which will cost you several hundred dollars.

Still, a new appraisal may not sway your lender:

- Even if you pay to get a new appraisal, be aware that many appraisers lowball the appraisal to protect the lender. (Lenders are the real, repeat customers for real estate appraisers, who, in turn, can steer other mortgage shoppers to them or away from them.)

- New rules that went into effect in 1999 make it easier to cancel PMI, but these rules apply only to new loans, not loans that were written before the effective date of the changes.

Tip: If your lender refuses to drop your PMI, consider refinancing the loan. Even if the interest rate isn't lower than you are currently paying, you will save money because you no longer will have to pay for PMI.

Should You Jump at a "Jumbo?"

Within a few months of issuing a mortgage, your mortgage lender will probably sell your loan in the secondary market to either Freddie Mac or Fannie Mae (the federally chartered agencies that buy mortgages and keep money flowing back into the mortgage market). But these agencies will only buy "conforming" mortgages that meet a variety of criteria. One criterion is that the mortgage cannot exceed a certain sum (currently, $240,000). If you need to borrow more than that amount, you will pay a premium—typically, ¼ percent to ½ percent higher interest. With rapidly rising home prices, many middle-class home buyers are now being forced into this "jumbo" mortgage category and are paying a higher interest rate.

If you are buying a relatively expensive home (in a price range that might require a nonconforming mortgage), here are two ways to avoid paying a higher, jumbo interest rate:

1. Put down a bigger down payment (more than 20 percent) to get your mortgage below $240,000, the "conforming" mortgage cutoff amount.
2. If you don't have the extra cash needed for a larger down payment, consider taking out two loans. One would be a "conforming" mortgage (not exceeding the current $240,000 cap), and the second mortgage would complete your down payment. You will pay a much higher interest rate on the second mortgage, so try to pay it off quickly.

What Is the Bite from Some Biweekly Mortgages?

With a biweekly mortgage, you'll pay one half of your monthly payment 26 times a year, so in essence, you'll pay the equivalent of 13 monthly payments instead of 12. Many lenders charge several hundred dollars to set up this payment schedule. Some unscrupulous third parties may offer consumers the option of setting up a biweekly mortgage, but instead of forwarding the money to the lender, they abscond with the homeowner's money.

You can do this yourself by making one extra payment a year (13 monthly payments instead of 12). You'll shave several years off your mortgage, and you'll save on the interest. Or, calculate one-twelfth of the amount due each month, and add it to your monthly mortgage payment. (Or add on as much as you can afford each month.) You'll shave years off your loan, and save thousands in interest payments. But remember: If you make *any payments early,* they come off the *end* of the mortgage. You cannot skip payments because you've paid ahead. You still have to fulfill your mortgage payment schedule. And, by paying any money early, when you finally pay off the mortgage (or sell the home) you may get hit with a prepayment penalty (typically 1 to 2 percent) for every dollar you paid ahead of schedule. So get *any* prepayment penalties waived—in writing—before you pay any money ahead of schedule.

STEP 3 EXPLORE CREATIVE WAYS TO FINANCE FOR LESS.

Here are some savvy mortgage shopping tips.

- *Ask the seller for financing.* It's quicker than going through a bank or mortgage company. You won't pay loan processing fees or mortgage origination "points." Sellers may be more lenient than banks in financing a buyer with less-than-perfect credit.
- *Negotiate better terms with your bank.* Banks are fighting for business and will often meet or beat competitors' interest rates, application fees, points, survey fees, and so on. If you have bank accounts, certificates of deposit, or credit cards, or do other business with the lender, ask for preferred customer terms: lower fees and a lower interest rate. Many banks will shave something off the mortgage cost if you agree to pay your mortgage with an automatic debit from a bank account (at their bank or elsewhere). Ask under what conditions you might qualify for better terms.
- *Get prepayment penalties waived.* You may want to pay down or pay off your loan early, but many mortgages charge penalties of 1 or 2 percent or more for the privilege. Get that clause struck from the mortgage document before you sign.
- *Add a reamortization clause.* I mentioned earlier that even if you make additional payments on your mortgage, you can't skip (or lower) your future monthly payments. Ask the bank to add a clause: If you make an additional payment of at least $2,000, the

bank will reamortize your loan (recalculate your payments based on the lower outstanding balance). You will still owe the same number of payments, but the monthly amount due will be reduced.

- *Check into special programs if you are self-employed.* If you cannot qualify for a traditional mortgage, ask about special programs that offer mortgages (typically, for 75 percent of the value of the home) for self-employed people.

STEP 4 BE WARY OF MORTGAGE RED FLAGS.

Some loans have hidden fees and other red flags that could force you into a foreclosure.

"Teaser" rates.   An adjustable rate mortgage that starts at 4 percent, with a 5 percent cap, may not peak at 9 percent (4 percent + 5 percent). The 4 percent may be a "teaser" rate. The real rate for the first year may actually be 7 percent, so the loan (with the 5 percent cap) peaks at 12 percent (7 percent + 5 percent). Get all terms of the loan in writing, including how high the interest rate can go, before you sign your agreement.

Negative amortization loan.   The interest rate on this loan floats, typically, for five years. At the end of the fifth year, the interest rate is fixed at the then-current rate. If it has gone up since you took out the mortgage, the lender will make up for any shortfall by *increasing the balance on the mortgage.* (If you took out a loan for, say, $95,000, you may now owe $102,000). Even though you've been paying on it for five years, you may now owe more money than the home is worth.

Hybrids.   These newer types of mortgages often begin with a fixed-rate loan for the first three to ten years, and then adjust based on market conditions at the end of that predetermined time period. If interest rates have gone up significantly by the time your rate is due to adjust, you run a risk that you may not be able to afford the new higher payments and could be forced to sell your house. Unless you are certain that you will be getting a significant increase in your income or that you will have sold the house before the initial rate expires, these hybrids can be very risky.

Balloon mortgages.   These mortgages amortize payments the same way 30-year mortgages do, but the whole balance must be repaid in three, five, or seven years. If you can't refinance when the balloon is due, you could be forced to sell your house. Avoid balloons.

◀ **Call provisions.**   For the same reason (i.e., the bank can demand early repayment, an early "call," of the loan), avoid loans containing these provisions.

STEP 5 GET TO THE POINT WITH POINTS.

One mortgage "point" equals 1 percent of the loan (mortgage) amount (on, say, a $150,000 loan, one point would equal $1,500). When you pay points, you're paying some interest in advance, in exchange for getting a lower interest rate over the life of the loan. By paying two points, or $3,000 in this case (2 points × 1 percent of $150,000), you might get a break of $\frac{1}{8}$ percent for each point, so you would get a $\frac{1}{4}$ percent lower mortgage rate. Is buying down your mortgage rate by paying points up front a good idea?

On the plus side:

- You only pay the points once (when you take out the mortgage), but you get a lower interest rate for the entire life of the loan.
- You may get to write off the points on your taxes in the year you buy the house. The alternative is to amortize the amount, deducting a fraction ($\frac{1}{30}$ of each point paid on a 30 year loan) each year, over the life of the loan.

On the minus side:

- For each point you pay, you may buy the interest rate down only $\frac{1}{8}$ percent, so it would take you about eight years to recoup that one point (1 percent) interest you paid ahead (when you took out the mortgage). Homeowners, on average, keep a mortgage less than eight years, so unless you expect to own the house longer, you might be ahead by paying the $\frac{1}{8}$ percent higher interest while you hold the mortgage, instead of paying the points.
- Paying a point or more up front, in order to buy down (lower) your mortgage interest rate, may not be the best use of this money. For instance, if your mortgage is for a little over 80 percent of the appraised value, and your lender is requiring that you buy PMI (private mortgage insurance), why not use the money earmarked for buy-down points to increase your downpayment to 20 percent instead? You can then avoid paying the PMI now and for the life of

the loan. (See page 251 for more information on PMI, especially when you can or cannot get it canceled.)

Cut Your Real Estate Taxes

Real estate taxes seem to go up for almost any reason. When housing prices are rising, following a banner year for home sales, property taxes go up. But when housing prices are dropping, due to sluggish demand or high interest rates, real estate taxes still often rise.

 ### DETERMINE WHETHER YOUR HOUSE IS OVERASSESSED.

If your tax bill has gone up, don't automatically write a check for the higher amount. Your home may have been overvalued, and you may get some tax relief by contesting the bill. Understand that the tax rate (also called the mill rate) is not negotiable, but the assessed value of your home (what your town says that your house is worth) could be reduced if it has been figured incorrectly.

Before you dismiss this sum as small change, consider this: Any error in this year's bill will be compounded in future years, because most towns rarely do full assessments based on door-to-door inspections of homes. Instead, new assessments are usually based on percentage changes from the prior year's bill. Many homeowners (estimates are as high as 45 percent) who contest their bill do get their taxes lowered.

If you haven't sold your house or made pricey renovations, why would your home suddenly become overvalued? Possibly because of what I call "guilt by association." Say your neighbors are in the process of doing extensive renovations, but you're not. The property assessors may assume that all the properties in your neighborhood have been improved.

Or, if you've fallen behind on repairs, and your municipality's assessors only did a "drive-by" appraisal (they literally judge the value of homes from the comfort of their cars), they can't see your backyard, or what your house looks like inside.

ASK ABOUT THE ASSESSMENT RATIO.

Know the assessment ratio for your town. If your home's market value (what it would sell for) is $200,000, but your assessment is only $180,000, you still could be overassessed. Many municipalities use only a *partial assessment,* not the home's full value. If the assessment ratio is, say, 75 percent, your assessed value should be $150,000 (75 percent of $200,000), or $30,000 less than the $180,000 assessment you received.

STEP 8 SEE HOW YOUR HOME'S ASSESSMENT COMPARES WITH YOUR NEIGHBORS'.

A little investigating could save you a bundle in real estate taxes. Start by calling your local government's tax office and asking where you can research the tax records. In most towns, homeowners can look them up at the courthouse or the local library. Your mission is to find your "property record" card and look for errors that could be causing you to pay more than you actually owe. Here are two red flags to look for:

◀ **Misstating dimensions.**   Overstatement of the square footage of your home. Overstatement of the number of rooms or bathrooms in your house.

◀ **Listing non-existent amenities.**   Incorrect listing of features, such as classifying your carport as a garage, or your half-bathroom (without a shower or tub) as a full bathroom. Incorrect inclusion of features that you don't have, such as central air conditioning, a working fireplace, or a pool.

Next, you want to find out how much your neighbors, who have similar homes, are paying in real estate taxes. Real estate assessments and taxes are part of the public record, so when you look up your home, you can also check out similar homes in your area.

Before you research the records, drive around your neighborhood and jot down the addresses of other homes that are similar to yours (in age, size, and architecture). Also note how their yards compare to yours, in terms of size, slope, and usable space.

If a similar house has more usable land, the assessment for that property should be higher than yours. How much higher? That's hard to answer. Property assessments are often called an art form, but they are really a subjective measure. If you have an architecturally unique property, it might pay to hire a professional appraiser to value your house and land. But be aware that you'll pay a few hundred dollars for this report, and it may or may not help your case.

STEP 9 FOLLOW PROCEDURES FOR CONTESTING YOUR REAL ESTATE TAXES.

- Check the property record card for accuracy.
- Get "comps"—assessments for comparable houses in your area.
- Find out the assessment ratio—the percentage of a home's value that is taxed (it's often less than 100 percent, but is determined by the community).
- Check procedures and time frames for filing in your community.
- Bring to the hearing any documentation that supports your case: appraisals, photos, or land surveys.
- Ask for a specific dollar reduction in your appraisal. Don't just say you want your taxes cut.
- Organize your materials and be succinct. You'll only get a few minutes to make your case.
- Consider filing an appeal to a review board if your request is denied.

Does it pay to contract with a hired gun to plead your case for you? If the hiree charges by the hour, probably not. But many attorneys work on a contingency basis—they typically get one-third to one-half of any tax reduction amount. A reduction this year would lower your taxes for years to come, and you could end up saving thousands more than you would pay the attorney.

There is a potential downside to contesting your real estate taxes: Your taxes could go up. But only about one in ten people who contest their bill suffer that fate. Don't make a frivolous complaint, but if you feel you are paying more than you owe, and the facts support your case, take a shot. Contest the bill.

Chapter 25

Don't Doom Your Remodeling Project Before It Begins

You can get your remodeling project done on time and within budget, but it takes some planning and good time-management.

Rick and Doreen's Story

Rick and Doreen Evans gave a $5,400 deposit to a contractor when he began installing their replacement windows. The $5,000 balance was to be due after the work was completed. The Evanses were not happy with the final job: Rick said the trim looked sloppy. But the contractor refused to do any more work until he was paid the rest of the money.

The Evanses decided to get a second opinion from a contractor that was recommended by their bank. The results were bad. The first contractor had removed load-bearing window headers, so it will cost the Evanses more than $10,000 to get the windows and walls shored up.

Their mistake was a common one: believing the contractor when he said they did not need a building permit for their "small project."

Whether you're patching a hole in your roof or adding a second story to your entire home, renovations typically take longer and cost more than estimated or planned. They can also take a huge toll on your family life.

What causes many of the problems? Over the past few years, I have asked dozens of homeowners why their projects didn't progress as planned. Here are the most common reasons they gave me:

- They did not start with a clearly defined project.
- They ran short of money before the project was completed.
- The contractor never saw eye-to-eye with them on what the project entailed.

The following eight steps will let you learn from other homeowners' missteps and not doom your own project before it begins.

DECIDE WHAT YOU WANT.

Some home renovations are better investments than others. For instance, adding living space or a new bathroom or bedroom, and updating a kitchen have traditionally yielded higher returns than other changes. At the other extreme, overimproving your home, so that it's bigger or has more expensive features than your neighbors' houses, can be a financial mistake.

Don't create the castle of the neighborhood unless you plan to live there for years. If you think you might be overimproving or might have to sell the house in the next few years, hire a home appraiser to assess your home now and to project its value, relative to the value of your neighbors' homes, if the proposed improvements are made.

If you're contemplating a home makeover, job one is to do your homework. Read magazines that focus on exterior and interior design, and visit showrooms, so you will know exactly what you want. Get advice and referrals from homeowners who have done similar projects.

STEP 2 **CHECK OUT SEVERAL CONTRACTORS.**

Your phone book's yellow pages are filled with names of home improvement contractors, but personal referrals are often more reliable. Interview four or five contractors. Get detailed proposals from at least three of them. If your research points to certain materials that you *know* you want, such as a certain brand of window, make sure the name of that brand of window is listed in the proposal (along with stock or part numbers and dimensions).

Then check out the contractors. Call your local consumer affairs office to make sure the candidates are licensed and the license numbers are genuine, not copied from the phone book. Call the Better Business Bureau to see if there are outstanding complaints against any of the contractors.

Get referrals from each contractor and call the homeowners listed. Ask each one how the work went. Did it proceed on schedule? Were cost estimates accurate? Were there things the homeowners now wish they had done differently? Don't forget to ask, "Would you hire this contractor again?" You could get a rave review or you may get an earful. Either way, you'll have more information when making your decision.

After you've narrowed your choices, get in your car and start visiting job sites in progress. Look carefully. Do the workers seem to be getting along with each other, or do you feel tension in the air? Have they contained the clutter to the work area, or is there a potential safety/health hazard? Is loud music blaring while they're working? Are their trucks and tools spilling over onto the street or neighbors' property?

As your scrutinize the bids, be sure you're not comparing apples to oranges. You need bids with identical features; otherwise, the price comparisons are meaningless. Have each contractor *itemize everything,* down to smallest details. (One plumbing contractor I hired gave me the tub faucet I specified but substituted a cheap stopper.)

Here are three red flags to look out for:

Low bid.   A bid that's much lower than the others could mean that the contractor (1) is using inferior materials, (2) won't be around to make needed repairs after the work is done, or (3) plans to have a big cost overrun after starting your project.

No permits.   They may tell you that without building permits your property taxes won't rise, because no one will know that you're having work done. Don't believe it. Dumpsters and trucks parked at or near your house are telltale signs that work is being done, and there's almost always an annoyed neighbor who is more than happy to turn you in. The contractor should get all necessary permits.

No inspections.   The real reason the contractor may not want permits is so that the work will avoid getting inspected. It's better to discover shoddy or inferior work early, before walls are closed in and repairs would cost more to make.

STEP 3 PUT EVERYTHING IN WRITING.

Include the dates the contractor will start and complete your job. Structure the payment schedule carefully, so that payments will be made at the end of phases, and only after the work passes required inspections.

Tip: The advantage of inspections after completion of various phases is that you will find out whether your project is up to code *before* the structure is closed in. If it falls short of code requirements, the workers are still on the job to correct any problems. If they refuse, you still have the money to pay another contractor to fix the leftover problems.

STEP 4 KEEP THE DOWN PAYMENT LOW.

Pay no more than 10 to 15 percent of the total project estimate before work begins. Reputable contractors usually have credit accounts with suppliers. If your contractor claims to need more money up front to pay for materials, that could be a sign of financial trouble. Contractors that have financial problems are more apt to cut corners.

Unscrupulous contractors often ask homeowners for big down payments and then don't show up to do the work for weeks or months—if ever. Don't make a down payment until the first full day of work on your project is under way.

Always have a reserve of enough cash to hire someone else, in case your contractor can't or doesn't finish the job. Hold out 15 or 20 percent for payment at the end of the project, when you'll know whether you are satisfied with the work. To speed up completion of your job, offer a cash bonus if the work is completed ahead of schedule *and* within budget.

As many homeowners have discovered, small projects can easily mushroom into big ones. Be sure that you've built in a large enough cash cushion to cover unexpected problems that may develop as the project progresses.

MAKE SURE THE REMODELER CARRIES ADEQUATE INSURANCE.

Accidents do happen, so it's important to know whether your remodeler carries proper insurance protection:

- Liability insurance, to pay for any damage the workers may do to your property or your neighbors' properties.
- Worker's compensation and disability insurance to cover medical costs and lost wages if workers get injured on the job.

Get copies of the contractor's policies, and tell the insurer(s) to notify you in writing if the insurance gets canceled.

PUT ALL CHANGES IN WRITING.

Perhaps the biggest surprise for homeowners is a final bill drawn up for thousands more than the original contract. The culprit, typically, is verbal, mid-project changes. To avoid any surprises, stipulate that the contractor can make no changes without your *written* approval via a "change order." The change order should include the *total* price of any changes: increased costs for new or additional materials, plus credits for materials that were in the original bid but are no longer included in the revised plan.

ASK THE SUBCONTRACTORS WHETHER THEY HAVE BEEN PAID.

You wouldn't want to pay for a remodeling job twice, yet many homeowners do. They find out, years after a job is completed, that even though they paid the general contractor—and have the canceled checks to prove it—the contractor pocketed all the money and never paid the subcontractors, such as electricians, masons, and plumbers.

When they don't get paid, these subcontractors can place a "mechanic's lien" on a homeowner's property. This might mean that before you could sell or refinance your property, you would have to pay for the work *a second time*.

How can you prevent a mechanic's lien against your property?

- Include the names of the general contractor and the subcontractor on your checks, so that the subcontractor has to sign it before it can be cashed by the general contractor.
- As you hand over money to the general contractor, have each subcontractor sign a "release of lien." That will give you signed proof that the subcontractors were paid.

CHOOSE THE BEST FINANCING FOR YOUR SITUATION.

If you need to take out a loan to pay for your project, you may be planning to borrow against your home's equity. But would a home equity "line" or a home equity "loan" be better for you?

With a home equity line of credit, you get approved for, say, $75,000, and you can draw on that as you need it, so you'll only pay interest on the money you have already borrowed. The downside is that there can be a lot of fees (such as application or activation fees), and the interest rate is usually variable, so your monthly payments could rise if interest rates do.

With a home equity loan, you'll typically be charged fewer fees. The interest rate is usually fixed, so your payments won't rise even if interest rates soar. The downside here is that you'll borrow the whole sum at the beginning of the project, and you'll have to pay interest on the entire amount even if you have no need for all of it yet.

If your credit is not good, you may have to turn to the contractor's ability to get a bank loan to pay for your project. But you'll lose bargaining power. The contractor already has the money, so you can't withhold payment if you're dissatisfied with the work.

A Few More Remodeling Tips

- Leave skilled work to skilled craftspeople. Many homeowners think they can save money by doing some of the work themselves. But unless you're skilled in various trades, leave the carpentry, electrical wiring, and plumbing jobs to the professionals.
- Give careful thought to the possibility of taking on the role of general contractor. Some homeowners who have been able to save money by successfully assuming this role say that there are three prerequisites: (1) good organizational skills, (2) lots of spare time to manage the project, and (3) the ability to get along well with others.
- Stay away from fix-it people who "just happen to be in your neighborhood" and ring your doorbell to say that they have some leftover materials (driveway black top is a common one) and can do the job "below cost" if you hire them to do the work today. Don't believe it. The materials are usually not what they are touted as (motor oil is the typical, substandard substitute for blacktop), and the job will look good only long enough for your check to clear the bank. Hire contractors you seek out (not those who seek you out) after you have thoroughly checked their references.
- Weigh the pros and cons of hiring an architect. When do you need one? There's no hard and fast rule, but, in general, an architect is a good idea if the project exceeds $50,000 or if you're changing the roofline or the front of the house. A licensed architect can often come up with a more aesthetically pleasing design and can cut the chances that your neighbors will try to put a stop to your project.

Chapter 26

Sell Your Home Quickly and for Top Dollar

Tom and Ann's Story

When Tom got transferred to a job in another state, he and his wife Ann knew that they would need every cent they could get from the sale of their current home. Real estate agents in their hometown had recently jacked up the sales commissions from 6 percent to 7 percent of the selling price, so Tom and Ann decided to sell their home themselves.

They placed ads in the local newspaper and held open houses every weekend. Three dozen families snooped through their home—and closets—on the first weekend. None came back. Five weeks later, one couple made an offer—14 percent below the asking price. (The buyer had subtracted the 7 percent commission that an agent would have gotten, and adjusted the price down based on a personal estimate of "needed repairs.")

With no other prospects in sight, Tom and Ann negotiated the price up to $95,500, and then accepted their only offer. Six weeks later, after failing to qualify for a mortgage, the buyer demanded his deposit back.

Like most people who list property themselves, Tom and Ann threw in the towel and signed on with an agent. By then, it was late summer; the prime selling season had passed.

How can you sell your home faster and for top dollar? For starters, here are some tips if you're selling your home on your own:

- If you're listing it yourself, to be on the safe side, skip the open house. Show your home by appointment only, and insist on seeing the visitor's driver's license and jotting down his or her name and address—before you begin the house tour.
- For a few hundred dollars, do-it-yourself agents can help you list and advertise your home. But you'll get only minimal assistance, and you will still need an attorney and knowledge of the mortgage market in your town.
- If any real estate agent brings you a qualified buyer, you can sign up with that agent for a one-shot listing. You will owe a commission (typically, 2½ to 4 percent) only if the agent sells your home.

AVOID COSTLY HOME-SELLING BLUNDERS.

Most home buyers would never entertain the notion of buying a house without some assistance from a real estate agent; yet, when it comes time to sell, many homeowners think nothing of going it alone. Paying a real estate agent to list and market your home can be a costly agreement. Depending on where you live, you can expect to pay an agent 5½ percent to 7 percent of the selling price. So, many home sellers say to themselves, "I can pocket more by doing the legwork myself." But a good real estate agent can do a lot more than hold an open house and slap a "For Sale" sign on your lawn. The agent can actually help you net more money at the closing, and sell your home sooner. Here are eight home-selling blunders and ways to avoid them.

- *Blunder 1. "For Sale by Owner" (FSBO), when you don't have the time or interest.* You save the commission, but selling takes a lot of your time, and most FSBOs are ultimately turned over to real estate agents. By then, valuable time has been lost. And expect prospective buyers to low-ball their offers so *they* can pocket the commission savings.
- *Blunder 2. Asking too much or too little for your home.* Ask too little and you leave money on the table. Ask too much and your home doesn't compare well with others on the market and won't sell. To set a fair price, check comparable sales. (If you work with an agent, he or she will do this for you.) Also check the tax records. Your local government can tell you how to access this free information.
- *Blunder 3. Not "shopping" for a real estate agent.* Some agents make a good pitch but do little once they get your listing. Compare the agents' marketing plans for your home. Don't choose an agent just because he or she suggests a higher "asking price" for your home (the amount may have been pulled out of thin air). Get references. Call previous home sellers and ask, "Would you list your home with this agent again?" From the responses, you'll discern the good agents.
- *Blunder 4. Negotiating a reduced commission up front.* This strategy discourages agents from marketing your home. (They will spend more time on homes on which they will earn *full* commissions.) Don't negotiate commissions until they have brought you a low offer. Then you can start dickering to close the price gap and the deal.

Tip: Offer a "quick sale" bonus of $200 to $600 to any agent who sells your home, at your price, within three weeks of your house's going on the market.

- *Blunder 5. Signing a lengthy contract.* Most sales are made within two weeks of a listing or just before the listing expires. Never sign for more than 90 days; you can always extend the contract, but it's hard to dump a complacent agent. If your agent hasn't delivered what was promised, talk to the broker who owns the agency, and ask to be assigned to a more proactive agent. If the second agent doesn't work out, ask to be released from the contract.

Tip: To keep your agent's attention, add a clause that allows you to terminate the contract with 24 hours' notice.

- *Blunder 6. Letting the agent put a lock box on your door.* This arrangement is convenient for the agent, but some agents think nothing of lending their lock-box keys to customers they barely know. If you won't be home when your agent is showing the house, personally leave the house key with the agent, or a neighbor who will be home and refuse to allow a lock box.
- *Blunder 7. Not disclosing defects.* Is your home's foundation cracked? Is there radon in your home? Lead paint? If you know it, disclose it. The laws have gotten stricter and can be used by a buyer to reverse a sale if the seller misrepresents any facts.
- *Blunder 8. Letting the buyer move in before the closing.* They'll find flaws (real or perceived) and will either refuse to close or will insist that you fix them or lower the price.

Spruce up the property before you try to sell it. Go for curb appeal (a tidy lawn, shrubs and blooming flowers by the front door). If necessary, paint inside and out, using neutral colors. Get rid of the clutter in rooms, closets, and the garage. Make sure everything smells clean and fresh.

STEP 2 PROTECT YOUR INVESTMENT.

If you lend money to the buyer, be sure to record your loan as a lien against the property. This record prevents the buyer from selling without your knowledge or from using the property as collateral for another loan. Check the buyer's credit report ahead of time. (Your bank or real estate agent can help you.)

WRAP UP YOUR RIGHTS.

If you are offering the buyer a "second" mortgage (because the buyer doesn't have a big enough down payment), insist on a "wrap-around" loan that requires the buyer to make the monthly payments for the first and second mortgages to you. You then pay the bank that holds the first mortgage. Otherwise, the buyer could fall behind on the first mortgage, the bank could foreclose, and you might not find out until after the house is auctioned off and your second mortgage is wiped out.

STEP 4 GET RELEASED FROM YOUR LIABILITY.

If you let the buyer assume your mortgage (or buy your home "subject to" your mortgage) and the buyer defaults on the loan, you would have to make up the loss to the mortgage company. Insist that the mortgage company must release you from the loan before turning it over to the buyer.

Start and Manage an Investment Portfolio with Only a Few Dollars a Month

Congratulations! You've been working hard and are on your way to financial self-reliance. You've freed up cash by cutting back on overpriced items you didn't need—or by finding merchants who sold them cheaper. You've asked for and gotten yourself positioned for a raise at work. You're taking advantage of employer-paid benefits, so things like insurance are now being paid for (or at least subsidized) by your employer. You're also taking advantage of other benefits, such as the flexible spending account, and you now use *pretax* dollars to pay for necessities such as out-of-pocket medical costs. You've cut your credit card and bank costs, and you may even have renegotiated a lower rate on your mortgage.

You've accomplished a lot. And now that you've freed up money, it's time to shift into high gear and start making your money work for you via some well-chosen investments.

You can be a bull or you can be a bear, but don't be a pig. Greed is unattractive. It can also devastate your net worth. Greed can drown out the inner voice that is trying to tell you that you are about to make a bad investment. To make money over the long haul, you need to do your homework and have realistic expectations. In this solution I'll show you ways to start an investment portfolio with as little as a few dollars a month.

Chapter 27

Make Your Money
Grow with Investments
That Are Right for You

"I inherited some money when my uncle died, and I know I should invest it," says Ryan Patterson. "But I really don't know anything about the stock market, so I'm afraid I'll buy the wrong stock at the wrong time and end up losing my money."

Ryan's concern is one I frequently hear. Whether you get a onetime windfall (from an inheritance or a big bonus from your employer) or have been methodically saving money for months or years, sooner or later you need to make some investment decisions so that you can get closer to reaching your financial goals and achieving what you want out of life.

STEP 1 LEARN THE SECRETS TO BUILDING A WELL-DIVERSIFIED PORTFOLIO.

LLOYD'S LAW

The way to wealth is by investing your hard-earned money in good-quality financial products—products that you have thoroughly researched—so that your money can start working for you.

Let's focus on ways to multiply your money—without taking undue risk.

No one is born knowing the ins and outs of financial markets. Despite what they might like you to believe, stockbrokers, industry analysts, and highly paid portfolio managers cannot regularly and accurately predict where stock prices are headed.

Of more concern is the fact that a lot of self-described financial planners who offer to "help you make financial decisions" are likely to give you advice that is better for them than for you. The planners may actually be insurance salespeople, stockbrokers, or convicted confidence artists who get a commission from selling a product that may or may not be in your best interest. How can you protect yourself? By learning the ten secrets of smart investing. Are you ready? Here goes.

- *Secret 1. Stick with simplicity.* I have never met anyone who regretted investing only in things he or she understood and could explain in one or two sentences. Some scam artists ply their trade by deliberately trying to confuse and deceive unsuspecting customers. How else would they convince reasonable people to buy risky or worthless investments?

  From penny stocks to wireless cable, scams can be low-tech or high-tech, and scamsters know that many customers will be too timid to ask a lot of questions. Consumers fear that asking questions would make them seem uneducated; instead, it would show that they were smart enough to suspect that they were being set up. Don't fall for a fast pitch. Only invest in things you understand.

  No one ever likes to admit having been scammed, but, sadly, it happens more often than most people think it does. I constantly hear from people who invested some or all of their life's savings on a deal that was touted as "a sure thing" by a friend, relative, coworker, or self-described financial planner. More often than not, the deal brought only a big loss for the trusting consumer.

- *Secret 2. Don't put all your eggs in one basket; diversify.* Don't sink everything into just one type of investment vehicle, such as a stock, bond, or mutual fund. Diversify; buy many types of investments. Balance your portfolio and decide on percentages for owning stocks, bonds, cash, and real estate (your home may be your only investment in real estate), based on your age and how much risk you can take. Risk comes in two forms: (1) how much money you could lose in an investment, and (2) how much market fluctuation you can stomach. When you're young, you can afford to take more risk because you have more years to recoup if the market takes a big dip. By being diversified, you can get in on the growth in good times, and keep bad times in certain sectors of the economy from wiping you out.

Tip: If you have only a small amount to invest, you can get instant diversification by buying a few shares in a good-quality, "balanced" mutual fund that invests in a wide range of stocks and bonds.

- *Secret 3. Know what you need the money for, and when. Set goals.* The sooner you will need the money, the less risk you can afford to take and the more conservative you should be when choosing an investment.

- *Secret 4. Avoid market timing—trying to buy low and sell high.* Markets go up and markets go down, but no one can accurately predict *when.* The big downside to market timing, as many investors belatedly discover, is that you're likely to lose not once, but twice. First, when prices are dropping and investors want to sell, many sell late, *after* prices have plummeted. Then, when prices begin to rise, they miss out again. They buy back late—not at or near the low, but long after the stock price has shot back up. Trying to time the market isn't really investing—it's gambling.

- *Secret 5. Don't fall for the flavor of the month—the investments that everyone's talking about.* Whether it's stock in an Internet company or in a genetic engineering firm, people who get in late—when these investments are all anyone's talking or writing about—usually lose, and lose big time.

- *Secret 6. Don't buy investments solely to avoid taxes.* Many consumers get a much smaller return on their money than they should be getting, based on their goals and risk tolerance. Why? Because they chose tax-advantaged investments (such as tax-deferred investments, or investments that are exempt from federal or state tax) that aren't right for them. If you stashed $100 in your mattress today, a year from now you would owe no taxes, but your money would not have grown at all. It would still be $100 (although, thanks to inflation, it would buy less than it could a year earlier).

LLOYD'S LAW

When choosing investments, focus on the after-tax return (what you have left after paying taxes), not just the amount of tax you avoid.

Some tax-advantaged investments, such as cash-value life insurance, tax-deferred annuities, and tax-free municipal bonds, often come with onerous restrictions on when and how you can withdraw your money. Taxes should be just one consideration. You also need to know and compare all characteristics of investments—including risk, ease of selling, and potential gain—before you decide to buy.

- *Secret 7. Research investments yourself, and steer clear of hot tips from friends, coworkers, or strangers.* If their advice is such a moneymaker, why are they sharing it with you or anyone else? Also, be leery of investing advice on the Internet. It's often hard to tell where the advice and supposed testimonials are *really* coming from. Con artists, disguising themselves as successful investors, often try to hype their scam. To make money over the long haul, choose your investments carefully and research them thoroughly.

- *Secret 8. Invest on a regular schedule.* No one knows when prices will suddenly rise or fall, so the best way to hedge your bets—and lower the average cost of an investment—is to "dollar-cost-average": Invest the same number of dollars every month (or quarter, or at some other regular interval). When share prices go up, you will be buying fewer shares at the higher price. If they go down, you will be buying more at the lower price.

  Consider signing up for an automatic investment plan—say, with a good mutual fund—so that it becomes a no-brainer to keep investing. You won't see the money or be tempted to spend the money on something else.

  If you just can't resist going with a hunch or a risky investment, then limit the amount of money you "play with" to no more than 10 percent of your investments. Then go ahead and buy and sell—until this money is all gone.

- *Secret 9. Understand financial risk—and how much you can afford to lose.* When you're looking to invest money, it's easy to focus on the upside—how much you stand to earn. But before you make an investment, you also need to understand how much you could *lose* if things turned sour—and whether you would have enough time to recoup any loss before you needed the money.

  All investments come with some risk; for some, the risks are obvious. A bad investment may not grow, but you also could lose all or part of your initial investment. Here's the good news: You can limit the downside potential by doing your homework before you invest, and by diversifying in several types of investments. If one goes down, others may either go up or at least not drop as much. The simplest way to limit your downside is to buy shares in a good, diversified mutual fund.

- *Secret 10. Keep some "ready cash."* You may need to get your hands on some money in a hurry, if you suddenly lose your job or have a family crisis, so never invest your "last dollar." Otherwise, you might be forced to sell just when prices are temporarily—but heavily—depressed.

Mutual Funds

Stocks have historically been one of the best investments for money you won't need for at least five years. Professionally managed mutual funds are an affordable way to get in on this stock market growth. The funds allow you to diversify even a small investment by owning fractions of shares in many companies.

A mutual fund manager pools money from thousands of investors and then buys a variety of stocks—and, possibly, bonds and other types of investments, depending on what kind of fund it is and what its goals are. Before buying or selling any of these securities, a good fund manager investigates the underlying company: what the business actually does; what its prospects are in the short term and longer term; where its share price is, relative to its projected earnings.

All of a fund manager's investments together are called a *portfolio.* In addition to stocks and bonds—and, possibly, real estate, gold, or other investments—the manager might be holding some cash. Why? Because, suspecting that the market is heading down, he or she wants to lock in profits and protect the fund investors' money. Also, if a well-researched bargain comes along, the cash can be used to snap it up.

Most mutual funds require initial investments of at least $500, but many funds will lower that requirement to as little as $100 if you sign up for an automatic investment plan. The plan authorizes them to withdraw a fixed amount from your bank account on a regular schedule.

Here's a no-brainer investing tip for beginners: Consider investing in a no-load (meaning no fee for buying or selling shares) "balanced" mutual fund that contains a variety of good-quality stocks and bonds.

By choosing the right mutual funds, buying individual stocks when you're ready, and including bonds in the mix, you can build a diversified portfolio.

STEP 2 CHOOSE THE RIGHT MUTUAL FUNDS FOR YOUR SITUATION.

There are thousands of mutual funds to choose from. Whether this is your first investment or an addition to a large portfolio, a good mutual fund can give you instant diversification. But, as a growing number of individual investors are beginning to discover, a mutual fund's costs can eat into its return, and buying shares in last year's hot fund may yield only mediocre returns during the next year. By avoiding the following blunders, you can increase your chances of finding mutual funds that can go the distance and get you to your goals.

- *Blunder 1. Throwing money at last year's top performers.* Funds in the top ten for their category (growth funds, income funds, and bond fund are three of the many categories) are often good places to *start* your search for a fund that can go the distance, but you need to investigate further. What got them to the top in one year may have been a fluke, or they may be taking undue risk, which yields a higher return when the market is rising but can lead to a big, *big* loss when the market slides.
- *Blunder 2. Comparing apples to oranges.* If, say, a long-term growth mutual fund had a 28 percent return last year, you might think that's pretty good. But, not so fast. *You need to compare its performance to the performance of other funds in that same category.* If the returns on the top ten long-term growth funds ranged from 39 percent to 55 percent last year, that 28 percent return was less than spectacular.
- *Blunder 3. Taking mutual fund advertisements at face value.* A lot of mutual fund ads boast: "We're #1." But how can so many all be in first place? Only by taking liberties with their measurement criteria can so many (falsely) claim so much. For instance, how did they measure their fund's performance—over a year, or over just a five-day period when the market did very well? To make their performance look even better, many funds will suspend expense charges for that short period. The claims you see in most mutual fund ads are often just window dressing. Go to the library, surf the Internet, or look up mutual fund performance in journals such as *Consumer Reports, Money* magazine, and *Morningstar.*
- *Blunder 4. Not knowing a mutual fund's goals.* Don't go by the name (such as "income fund" or "growth fund"); that may no longer be its actual goal. Read the fund's prospectus to see what the fund manager is really trying to accomplish, and what kind of investments the fund manager is making.
- *Blunder 5. Not knowing a fund's loads and other fees.* A load is a sales charge to buy shares (a front-end load) or to sell shares (a back-end load). Plus, there can be several annual fees that you will pay, year in and year out, as long as you own shares in the fund. A fund's expenses eat into its returns, so look for a fund that has relatively low expenses compared to others in its fund category.
- *Blunder 6. Thinking you're diversified when you really aren't.* If you're investing in several different mutual fund companies—say, Fidelity, T. Rowe Price, and Vanguard—but all the funds are "Blue chip" or "growth" funds, then you're not really diversified. They

could all be investing in the same (or same types) of stocks. To diversify, you would need to be in different types of funds, such as "growth," "small capitalization," and "international" funds.

- *Blunder 7. Assuming that "life-cycle" or "lifestyle" funds reflect your lifestyle and goals.* These funds do give instant diversification, but your lifestyle (and needs) may be quite different from the predetermined ones that the fund is targeting. Customize your investments to fit your lifestyle needs. Once you know what you're doing, diversify yourself instead.
- *Blunder 8. Not investing regularly.* Dollar-cost average. If you invest, say, $100 each month, you'll end up with more shares when prices are lower, and fewer shares, if prices go higher.
- *Blunder 9. Not reinvesting dividends and capital gains.* Reinvestment can increase your return.
- *Blunder 10. Not weighing costs before deciding where to buy mutual fund shares.* You may be able to buy mutual fund shares from banks, traditional stockbrokers, or online brokers, or directly from the mutual fund company, but where you buy may affect how much you will pay. You'll often pay lower commissions and sales fees if you buy directly from the mutual fund company. More of your money will then be going to work for you—not toward someone else's sales commission.

Tip: Avoid the "December tax surprise." Every year, unsuspecting mutual fund customers send in money to a mutual fund to buy some shares, but a few weeks later, they get some of their money returned, along with a tax bill. Why? Because the fund has issued its capital gains and/or dividends distributions, and both are taxable transactions. Customers realized no gain, but they still owe tax. This problem is compounded even further if a load (sales charge) was paid when these new shares were purchased. Before you send money during the last quarter of the year, be sure to ask the fund manager what date is the "ex-dividend date," and don't invest until after that date.

STEP 3 LEARN THE INS AND OUTS OF INDEX FUNDS, TO UNDERSTAND WHAT AN INDEX FUND CAN AND CANNOT DO FOR YOU.

High-quality, professional money management at an affordable price is the draw for many mutual fund customers. They turn over their investment money to a fund manager who, they expect, will know (based on his or her firm's research and by speaking with industry experts) which stocks to buy or sell, and when. That's known as an actively managed fund. At the minimum, investors expect that the fund will beat the market averages.

But, in the late 1990s, returns on many actively managed funds not only didn't break any records, they couldn't even keep up with market averages. When that happens, investors (and financial analysts for that matter) openly question why investors should be paying for a professional fund manager to manage their money, when a fund that just picks investments that would mimic the performance of a particular index could improve their return and cut their costs.

There are many indexes to choose from. Among the popular ones that many mutual funds try to mimic are:

- S&P 500 index invests in 500 large, blue-chip companies in major industries.
- Wilshire 5000 index casts a broader net and includes large and small companies that are regularly traded.
- Russell 2000 index concentrates on stocks of smaller companies—also called "small-cap" (small-capitalization) stocks.

A Closer Look at S&P 500 Index Funds

One of the most popular mutual fund indexes is the Standard and Poor's 500 (S&P 500), which invests in 500 large, blue-chip stocks. A fund manager for a mutual fund that "indexes" the S&P 500 invests in all the companies in that particular index.

Pros:
- *Diversified.* These funds invest in all 500 big, blue-chip companies. If some don't do so well, you can hope that others will do better than you would by investing in just a few companies.
- *Lower expenses.* Because there are few changes in the stocks included in the index (few companies go in or out of this group in the course of a year), your fund won't incur a lot of expenses from the fund manager's buying or selling stocks in the portfolio. And lower turnover in the portfolio helps your tax situation.
- *Lower taxes.* A surprise to many people when they invest in mutual funds for the first time is the yearly tax hit. When the fund manager sells some holdings during the year, you have to report

capital gains on those sales on your tax return for that year, even though you haven't sold any shares in the mutual fund. By contrast, if you are invested in individual stocks or bonds, you don't have to worry about paying capital gains until you actually sell the shares. With mutual funds, you have to pay as you go each year.

- *One hundred percent invested, so no cash cushion.* Index funds are required to stay fully invested in stocks, so you will be able to catch any rise in those stocks. Unlike with other types of funds, you won't miss out on potential growth because your fund manager was holding onto some cash for a rainy day or a buying opportunity.

Cons:

- *Betting on bigger companies.* Because the S&P 500 only includes big, blue-chip companies, you miss out on potential growth in smaller companies or specific industry sectors.
- *No cash cushion.* One of the things successful fund managers in other types of funds can do is sell when they think prices are on the verge of dropping. But index fund managers can't hedge in cash, so they (and you) will take the full brunt of a fall.

Consider index funds as *part* of your investment strategy, along with other conventional funds that invest in, say, health care, foreign countries, or whatever you choose to buy after doing your own research.

STEP 4 CONTEMPLATE ADDING FOREIGN INVESTMENTS TO BOOST YOUR RETURN AND LOWER YOUR RISK.

An index fund will never beat the market, so putting all your money into one (or more) index funds is not a good strategy. To get more diversification, you might want to consider investing, say, 5 or 10 percent of your assets in foreign countries—again, through well-managed mutual funds. You can invest in specific parts of the world, such as the Pacific Rim, Latin America, or Europe, or you can go for an international fund that invests in stocks in many continents.

To get in on the ground floor of international investments that could be on the verge of taking off, some investors like to put a little of their money into "emerging market" funds. But here are some risks you should consider before you buy shares in mutual funds that invest in other countries:

- *Currency fluctuation.* If the other country's currency shifts relative to the dollar, that will affect the value of your investment.
- *Political turmoil.* Labor strikes and toppled governments are just two worries for investors in other countries.
- *Price fluctuation.* As with other investments, the price of the underlying investments in emerging markets will affect the value of your holdings.
- *Panicky fund managers.* As with any mutual fund, some managers of foreign-investment funds panic and sell shares at depressed prices to raise cash, just in case some investors want their money in a hurry. Some analysts say that this is more apt to happen in riskier, emerging market funds than in other types of funds.
- *You may already be invested—and not know it.* Many domestic growth or income funds have some foreign holdings. Why? Because when many fund managers search for better returns, they turn to foreign markets, and you may not realize it. It's not enough to read a fund's prospectus. If you're concerned that your fund is too highly leveraged in foreign countries, you might want to call the mutual fund you're involved with (or thinking of investing in), and ask how much exposure the fund has in foreign markets.

When you invest in any mutual fund, be sure to read the fund's prospectus and understand the fund's current goals and all fees. As your wealth starts to grow, sooner or later, you might start toying with the idea of investing in individual stocks. In Step 5, I show you the basics of investing in stocks, and some ways to keep commissions from devastating your returns.

STEP 5 — CONSIDER BUYING INDIVIDUAL STOCKS WHEN AND IF YOU ARE READY AND WILLING TO DO YOUR HOMEWORK.

Buying shares of mutual funds is an easy way to invest money and get instant diversification, but mutual fund fees can significantly eat into your returns. If you have more than $10,000 to invest and you are willing to do your homework, buying some individual stocks may be worth at least considering.

When you buy stock in a company, you actually become a part owner of that company, and you stand to gain if that company does well. However, you could lose some or all of your investment if the company does poorly or goes broke. I cannot stress enough the importance of doing your homework before you buy and while you hold investments.

Know the Advantages of Individual Stocks

Let's look at some of the advantages of individual stocks and compare them with mutual funds:

- *Taxes.* Mutual funds are required to distribute capital gains every year, so you typically have to pay capital gains tax on your shares every year even if *you* don't sell any shares. By contrast, with individual stocks, you would owe capital gains tax only in years when you sell shares of stock at a profit. (This can also simplify filling out your tax forms.) Whether you have stocks or mutual funds (or any other investments), keep good records of when you buy or sell shares, or when you're reinvesting dividends.
- *Fees.* With mutual funds, your account is debited yearly to pay a variety of mutual fund fees. There are no comparable management fees with individual stocks.

Investigate Before You Invest

You should choose stocks based on a company's potential to make money in the future. But before you try to predict the future, investigate the company itself. How has the company done in the past? Before you buy a stock, you need to do some research. For instance:

- See what the company says about itself. Check out its Web site and its annual report. Ask your stockbroker for company information and in-house analysis of any company the broker recommends. Contact the company's investor relations department, or go to the business room of the local library and research the company's financial reports.
- Read up on the company, especially its stock price range relative to the industry in general. Check out the *Investor's Business Daily, The Wall Street Journal, Barron's,* and the business section of your local newspaper (if the company is located in your area). Peruse the Web sites of personal finance magazines, such as *Money* (www.money .com), *Kiplinger's Personal Finance* magazine (www.kiplinger.com), *Smart Money* (www.smartmoney.com), and *Fortune* (www.fortune .com) for more analysis.

- See what Standard and Poor's has to say about the company—look up the monthly *S&P Stock Guide* and the annual *S&P Stock Reports*. You can find both of these in most public libraries, or go to Standard and Poor's Web site at (www.standardandpoors.com) for more information. Look at the company's earnings, its price-to-earnings (P/E) ratio (if the price has already shot up relative to earnings, you may have missed the opportunity), its book value, and its total return. No company performs in a vacuum; investigate the company's industry. Is it strong? How would it do if the economy hit the skids?
- Put the information in perspective by checking out a stock's historical performance in *Value Line*. You can find this at the library or click on the Web site (www.valueline.com) for additional information. While at the library, also look at *Moody's Manuals* or their Web site (www.moodys.com), for more information on dividends and stocks.

Diversify with Just a Handful of Individual Stocks

One of the reasons people invest in mutual funds is so that they can have instant diversification. How many individual stocks would you need to buy, to achieve diversification? Research shows that owning stocks of as few as a dozen large companies in different industries can offer you the benefits of diversification. But with just a few stocks in your portfolio, you have to choose these stocks very carefully. Begin by finding stocks that have:

- Steady growth—look for companies with annualized earnings increases of at least 10 percent per year over five years.
- Big assets—at least $3 billion (share price × number of shares they've issued), because companies of that size rarely fail, and they don't usually falter for long because they have enough money to keep going even through short patches of bad times.
- Good value—fairly priced, relative to its past and projected earnings.

Create a Diversified Stock Portfolio Within Twelve Months

You don't know whether share prices will rise or fall, so don't jettison dollar-cost averaging when you move into individual stocks. Here's one way to apply the same principle when you're buying stocks in individual companies:

- Choose the 12 stocks that will make up your portfolio for the next year (using the principles listed above).
- Write down the total amount of money you will invest during the year, and divide that number by 12, to figure out how much you will invest each month. If you have, say, $12,000 to invest over the year, you will want to invest $1,000 ($12,000 divided by 12) each month.
- In January (or month 1, if you're not starting at the beginning of the calendar year), buy $1,000 worth of shares in Company 1.
- In February (month 2), buy $1,000 worth of shares in Company 2.
- Continue the same purchasing schedule over the next 10 months so that by the end of month 12, you own shares in all 12 companies.
- In month 13, start the cycle over. Invest $\frac{1}{12}$ of that year's amount in Company 1. Continue to invest each month in the same rotation as in the first year.

You will be diversified, and your method will be something akin to dollar-cost averaging, but with individual stocks.

DRIP Your Way to Wealth

When you buy just a few shares of individual stocks, brokerage commissions can eat up your profits. To hold down your costs, consider companies that offer a dividend reinvestment program (DRIP). Through a DRIP, you can not only reinvest dividends, but also can buy new shares directly from the company, without paying a commission to a stockbroker.

Warning: Not all DRIPS are free. Some companies have realized that profits can be made by charging their investors recurring and one-time fees for the following services: setting up a DRIP account, maintaining an account, and reinvesting dividends. Be sure to ask about the fees before sending in money or authorizing dividend reinvestment services.

Even if you can add shares of a company's stock to your portfolio by signing up for a DRIP, in many cases you'll need to buy your initial shares through a stockbroker or over the Internet, not directly from the company. If you buy your initial shares through a stockbroker, be sure to register the shares in your name—*not in the name of your broker*. Two Web sites where you can buy your initial shares inexpensively are: Waterhouse Securities (www.waterhouse.com) and Sure Trade (www.suretrade.com).

Whether you invest in mutual funds or individual stocks, you should be in it for the long haul:

- Reinvest your dividends.
- Invest new money on a regular basis—say, $100 each month (or every quarter, as long as you keep it up).
- Diversify in more than one company and more than one industry or sector of the economy.

Sadly, stocks—or any investments, for that matter—have their limitations and come with their own risks. By adding some well-chosen bonds to your portfolio, you can effectively minimize your risk without seriously crimping your return. In Step 6, I cover the basics of bonds and show you how and where you can research and buy them.

STEP 6 UNDERSTAND HOW BUYING BONDS CAN CUT YOUR RISK.

A bond is nothing but an IOU—usually, from a corporation or a government. You lend the money for a set amount of time and the bond issuer promises to pay you back. In exchange for the use of your money, the bond issuer agrees to pay you a certain rate of interest. If held to maturity (months, years, decades), a bond should repay you the bond's full face value in addition to any interest you have been promised.

The important things to understand about bonds are:

- When interest rates rise, bond prices drop. Bond prices can go in the opposite direction of stock prices, so investing in some well-chosen bonds can diversify your portfolio and cut your risk.
- To get the highest yields when interest rates are rising, choose shorter-term bonds. Conversely, switch to long-term bonds when you believe that interest rates are going to drop.

What can go wrong with bonds? The company (if you buy a corporate bond) could go belly-up, so check the rating of the company's bonds before you buy. Look for high-quality issues—rated Aaa or Aa by Moody's, or rated AAA or AA by Standard and Poor's.

If an interest rate on a bond is exceptionally higher than the rate being offered for similar types of bonds, take it as a sign that there is some higher risk with this particular issue.

Learn the Lexicon of Bonds

Here is an overview of popular bonds.

Treasury Bills (T-bills). These short-term investments are offered by the United States Government and are very safe. They typically mature in three or six months. They are sold at a discount (for less than their face value, and that price is determined based on prevailing interest rates). You send, say, $5,000, and the unused amount gets credited to your bank account (you give instructions when you set up the account). With T-bills, you can:

- Purchase through the Treasury Direct program at this Web site: www.publicdebt.treas.gov.
- Reinvest automatically.
- Sell early through your bank or broker (although you will owe a commission).
- Avoid taxes until maturity, and even then, avoid state or local taxes.

Treasury Notes. These encompass a two- to ten-year time horizon. You can also buy them through the Treasury Direct program, with a $1,000 minimum purchase. You can resell them before maturity. They will not be "called," which means they can't be redeemed early by the Treasury. The buzz for T-notes improved when inflation-adjusted versions, called TIPS (Treasury Inflation Protection Securities), were introduced in 1997. The current interest rate on TIPS may be less than on traditional T-notes, but you'll likely get more at maturity, after inflation has been accounted for.

Treasury Bonds. These have maturities of more than 10 years; up to 30 years. Some T-bonds can be called early (redeemed), but the chances are small. If inflation picks up, you'll be sorry that you locked yourself in for such a long period.

Series EE Savings Bonds. These pay a variable rate and can be purchased at a denomination of $50 and up (you pay half the face value at purchase). They are easy to buy; many employers offer employee payroll savings plans that enable an automatic purchase of these bonds from your paycheck. You can also buy them at banks. Interest is credited monthly. You can sell these bonds before maturity, but you will be hit with a three-month interest penalty if you cash in the bonds within five years of purchasing them. For information, call (800) 487-2663, or you can buy bonds online at the Web site www.savingsbonds.gov.

Series I Bonds. These are inflation-indexed, so they pay a fixed interest rate, plus an additional interest rate based on the recent level of inflation. For information, call (800) 487-2663, or you can buy bonds online at www.savingsbonds.gov.

Municipal Bonds ("muni" bonds). Issued by city, state, or other municipal governments, these bonds are not taxed by the federal government and are typically exempted from state tax if you live in the state where they were issued. The appeal of these bonds is greatest with taxpayers in the highest tax rate brackets. You can buy individual muni bonds from a stockbroker, and muni bond funds from mutual fund companies and stockbrokers.

What can go wrong with munis? The local government could default. Don't laugh; some already have. If tax laws are significantly changed, these bonds would lose their appeal; you probably wouldn't be able to sell them before their maturity because nobody would want to buy them. If you sell these bonds for a profit, you would be subject to federal, state, and local capital gains taxes.

Bond Funds. These are professionally managed mutual funds that invest in bonds. Fund managers typically take out a relatively high fee for their services, and you can't hold your shares to maturity because the shares never mature. When bonds mature or are sold early, the manager buys replacements. So if interest rates rise or there are other problems in the economy, you could take a bath when selling these. Steer clear of bond funds that have much higher returns than comparable funds run by other managers—they are likely taking undue risk with investors' money.

Money Market Fund. Managers of these funds invest in government and corporate securities. These are not federally insured. The interest they pay is often slightly higher than you could get at a bank, but you need to focus on total return (including capital gains and dividends) when comparing competing money market funds or comparing other investments with money market funds. On the plus side, you can usually write checks against these accounts; they are completely liquid. Look for a money market fund with low fees.

Unit Trusts. These are unmanaged mutual funds. They keep the bonds they initially buy, so fees are typically low, but sales commissions are often relatively high.

Corporate Bonds. These bonds compare poorly with Treasuries. Why? You'll pay higher commissions to buy them, they are harder to sell early, they could be called early, and the corporation could go belly-up.

Junk Bonds. These are just bonds that have been branded with a risky rating; to make up for it, they come with a higher-than-normal interest rate. Historically, most have been less risky than their interest rate would indicate. But you could lose big—lose the income you counted on, as well as the amount of your initial investment—if these become worthless. If you choose to buy them, they should be a very small part of your portfolio.

Zero-Coupon Bonds. These bonds are sold at a discount and pay their face value of $1,000 at maturity. Their prices are very volatile over time, so they are riskier than other bonds if you must sell early. Also, you must pay tax on them each year, even though you don't receive money until they mature or you cash them in early. They may be called early. To avoid paying the tax due on these bonds each year, consider buying them for a tax-deferred account, such as a retirement account.

Know How Bond Funds Stack Up
Against Individual Bonds

You may get a higher yield in a short-term bond fund than in short-term Treasuries, because the bond fund may also have in its portfolio corporate bonds with higher returns.

Tip: Individual bonds come due at some predetermined date, so if you hold them to maturity, you should get the bond's face value. But bond funds never mature. Instead, fund managers periodically buy new bonds, sell old bonds, and replace bonds that were redeemed, so if interest rates have risen since you bought them, you could take a drubbing when you sell. Understand this before you buy shares in a bond mutual fund.

Investment Strategies for a Onetime
Lump Sum of Money

One strategy is to "ladder" to limit your loss or increase your bond gain. You can do it with bonds (or bank CDs). No one can accurately predict a fall in interest rates, so if you suddenly come into a lot of money, consider "laddering" some of it by investing it in an array of bonds with varying maturities. It's a way to increase your money choices in the future, and it potentially gives you a higher yield than investing a onetime windfall in only one time horizon.

Consider what I call "interest-rate averaging" for bonds; it's sort of like dollar-cost averaging for stocks and mutual funds. You'll be doing some instant interest-rate hedging for a onetime, lump-sum investment.

You can buy bonds that mature in one, two, three, four, five, and ten years. Your return will be a weighted average, equivalent to about what you would get if you put all your money in five- to eight-year bonds. (You give up something today, compared to what you could have earned.) As each bond comes due, you decide where to reinvest the money, depending on where short-term and long-term interest rates are.

If interest rates have risen as the one-year bonds come due, you can reinvest in one-year bonds, but you might want to put all (or most) of the money in longer-term bonds (which typically pay more). The following year, your original two-year bonds will come due. Again, based on current rates, you choose how long to tie up the money. Ultimately, you could end up with a portfolio of ten-year bonds, a portion of which will come due every year.

The good news is that this system can make up some of your ready cash because the bonds will come due periodically. If you need cash in a pinch, you won't have to sell off other assets prematurely.

The bad news is that if interest rates plummet, you could end up reinvesting the money in lower-yielding bonds. This is a bet that I could live with. It gives you some protection from an unexpected interest-rate drop.

Bond-Picking Strategies

- Choose high-quality issues—those rated Aaa or Aa by Moody's or rated AAA or AA by Standard and Poor's.
- Check into the possibility that a bond might be called early (before it matures). You would likely get the face value, plus a small premium. But if you paid a bigger premium to buy the bond (because interest rates had been dropping), you might not get back as much as you paid.

Warning: Beware of "dirty bonds" sold by brokers who call, out of the blue, offering you a "great deal" on some bonds. Here's how it works. They get a notification that a bond is about to be called early. They offer to buy the bond at the current higher price from one of their valued customers (so, that customer "won't get stuck"). They then try to pawn the bond off on you or another stranger they've never worked with before. Their favored customers get the higher price and you get left holding the bag on bonds—and ultimately taking a bath when they are called for less than you have just paid.

- Choose only high-quality bonds if you think you might need to sell them before they mature. The secondary market is stronger, so it will be easier to sell them at a fair price.

STEP 7 KEEP YOUR WITS WHEN THE MARKET TUMBLES.

It's not until the market tumbles that many new investors consider the possibility that stocks can go up and down—and down much more quickly than they went up. The choice for you, as an investor, is when (or whether) to turn your paper profits into real profits (or losses). (Yes, the market can drop, and you may still owe taxes on a gain; more on this coming up.) It's never too early to plan what to do if prices go south.

A "bear market" is defined as a drop in major stock indexes of at least 20 percent. Nothing tests an investor's resolve or basic beliefs more than a plunge in the market. The average investor—and most portfolio managers, despite their claims—cannot accurately predict where stock prices are headed, or when. But with the avalanche of business news on television, radio, and the Internet, and in newspapers and magazines, when prices go into a swan dive, even the most confident investor may begin to question his or her own best judgment.

It's human nature to get nervous when stock prices fall, or interest rates shoot up, or large layoffs are announced by a major U.S. corporation, or unrelentingly bad financial or political news is coming from a country that is a U.S. trading partner. But selling in a panic, after prices have already plunged, is rarely a wise choice. So, objectively, how can you avoid some common mistakes and cut your risk? Here are five questions to ponder when the gyrations in the market start making you queasy, and the actions you can take to reduce the queasiness.

- *Question 1. What do you need the money for, and when do you need it?* As we discussed in Secret 1, at the beginning of this chapter, the stock market can be a good place for some long-term money (money you won't be needing for at least five years). But as the months have marched on, you may have entered that magic five-year time horizon when, for instance, you will need to start paying for your child's college tuition or putting together a down payment for a house. If so, consider moving this money into a safer haven, such as a money market fund, a bank CD (certificate of deposit), or a Treasury bill (described earlier in this chapter). You won't get double-digit returns, but you won't jeopardize your principal, either.

- *Question 2. Is it time to rebalance your portfolio?* Even before you invested, you should have decided what percentage of your portfolio you want to have in stocks, bonds, other investments, and cash. You diversified your investments to lower your overall risk. For simplicity's sake, say you want 70 percent in stocks and 30 percent in bonds (the percentages you originally chose). If the stock market had a strong run up, you might now have 85 percent of your assets in stocks and only 15 percent in bonds. One way to rebalance your portfolio is to sell off some of your stocks, then take the profits and buy more bonds, to restore the 70 percent/30 percent stock-to-bond ratio.

  Choosing which stocks to sell isn't easy. One way to decide is to look at your holdings and ask yourself, "If I had the cash, would I buy this stock at this price?" If the answer is no, consider selling that stock.

- *Question 3. Is this a good time to sell at a loss for tax purposes?* Before you sell any investment, you should have at least a rough idea of the tax implications. If you sell shares of stocks or mutual funds, bonds, or other investments, for *more money than you paid,* you'll likely owe a capital gains tax—even if the price is now lower than it was just a week ago. Calculate your taxes before you sell. (Estimate how much you would get if you sold the shares today, then subtract from that amount what you paid for the shares. Did you make money? If so, did you own this investment at least a year, so that you might qualify for a lower capital gains tax rate? If not, it might pay to wait until you qualify for the lower rate, but be aware that prices could drop. You will have to weigh the trade-off.)

Tip: A loss—that is, selling shares for less than you paid for them—could have some tax benefits. You may be able to write it off against some capital gains you have from other transactions. But if you don't have enough gains to use up the loss, consider another tax option: writing off the loss against your income, up to $3,000. That would reduce your tax bill for the year. For more details, contact your tax adviser.

- *Question 4. Is this a good time to buy more at reduced prices?* "People like to take risk when they make money and don't like risk when they lose money," says Alexandra Armstrong, a certified financial planner. "Letting emotion take over is a big mistake."

   If you've been "dollar-cost averaging," remember why: to lower your average share price. You chose to buy fewer shares as the price went up, and more if they went down. So, consider a market drop to be a *buying opportunity*—a chance to buy more shares at a lower price.

   Note: If you've sold some stock to take a tax loss but you still want to own that stock for the long term, what can you do? You can buy it back at the new, lower price, but wait at least 30 days to avoid violating the "wash-sale" provision of the tax code.

- *Question 5. Is fear of the unknown keeping you up at night?* If you're worrying about your investments, it may be time to learn more about money and your investments. Consider consulting an objective fee-only financial planner, boosting your money IQ by attending a course at a community college, or reading some personal finance magazines (see Chapter 3 for more advice). More knowledge and information should allay your fear of the unknown. If that isn't enough to quiet your inner voice, consider cutting your risks by selling off some of your investments and putting that money in safer places.

   If you're going to start making investment decisions yourself, you're probably going to need to open an account with a brokerage firm. Do you need a full-service firm or will a lower-cost discount broker suffice? And are you ready to test your skills and start investing online? The next chapter will help you answer these questions *and* find and interview the right broker for you.

Chapter 28

Find a Compatible Stockbroker
or Online Broker

Do you need a stockbroker? You may not, if you don't have a lot of money to invest or if you only plan to invest, for now, in mutual funds (many of which you can buy directly through the fund company), Treasury securities, and some individual stocks. But if you plan to expand your investing horizons, then a broker could be just what you need. Are you looking for the hand-holding and advice of a traditional, full-service broker, or would a lower-cost, discounted one suffice—leaving you with more money to invest because you've saved on commissions?

STEP 1 DECIDE HOW MUCH HELP AND ADVICE YOU NEED.

Do you need a full-service stockbroker? If you understand the basics of investing and you have the time and desire to research and investigate potential investments, then you may not need a full-service broker. If all you want is someone to execute trades that you initiate, then a discount broker, or possibly an online broker, may be all you need.

How do they compare? With a full-service broker, you get a lot more than just execution of trades. The broker will likely provide you with research on companies that are suggested for you to buy or sell—through the broker, who, of course, will get a commission. He or she also will likely try to sell you on letting the brokerage firm manage your assets—specifically, with an account called a "wrap account," in which, the broker will suggest, you should keep your stocks, bonds, mutual funds, and, while you're at it, some cash. The firm may also give you a credit card or debit card "for your convenience." The fee for this account is typically 1.25 percent to 3 percent of your assets under management, but some of your trading fees may be waived. Full-service brokers will often discount their commissions, even without a wrap account, if you give them enough business, but you have to ask.

"But You Don't Look Like a Discount Broker!"

A new customer walking in for the first time might not spot the difference between a full-service broker (such as Merrill Lynch or Paine Webber) and a discount broker (such as Charles Schwab). The stock tickers tick by, and the furnishings probably look similar. But most employees at a discount broker work on a salary, not a commission. And although discount brokers may let you use their research facilities to analyze companies, what you choose to buy is just that—your choice. Unlike full-service brokers, discounters rarely make suggestions to you. A discounted broker is less like a traditional stockbroker and more like an order-taker.

How do you choose between discounters and full-service brokers? You need to decide what's important to you, and how many extras you will need. With a discounter, you can be nickel-and-dimed to death. For instance, discounters may charge low fees for trades, but if you lose your statement, you may have to pay $10 or more for a duplicate. A $10 advertised trade at a discounter may only be possible if you trade online, not by phone. The discounter may add surcharges for each transaction, on top of its advertised rate. A wire transfer of your money can get very pricey. You need to know the *total* cost for the services you use.

For up-to-date comparisons of charges and services for discount brokers and online trading, check out (at the library or online) financial publications such as *Kiplinger's Personal Finance* magazine, *Money, Smart Money,* and *Fortune.*

 CHOOSE A FULL-SERVICE BROKER PRUDENTLY.

If you've decided to choose a full-service stockbroker, you need to check him or her out before you hand over your money. Make sure that he or she is well-trained, experienced in working with clients in situations similar to yours, and not set on doing more trading than you want or need. Here's how to start your search:

- Get referrals from friends, coworkers, and other people in financial situations similar to yours (that is, similar income, investing goals, financial knowledge, and so on). You want a broker who has been in business at least 10 years. But someone who survived—and whose clients survived—the market crash of '87 might be a better choice.
- Cross off your list the name of any broker who works for a firm that is not covered by the Securities Investor Protection Corporation

(SIPC). The coverage would protect you from losses in your account up to $500,000 (up to $100,000 in cash). Note: Many brokers carry additional insurance to cover larger losses.

- Meet with the branch managers of the brokerage houses you are considering. Tell them a little about yourself: your financial goals, and the amount you have to invest. Then see whom on their staff they recommend.
- Steer clear of "the Broker of the Day"—the broker who automatically gets the next new client who walks through the door. You want someone who is simpatico, not the person whose number is up.

When you've got the names of a few potential brokers, conduct a phone interview with each one on your list. Ask the following:

- How long have you been in this business?
- What is your background? Any special financial certifications—Certified Financial Planner (CFP) or Certified Public Accountant (CPA)?
- Where did you go to school? When did you graduate, and with what degrees?
- Have you had any additional training since college?
- Where have you worked prior to this firm?
- What types of investments do you specialize in, and what types of investments would you suggest for me?
- What kind of research information will you give me about investments I already own?
- How do you charge for your services? Are you paid a commission on financial products, such as mutual fund shares I buy through you? What discounts am I eligible for?

Be sure to get names and numbers of references from the brokers, and *call them.* Cross off any broker who won't provide at least three names. Also get a copy of the broker's Central Registration Depository (CRD) report. (Call the National Association of Securities Dealers, at: (800) 289-9999.) It lists a broker's job history, any disciplinary actions, and a summary of customer complaints. Check that there are no discrepancies on this form, compared to what the broker told you.

Go with your gut reaction. Pay attention to the responses you get. Do you feel you were (or were not) listened to? Were you taken seriously and treated with respect? If in doubt, you'd be better off leaving your money in mutual funds or a bank rather than handing it over to someone who, your intuition tells you, is not a good match—and whose advice could cost you money in the form of lost investment return.

Brokers are in it for the money—theirs—and if it looks like you won't generate a good amount of commissions and other fees, a broker may not want you as a client. Often, large national brokerage houses are more willing to take on a small customer account than a smaller firm would be.

If you've decided to limit your investing (and homework) to companies in your geographical area, an established regional brokerage house might be in a better position than a national brokerage house to point you to up-and-coming companies with good potential.

STEP 3 HANG UP ON COLD CALLERS.

If you get a call at dinnertime, and the caller is offering you a hot investment, what should you do? Hang up. Run, don't walk from "cold callers," who typically buy your name and number from a list and then call you at dinnertime, offering some "great investment." Ask yourself: If the advice is so great, why is it being offered to a total stranger and not one of the regular customers? Is it because he or she has no regular customers? Or because the advice isn't any good?

Even if the caller says your name was passed along "from a friend of yours," don't automatically believe it. It could be a bluff. Or maybe your friend did give your name, because giving out YOUR name was the only way to get the salesperson off the phone!

STEP 4 SELECT THE TERMS AND CONDITIONS OF YOUR ACCOUNT WITH CARE.

Here are some red flags to guard against when you set up your account:

◀ **Discretionary account.** Your broker asks you for authorization to buy or sell securities in your account at *his or her* discretion, without having to get your permission. You may not like the investment decisions the broker makes, but you can be sure he or she will get a full commission for each of the trades. Don't let a broker set up a discretionary account for you.

◀ **Margin account.** Setting up a margin account lets you borrow against the value of some of your investments to buy additional investments. If these new purchases take a dive, you would either have to come up with the cash to meet your "margin call," or you would be forced to sell the securities that you borrowed against. If you must sell during a broad market dip, you may end up selling at a big, but temporarily discounted, price. If that's not bad enough, you may still owe tax on the sale of the depressed investments you were forced to sell. Unless you are a very sophisticated investor, just say no. If you don't have the cash to make an investment, resist the urge to buy it.

◀ **Unauthorized trades.**   These are investments that were bought or sold without your specific authorization. Keep confirmation slips, and reconcile your statements when they come in, to make sure that no trades were conducted that were not authorized by you. If any were, complain immediately to the broker and the branch manager. An honest brokerage house should reverse the trade and make you whole.

◀ **Churning.**   The broker convinces you to buy and sell—a lot! He or she gets a commission each time, on money that is coming out of your pocket. Keep notes of conversations with your broker, and jot down *who* instigated each trade. If your broker is suggesting too many changes, contact the branch manager. If you still feel that your best interest is not coming first, tell the manager that you will be closing your account and taking your business elsewhere.

Stick with a "cash account," where your transactions are paid and reconciled in cash within three days of a transaction.

If you feel that a broker has done you wrong, contact the National Association of Securities Dealers (NASD), at (800) 289-9999 or www.nasd.com; your state's securities regulations division (contact your local government for an address and phone number); and the Securities and Exchange Commission (SEC) at the following address:

SEC Division of Enforcement
Enforcement Complaint Center
Mail Stop 8-4, 450 Fifth Street, N.W.
Washington, DC 20549

STEP 5 KNOW WHAT YOU'RE GETTING AND GIVING UP WITH AN ONLINE BROKER.

William's Story

"I had started a small business a few months earlier, so I decided to sell off some stocks and use the money to buy office equipment. The plan was to place a few sell orders via my online broker as soon as the market opened in the morning. Apparently, I wasn't alone. Due to 'heavy trading volume,' I couldn't get my entire sell order to take. As I pounded on the keyboard, trying to unfreeze my screen, the market dropped more than 200 points within the first half-hour of trading. My profits were evaporating before my eyes.

"As I continued to stare at the immobilized hourglass on my screen, hoping for a confirmation or even a cancellation of my order, nothing happened. Panicked, I tried to send e-mails to my online broker with one hand as I dialed their customer service number with the other hand. The screen then flashed a couple of times and went blank. But what did that mean? Did my order take or didn't it? Not knowing what to do, I tried to cancel the order, but couldn't get back onto my broker's site.

"Their customer service number offered little in the way of service. I got busy signal after busy signal the first nine times I called. On the tenth call, at least I got through, but not to a person. Instead, I was stuck listening to bad music on the phone, interrupted every 63 seconds (I timed it) by a prerecorded, sickeningly sweet announcement saying that, 'Due to heavy calling volume, there will be a delay before speaking to a customer service rep. Calls will be taken in the order in which they are received, so please stay on the line. And have a nice day.'

"As I sat, on hold, I turned my TV on and nervously watched the CNBC ticker as my prices were plummeting! After more than two hours, the music abruptly ended and I heard several clicks, then the announcement, 'If you'd like to make a call, please hang up and dial again.' After holding all that time, I had been CUT OFF! It was 9:00 P.M. when I finally got a confirmation for three of my sell orders. But what happened to the other two? To this day, the broker has no record of them. This online fiasco cost me more than $7,600 in lost profits, and I needed that money to pay bills."

Do You Feel Lucky?

Online brokers have become a pivotal part of the do-it-yourself money movement. Convenience and cost saving are the major draws. You can place orders to buy or sell stocks 24 hours a day. Some online brokers are even trading shares in mutual funds. And with a growing number of firms offering online trading, a savvy consumer can make a trade for well under $10—a fraction of the cost to place the same order with a real, live person.

But convenience and cost savings notwithstanding, using an online broker is not for everyone. Novice investors—or even more sophisticated, experienced investors who don't have the time or inclination to check out potential investments—may need a little more handholding. With an online broker, they're on their own.

Consider this: If you buy a stock on the advice of a broker, but it turns out that the stock was too risky for your goals, you could have some recourse against the broker and, in some cases, might be reimbursed for your losses. But when you use an online broker, you choose what to buy and what to sell, and when to do it. Put simply: If you buy something that is too risky or not suited to your financial goals, you have no one to blame but yourself.

Grace's Story

"The ease with which I placed my online trades—by just making a few key strokes and pressing the enter key—seduced me into making more trades than I had planned and buying things I hadn't gotten around to investigating," confesses Grace. "I made some money at first, and gave myself credit for knowing a lot more about investing than I really did. In retrospect, I had just been lucky. Online investing was as easy as playing the slot machines in Las Vegas. Only you're not feeding in quarters or $1 bills. Instead, with an online broker, the no-armed bandit is devouring hundreds or thousands of dollars at a time, but you don't realize it because you don't see the money getting sucked up."

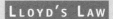 **LLOYD'S LAW**

If you don't know a lot about investing, and you aren't going to put in the time or effort to research potential investments, an online broker may be too risky.

STEP 6 COMPARISON-SHOP FOR AN ONLINE BROKER.

If, however, you have the knowledge, time, and patience to investigate investments yourself, and you feel that you are ready to trade online, here are some things to consider when choosing an online broker:

- *Research brokers' ratings.* Check out the performance numbers of online brokers, conducted periodically by personal finance magazines such as *Barron's* at www.barrons.com, *Kiplinger's Personal*

Finance magazine at www.kiplinger.com, or *Smart Money* magazine at www.smartmoney.com. These magazines and their Web sites will give you current information about the services offered by various online brokers, the fees they are charging, how comparatively well each is performing, and what types of customers would be best suited to use each of them.

- *Investigate their backup procedures.* We've all heard stories about things going wrong—a computer crashes, phone lines go down—so you need to ask about backup procedures. Before a heavy trading day or an unexpected crash of a broker's server gets in the way of your executing a trade, find out if a back up server is ready to handle large numbers of orders or other glitches online. Also ask whether you can reach a living, breathing customer service rep if necessary, and then verify the availability by calling ahead a few times to see how long it takes to get through, and how knowledgeable the people on the other end of the phone seem. But remember: Getting through on a slow trading day when there are no problems is no guarantee that you will get similar service during a problem situation.
- *Understand the fee structures.* Many online brokers charge different fees for different services. For instance, some charge more for a "limit order" (you place an order to buy, say, 100 shares of XYZ Corporation at no more than $20 a share) than for a "market order" (the broker will buy 100 shares at whatever the current price is).
- *Read the fine print before signing anything or sending money.* Scrutinize the new-customer agreement carefully before signing it or sending any money. If the agreement seems too vague, or lets the brokerage firm off the hook in situations where you feel it should take responsibility (if your password is stolen, or you are unable to execute a trade when you try to place an order), see what the competition is offering. There are over 100 online brokers to choose from, and some are more consumer-friendly than others.

STEP 7 **TAKE MEASURES NOW TO AVERT A PROBLEM LATER.**

What would you expect to have happen if your transaction(s) don't go as planned? Will the online broker make up for your loss when you couldn't execute your trade because you couldn't get through? Maybe, but to get *any* remuneration, you must be able to show that you exhausted *all* methods—online and by phone—to execute your order. Here are some steps to take to get your order through in the first place, or to bolster your case if you couldn't get through:

- *Create a paper trail.* Whether your trade goes through as planned or not, when you use an online broker, it's a good idea to document events as you go. Make a note of every order you placed—or tried to place. Write down the time as well as the outcome. Print out your computer screens, e-mails, and any other computer correspondence, and keep a phone log of customer service calls you make, including when you placed a call but couldn't get through. If you did speak with someone, jot down the name of the person, the time, the date, and what was discussed and agreed to.
- *Hedge your bets.* Consider signing up with two different online broker services, to give you a backup in case of an unforeseen glitch. Verify that if the Internet fails, you can make a tried-and-true phone order, and ask whether there is a nearby office where you could place an order in person.
- *Put extended hours to work for you.* If possible, place online orders during off-peak hours (early morning, or at night) when traffic is lighter.
- *Make sure your equipment is up to snuff.* Ensure that your computer, modem, browser, software, Internet Service Provider, and phone line are big enough and fast enough so they won't let you down in a crisis.
- *Proofread before hitting the "Enter" key.* Typos can be costly. An erroneous keystroke could cause you to buy or sell shares in a company other than the one you intended. Or if you planned to trade 100 shares but type 1,000 by mistake, guess what: You typed and "entered" it, you traded it. Once you hit the "Enter" key, you are on the hook for that transaction. Some consumers have made the same trade two or three times because they "didn't think it took the first time," so they entered the order again. In other cases, they thought they had canceled an order, but the original order went through without their realizing it.
- *Have realistic expectations.* With prices changing at the speed of light, you may miss a few big moves in the market. At the least, the prices you are seeing on your screen at any time may be a little behind the times, so you may miss the split-second high or low in price that you had wanted.

- *Complain if appropriate.* If you're having a recurring problem with an online broker, try to resolve it directly—and right away. The broker may fix the problem or compensate you for a loss that you can document was the broker's fault. If not, it might be time to change brokers.

Tip: Consider filing a complaint with the National Association of Securities Dealers (NASD), at www.nasd.com, if you feel your broker's performance was not up to the promises you were given.

A note on day-trading: It's very, very risky! A day-trader is someone who makes multiple stock trades (purchases and sales) in a day. At best the trader makes a small amount of money on each trade and then usually cashes out everything at the end of the day. But, for a growing number of day-traders who thought they knew what they were doing, day-trading has resulted not in profits, but in massive losses. Day-traders have literally gone into debt to the tune of tens of thousands of dollars or more. They've wagered money they never had in the first place, and will need years, or decades, to pay it off. And it happened faster than they could fathom it. My advice: Don't try it!

Make the Most of the New Retirement Realities

The biggest fear many older workers have is that they will outlive their money. The sooner you start saving for retirement, the better your chances for meeting your financial goals. But how much do you need? Where should you invest it? Why can't you rely on the predictions of some online calculators, which are provided at a growing number of financial planning Web sites? The answers to these questions are in this solution—plus, how to make sure you are taking full advantage of employer-offered retirement savings plans.

Chapter 29

Lay the Groundwork for a Comfortable Retirement

Joshua's Story

"The day I retired was the happiest day of my life. Don't get me wrong; I had a good-paying job, but I was tired of the commute. I was tired of the office politics. I was even getting bored with my work, so saying *Adios* was liberating, even though it was a bit terrifying. Roberta was a very supportive wife. We talked about where we wanted to live—in our same family home near our children and grandchildren—and we agreed on how we wanted to spend our time—mostly golfing and sailing.

"I am fortunate in that I'm collecting a pension from work, and we did manage to save some money over the years, but where are all the savings I was told I would see, once I retired? Our living costs not only haven't dropped—they've actually gone up.

"Granted, I no longer have the commuting costs. My clothing costs haven't dropped—they've risen too. I already owned a closet full of business suits, which I only wear now when I go to a coworker's funeral. Roberta and I have had to buy a bunch of new clothes for our new lifestyle. I admit, our hobbies aren't cheap. But, come on, those retirement planning brochures always tell you that your postretirement expenses will be about 75 percent of your preretirement expenses. Maybe, if you're content sitting in a rocking chair somewhere and watching life pass you by; but for anybody who still has a pulse, you'd better have a hefty bank account to support yourself.

"The biggest shock came when I calculated my taxes for this past year. The year I retired, my income actually went up. I had to pay taxes on my salary and mutual fund income, plus more taxes on some onetime payments (for unused vacation days and an unpaid bonus) from my former employer. To make matters worse, I've lost a bunch of tax write-offs I used to count on, for things like unreimbursed business expenses and contributions to my retirement savings plan. Since my income was so high, I couldn't even take the full write-off for the itemized deductions I still had. I was only allowed to take a fraction of them; gee, how come my Congressman didn't boast about *that* when he bragged about his efforts to reduce taxes?"

Sorry to say, those sunny estimates of easy, cheap living after retirement are no longer very realistic—if they ever really were.

Why Retirement Will Cost More Than You Thought

You've probably heard that when you retire, you will be able to maintain your current lifestyle but it will cost you just 65 percent to 80 percent of what it currently costs. And why not? Your out-of-pocket expenses should drop. Commuting costs to work will be gone, and you won't need to buy or dry clean work clothes, or pay to eat out at lunchtime. And one of the biggest savings, or so the argument goes, may be the old homestead. Most retirement models project that you can sell your home (for a tidy profit, of course) and move someplace where the living is easier—and much, much cheaper.

For earlier generations of retirees, that may have been true, but you can't count on that anymore. The old estimate was based on many assumptions about life expectancy, lifestyle, and tax laws, and those assumptions no longer apply. Here are some reasons why life after work comes with a heftier price tag than those old estimates would indicate:

- You may not want to relocate to a less expensive place. If you've got friends and family nearby, starting over in a strange town may not appeal to you. Even if you want to move, you may have trouble finding someone to buy your home.
- Finding a buyer for the homestead—and selling at a high price— will be harder as retirement nears. Because of an aging population and recent tax changes (home sellers are no longer forced to buy a larger home than they need, in order to avoid paying capital gains tax on their prior home), demand for larger, family-friendly homes will continue to shrink.
- Prices for nice homes in desirable retirement communities will likely rise. Finding a buyer for your old home may not be your only problem. As the population ages, demand for desirable retirement homes in sunnier climates will keep going up, so you'll not only get less for your old home but will have to pay more for your new one.
- Your share of health care costs is apt to keep rising. Guaranteed pensions aren't the only thing going the way of the dinosaur. An increasing proportion of retired workers are finding that they have to pick up more of their health care costs than in years gone by.
- Your income taxes may go up. You won't be able to take some of your work-life write-offs, such as deductions for contributions into

retirement savings plans [401(k) plans, IRAs, Keoghs, or whatever you've been taking]; your mortgage will be almost paid off; and you'll lose your exemptions for dependent children.

• An active retirement doesn't come cheap. If sitting in a rocking chair, whiling away the hours and days, doesn't really appeal to you, staying active in sports or other activities is going to cost you plenty.

So how much income will you need in retirement? A lot. Probably more than you would guess, and, unfortunately, maybe more than you may have managed to put away. But the situation may not be as dire as some financial service providers would have you believe.

Why Retirement Could Actually Cost Less Than You Thought

Some financial service providers run Web sites or provide other information that allow you to estimate what you will need for a comfortable retirement. They make it sound like a science, but it isn't. No one really knows how much you'll need, how high inflation will be, how well your investments will do, or what the market will be like if you choose to sell your house or to buy a new one. They also don't know what tax rates or other tax changes will apply, or what you can realistically expect from Social Security.

If you've visited one of these Web sites or followed the financial recommendations from a scurrilous financial service firm, you may have gotten skewed estimates of how much money you will need at retirement. It may look like you're going to need to save much more money than you thought, and possibly more than you will need. Why would they do this?

This is perplexing until you consider the following: These financial service companies are discounting—if not outright ignoring—money you will get from your employer (as a pension or other retirement savings) or from Social Security. Why omit these? Because they want to encourage consumers to save more money, but not for altruistic purposes. These companies want you to save with *them,* and guess what: These companies, using this mind game, will reap sales commissions and other money management fees from your money—and from your fear. To avoid getting snared by an unscrupulous firm, stick with reputable financial planning companies whose references you have personally checked out.

Tip: To get a more accurate estimate of the risk you may be taking with your retirement nest egg, check out the free calculator on the

Financial Engines Web site (www.financialengines.com). Unlike some calculators (like the ones discussed above, which project one number for the value of your investments), the Financial Engines calculator will tell you the likelihood that your retirement investments will get you to your financial goals. If this calculator shows you that you are taking more risk than you realized or are comfortable with, you can make changes now. The sooner you get your investments on track, the better.

The Secret to Retirement Planning Revealed

Now that I have your attention, the secret is: There is no secret. A comfortable retirement is like any other financial objective. You need to set some goals, see where you're starting from, and plot a course to get to your destination. Try the five steps in this chapter.

STEP 1 SET SOME GOALS.

Here are some questions to ponder while you're deciding what you want to do with the rest of your life:

- When do you want to retire?
- How do you want to retire? Will you take full-time retirement, or will you continue to work part-time? If so, for how long?
- How would you like to spend your retirement years? Doing extensive traveling? Taking part in pricey activities, such as golfing or sailing? Doing volunteer work? Starting a new business?
- Where would you like to live? If you'd like to stay in the same town, would you be staying in the same home? Moving to a retirement community that requires less work? Or just moving to a less expensive, smaller home, condo, or apartment that's easier to maintain? Would you prefer to move to another part of the country? How will living expenses there compare to your current ones?

STEP 2 TAKE A STAB AT WHAT RETIREMENT WILL COST.

Joshua's story illustrates that expenses don't automatically drop when you retire. Unless you make a serious effort at belt tightening, your living expenses probably won't drop much—if at all.

On page 309 is a revised version of the form you filled out in Chapter 2, where you tracked what a month of living expenses is *currently* costing you. Your task now is to use the form you already filled out as a base, and write in the amount for "Costs: Current." Then, in the new column ("Costs: Projected"), fill in what your estimated costs will be. You reach these new numbers by omitting or lowering expenses you think you will no longer have when you retire (no more commuting costs, lower dry-cleaning costs, no more union dues). Next, write down the activities you would like to do while you're retired. For instance, Joshua and his wife Roberta chose to spend their time golfing and sailing. Write down what you would like to do, then get estimates of what those activities would cost. Also, if you plan to move, what will your moving expenses be? Remember, if you move after you retire, you won't be able to take a tax deduction to cover moving expenses, because you're no longer relocating for work.

Projected Postretirement Spending Plan

	Costs	
	Current	Projected
Housing (mortgage/rent—first/second home)	$_____	$_____
Utilities (electric, gas, water, phone)	$_____	$_____
Taxes (include lost deductions)	$_____	$_____
Credit card	$_____	$_____
Student loans	$_____	$_____
Obligations you must pay (alimony, child support)	$_____	$_____
Bank fees (ATM, others)	$_____	$_____
Insurance (health, home, car, life, disability)	$_____	$_____
Medical/Dental	$_____	$_____
Food (meals, snacks)	$_____	$_____
Clothing (purchases, dry cleaning)	$_____	$_____
Transportation (car payments, gas, tolls)	$_____	$_____
Magazines, newspapers, books	$_____	$_____
Gifts, charities	$_____	$_____
Personal (toiletries, allowances)	$_____	$_____
Entertainment	$_____	$_____
Sports and hobbies	$_____	$_____
Vacation	$_____	$_____
Relocation costs	$_____	$_____
Line "C." Total Spending	$_____	$_____

To determine the monthly amount for vacations and other occasional items, take the yearly totals for those categories and divide by 12.

Some possible expenses to consider:

- Hobby costs (be sure to allocate money for lessons to learn new hobbies, as well as for the equipment you will need).
- Moving costs to relocate to a new town.
- Second-home costs, to purchase or rent a vacation home.
- Lost tax deductions—you won't be making new deposits to your retirement savings plan unless you start a business or take another job that qualifies you to make new deposits; your mortgage is probably almost paid off; and chances are your kids have grown up and no longer qualify for personal exemptions.
- Clothing costs for your new lifestyle.
- Taxes related to mandatory withdrawals from IRAs or other retirement savings plans. Most, if not all, of this money was tax-deferred when it was deposited, so it's fully subject to tax when it's withdrawn.
- Taxes on some of your Social Security earnings, if you're also earning other income.

You can subtract some things that won't apply anymore, such as:

- Commuting costs; lunches out every day.
- Dry cleaning/purchasing business clothes.
- Union dues.

 TAKE A STAB AT WHAT YOU WILL EARN.

Sources of retirement income have often been likened to a three-legged stool. The three legs are: Social Security, pension, and private savings. But with pensions becoming a dying breed and the Social Security crisis putting a potential crimp on payouts, most people now assume that some money will have to come from someplace else. For a growing number of retirees, postretirement work is filling their needed income gap.

- Check your projected Social Security benefits (Line "A" on page 311). Call the Social Security office at (800) 772-1213 (or visit the Web site at www.ssa.gov) to order a form called "Request for Earnings and Benefits Estimate Statement." Verify that your earnings records are accurate, and analyze the projected benefits to see when it might make financial sense for you to retire.

Tip: If you owned a small business at the same time you were working for an employer, double-check the figures on file with the Social Security Administration. I have discovered that during the years when workers get paid Social Security through an employer and through their own businesses, they may only have gotten credit for the self-employment Social Security payments they made themselves (calculated on Schedule SE of the federal tax return). When the IRS's scanner finds this one Social Security figure, it apparently stops scanning for any others. Social Security may have totally overlooked any other amount your employer and you paid through work (listed on your W-2).

- Check your projected pension (Line "B" below). Stop by the benefits coordinator's office at work, and get a copy of your pension records. Check them for accuracy. Also, you may have some pension money from a full-time or summer job you had years or decades ago. Over the years, some private pension funds have closed while they were still holding onto former employees' pension money. To see if you have some money that you either forgot about or didn't even know you had coming to you, check The Pension Benefit Guaranty Corporation's Web site at www.pbgc.gov.

To estimate your income more precisely, fill out the following form.

Projected Postretirement Income Plan

	Line	Amount
Social Security income	A	$_____
Pension income	B	_____
Salary	Z1	_____
Other earned income (from work)	Z2	_____
Retirement savings income [401(k), IRA, Keogh]	Z3	_____
Unearned income (dividends, interest, royalties)	Z4	_____
Rental income	Z5	_____
Annuity income	Z6	_____
Alimony (income only; not payments)	Z7	_____
Line "Y." Total Income (sum of above items)		$_____
Subtract Line "C," Postretirement Cost—Total Spending		–$_____
Savings or Shortfall ("D")		$_____

Add your projected Social Security income ("A"), your projected pension income ("B"), and all other income ("Z1–Z7"). From that total, subtract ("C"), your estimated postretirement cost. The difference ("D") is the shortfall, if any, that you will need to fill with personal savings and/or postretirement income. The formula:

$$D = C - (A + B + Z)$$

translates to:

$$\text{Projected shortfall (or surplus) (D)} = \text{Cost (C)} - \left[\begin{array}{c} \text{Social Security (A)} + \text{Pension (B)} + \\ \text{Other income (Z)} \end{array} \right]$$

Bottom line: It's safer to estimate that your expenses won't drop much, if at all, after you retire. For now, figure that life in retirement will cost between 80 percent and 100 percent of what it costs you during your working years. If this estimate turns out to be high, you'll just have more money to play with when you retire.

STEP 4 PLAN FOR A BIRTHDAY GREETING FROM WILLARD SCOTT.

Maybe you won't live to 100 (so Willard won't wish you "Happy Birthday" on *The Today Show*), but the fact remains, more people are living to an older age. The new problem created for retirees: living longer than they budgeted for, and longer than their money lasts.

The old advice was simple: When you're ready to retire, cash in your stocks (they were supposedly too risky) and buy bonds. You can then live "safely" off the income.

That advice might have made some sense when people only lived a few years after they stopped working. Now, it's not unusual to live decades after retirement. So, for a growing number of retirees, an overriding concern is: "Will I outlive my money?" Living off bond income will only cut it for the wealthiest retirees.

Why shouldn't you put all your money into bonds during your golden years? Two of the biggest foes you will be facing are inflation and taxes. And, unfortunately, your income from bonds and other safe postretirement investments, such as money market accounts, won't be big enough to keep you ahead of this dynamic duo. Your nest egg will get chipped away.

Inflation and taxes are the one–two punch that poses a constant threat to your nest egg. They can not only erode your spending power, but deplete your life's savings. Retirement should be a time of relaxation, not years spent fearing that your money will run out before you do.

For planning purposes, assume that you will live at least to age 90. (Even cash-value life insurance companies often assume that policyholders will die before that, so if money coming from your life insurance is part of your retirement nest egg, double-check the assumptions.) Better to find out as soon as possible, when you still have years (or decades) to build your nest egg.

STEP 5 FIND WAYS TO IMPROVE THE QUALITY OF YOUR GOLDEN YEARS.

Where should you focus your efforts now? Toward making your projected shortfall ("D") equal to zero or less. Actually, you should target to have a surplus in "D." Here are some ways to accomplish this plan.

- Save more. As we discussed earlier in the book, the easiest way to save more is by paying yourself first. There's no getting around it—building a surplus means saving more. Make saving your first priority. Put a little away before you do anything else, including paying bills, and absolutely before buying luxuries (or those day-to-day money wasters you can't even recall). There are loads of how-to ideas in Chapter 2.
- Spend less. Your goal always is to spend less than you make. And what's leftover can add to your savings. (See Chapter 2 for more cost-cutting tips.)
- Earn more. This could help create a surplus in two ways. If your earnings go up and you keep your spending constant, you'll have more left over in each pay period. If your earnings rise, depending on how your pension from work is calculated, your retirement income might also be larger.
- Consider postponing retirement a year or more if your employer will go along. Your last years of work, prior to retiring, will likely be your highest earning years, so retiring early could cost you a bundle in lost income.
- Understand your postretirement health coverage before you agree to retire. Many companies are cutting back or eliminating their health insurance for employees and retirees. Age and preexisting

conditions can make it hard to get health insurance on the open market, so postponing retirement until you qualify for Medicare (at age 65 currently) may make sense. It also eliminates the risk that your former employer could change or eliminate your coverage after you retire, but before you qualify for Medicare.

- Invest more aggressively. Don't take undue risk, but by investing too conservatively, you might be letting money slip through your fingers. Your investing plans are your best weapon against the enemies of taxes and inflation. Consider hiring professional help. The fee for one hour with a qualified financial planner could be money well spent. (See Chapter 3 on working with a professional financial planner.)

- Don't rule out going back to work after retirement. A lot of people dream of a long and early retirement, but, for millions of retirees, the thought of it greatly exceeds the reality. It turns out to be unrealistic—or, more importantly, a boring choice. If retirement is less interesting or fulfilling than you had hoped, try something else. Spend your golden years doing something you enjoy, and spend them with people who appreciate you.

You have decades of job and life experience to share—and, at last, lots of employers are starting to appreciate older workers. Don't hold out for the highest dollar; job satisfaction may be more important than salary at that time in your life. Because you may not need costly employee benefits, such as health insurance, you may be more appealing to a potential employer than other, preretirement candidates. Don't constrain yourself to the same field. Maybe you have a hobby or other interest that was impractical as a first career but could be great fun (and a good way to earn some money) as a bonus career.

Chapter 30

Maximize Your 401(k), IRA, Keogh, and Other Retirement Savings Plans

Pensions and Other Employer-Offered Plans

Tyler's Story

"When I accepted a job offer at another company, I knew I would have some regrets. It would be tough to say goodbye to my friends at work, and my employer had been good to me over the past six years. But I figured an $8,000 raise and a better benefits package than I was currently getting would go far to ease my mind. What I hadn't taken into account, however, was that I would have to repay the loan I had taken against my 401(k) last year, when I left the company.

"Coming up with the cash quickly would be tough, but the other option wasn't much better. If I couldn't repay the loan, I would have to pay income tax on the loan balance, as well as a tax penalty, because I'm only 33 years old. While she was calculating my tax bill, the benefits coordinator at work said she also wanted to remind me that I would *not* be allowed to keep all of the money my employer had been paying into my 401(k). When I asked why, I was told it was because the company has a three-year vesting policy, and almost $12,000 of the money in my account hadn't been there that long. I hope the new job is worth it, because it's costing me money to go there."

In this chapter, we'll discuss defined benefit plans, defined contribution plans, 401(k) plans, ESOPs, IRAs (traditional and Roth), Keoghs, SEPs, SIMPLE IRAs, and variable annuities.

 UNDERSTAND THE DIFFERENCES BETWEEN TRADITIONAL PENSIONS AND NEWER RETIREMENT SAVINGS PLANS.

Defined Benefit Plans

For our parents and grandparents, planning for retirement was fairly simple. If they faithfully worked for a decent employer for many years, in addition to receiving a gold watch, they were taken care of via a company pension. Based on their salary and number of years of service with the company, they were guaranteed a set amount of money each month for the rest of their life.

Aside from their years of loyal service, they made no other contribution. The pension was "on the house," so to speak.

This type of plan is a "defined benefit" plan. Your employer might promise to pay you a pension for life. The size of the pension is often based on the average of an employee's wages in the past five years of work, before retirement, and then multiplied by the number of years of service.

Since benefits are back-end loaded, workers who stay with one employer for decades tend to come out better than those who change jobs frequently. To keep inflation from chipping away at your standard of living, some of these plans also have a cost-of-living adjustment every year or so.

LLOYD'S LAW

Don't change jobs capriciously—until you've crunched the numbers—if you are covered by a traditional pension plan. Leaving your present employer could cost you pension money that you may never recoup at your next job.

Your benefits coordinator can provide you with a projection of your pension payouts based on a variety of scenarios.

Note: Some employers have been swapping their decades-old traditional pension plans for a different type of pension, called a "cash-balance" plan. With this newer type of plan, each year your employer might contribute, say 4 percent of your yearly earnings, plus a small interest payment on that money, into an account earmarked for you.

Cash-balance plans tend to be less expensive than traditional plans for employers and are often a better deal for younger workers, with fewer years of service. They are more portable than traditional pension plans. Vesting often occurs with five years of service, so a departing worker can usually roll the money into an IRA, or, possibly, into a plan offered by a new employer.

Older workers, with decades of service, and whose salaries have shot up in their last few years of employment, can lose tens of thousands of dollars, or more, when their employer switches to this method.

Tip: If your employer switches pension plans, ask the benefits coordinator to provide you with projected payouts using the old and new methods. In response to pressure from older workers, some corporations have allowed older workers to keep their higher-paying, traditional pensions.

Defined Contribution Plans

A different kind of retirement plan has become increasingly popular in the past few years. Workers are no longer promised a certain pension for life; instead, an employer merely promises to make a certain contribution to a retirement savings plan. The amount received at retirement will depend on where the money was invested (and how the investments did) and won't be known until the employee retires.

Employee Stock Option Plans (ESOPs), 401(k) retirement savings plans, 403(b) plans, 457 plans, stock-bonus plans, employee Keogh plans, and Simplified Employee Pensions (SEPs) fall into this category. They are "defined contribution" plans. Because only the contribution, not the benefit, is known ahead of time (or "defined"), the onus is on you, the employee, to make sure that you will have enough money to live on during retirement.

LLOYD'S LAW

Where your money is invested during your working years is going to make a big difference in how much you'll get at retirement.

STEP 2 MAKE THE MOST OF YOUR 401(K) RETIREMENT SAVINGS PLAN.

LLOYD'S LAW

What you don't know about 401(k)s can cost you your nest egg. When it comes to investments, you've no doubt been cautioned, "Don't put all your eggs in one basket." But if you're putting money into your employer's 401(k) retirement savings plan and it's being invested in your employer's stock, you could be risking your career and a secure retirement—and not even realize it. More on this later in this section.

Q: What are 401(k) plans?

A: These are retirement savings plans offered by many employers. As an employee, you can put in pretax earnings (up to a certain yearly limit, currently around $10,000). The money will grow tax-deferred, and some employers also will contribute cash or stock, matching all or part of your contribution. You may also be allowed to add after-tax money. (Your contribution won't be deductible, but will grow tax-deferred.) Make the maximum contribution to your company's 401(k) retirement savings plan each year.

Q: Who chooses where my money will be invested?

A: You choose from among the choices offered by your employer—typically, stock or bond mutual funds, money market mutual funds, or your company's stock. You can switch between investments, subject to the rules of your plan.

Q: Should I show loyalty to my employer by investing in the company's stock?

A: You have to look at your whole portfolio—all of your investments, both outside the plan and in. If the 401(k) is your only investment, you're already taking a gamble: *Your job security and financial security are all dependent on your employer.* If your employer offers company stock as its matching contribution, then forgo company stock for your contribution, unless you've got a large, well-diversified portfolio outside of this plan (including some mutual funds, stocks, bonds, and money market accounts).

Tip: If your employer will only match your contribution if you invest in company stock, consider investing in company stock and then transferring to something else after vesting of your employer's contribution has occurred.

Q: How can I make the most of my 401(k)?

A: By keeping these strategies in mind:

- Max it out. Especially if your employer is matching your contribution dollar-for-dollar or even 50 cents for every dollar you contribute, you want to get the full benefit. Think of it as free money, a recurring bonus.

- Invest aggressively, but within reason. You don't want to take undue risk, but if you have a number of years (or decades) until you plan to retire, don't sock all your 401(k) money away into bonds or money market funds that yield just 3 percent or 4 percent growth a year. You need more growth potential—such as from the stock market—so that this nest egg will grow enough to more than offset taxes and inflation by the time you retire, years or decades from now.
- Invest your money and forget about it—or at least don't obsess over it. Your company plan may give you an 800 phone number to access your account, but don't keep making changes to your investment mix. Even more than individual investments, you want to invest this money for the long term. Don't try to time the market. This investment grows tax-deferred, so you will actually amplify your *lost return* by trying to time it. Review your plan's investment choices and the performance of your investments at least once a year. But to maximize your retirement savings, it's best to leave your money in the plan, and don't change your investment choices too often. The market will have ups and downs. Steady investors do better over time than those who try to time the market.
- Read your plan statements closely. (You should get a statement at least once a year.) Double-check that your contributions (and your employer's contributions) have been posted correctly, and that the money is invested in a timely fashion.

Q: If I need cash in a hurry, is it a good idea to borrow against my 401(k)?

A: No. It should be one of the last sources you consider. You pay the interest to yourself, and it's often at a relatively low rate (typically the prime rate plus one or two percentage points). So it sounds like a good place to borrow, but it costs more than most people realize. Here's why:

- You'll usually be charged a setup fee—a $50 charge is common.
- You will repay the loan with *after-tax* money, even though the money you borrowed had *not* been taxed. For simplicity sake, if you are in the 28 percent tax bracket, you will need to earn $1.28 to repay each dollar you borrow.
- The interest rate that you pay to yourself on the borrowed 401(k) plan money, while low compared to other types of loans, is not the relevant interest rate to consider. You need to look at *what the*

money would have earned if it had stayed, untouched, in your 401(k) plan. If the money is invested in a mutual fund earning 18 percent, that is the cost to consider when weighing a 401(k) plan loan against other loan sources.

Tip: Look into low-cost credit union or bank loans instead.

Here are a few things to keep in mind if you *must* borrow from your 401(k):

- Be sure to tap the lowest-yielding investment in your 401(k) portfolio.
- If you're borrowing for a down payment on a home, ask to secure the loan with a lien on your home. (This loan would be recorded against your property on your local government's records, just like your first mortgage.) In that way, the interest on your loan should be tax-deductible.
- Be sure to pay back any loan before leaving the company, or you will likely have to pay tax, plus if you are under age 55, a 10 percent tax penalty. Note: If you are leaving the company because you quit, were fired, or retired, the age when the 10 percent tax penalty is waived is not 59½.
- If your employer matches your contribution, keep making new contributions to your plan even while the loan is outstanding. Borrow extra from your 401(k) if you have to, so you will have enough to continue making these new contributions.

Q: If I leave the company, can I take all the 401(k) money with me?

A: You can take out your contribution, and the money it earns is yours to keep as well. But you need to ask when the employer's contribution becomes vested; that's when the money your employer contributed belongs to you as well. Some employers vest their contribution immediately. Others make employees wait a year or more.

Q: If I leave the company, where else should I consider reinvesting the money?

A: You can reinvest the money, either in your new employer's retirement savings plan (if it's allowed by both your new and old employers) or in an Individual Retirement Account (IRA). Remember, if you are under age

55, don't spend the money, or you will not only likely owe taxes, but also a penalty.

Tip: If you are transferring the money to an IRA, don't take possession of the money. Have a check sent to the IRA trustee. (Ask the bank or investment company that will be holding the IRA for you for contact information, including the contact name and address.) Otherwise, 20 percent will be withheld for taxes. Unless you make up the 20 percent from your own pocket, you will also be taxed on the 20 percent (it will be considered an early withdrawal). If you are under age 55, you are also subject to a 10 percent penalty.

Q: How fast can I get access to my money?

A: An employer can keep your money until you are age 65 or have been participating in the plan at least ten years (whichever comes later), so it could take weeks, months, or years to get the money in hand. Your other option is to leave the money with your former employer, but only do this if you are satisfied with the plan and with your employer's financial stability.

Q: If I die, will my spouse get the money?

A: Yes, unless your spouse has waived his or her rights by signing a statement to that effect on the enrollment form. If you are unmarried, the money goes to your designated beneficiary.

STEP 3 SEE HOW YOUR 401(K) PLAN STACKS UP WITH OTHERS.

How good is your plan? No two 401(k) plans are the same. They can vary greatly in terms of options and service. The better plans provide all or most of the following:

- Employer matches, with 50 cents or more, each dollar the employee contributes.
- Employee can direct all investments, his or her own contribution *and the employer's contribution.*
- Employee has multiple investment choices—six or more.

- Employer's contribution is immediately vested. (You wouldn't have to give any money back if you were to leave the company.)
- Employee has immediate access to current account information, online or by automated phone, including current account balance(s).
- Employee can reach a live customer service rep by phone and can place a trade order.
- Employee has the option to change investment mixes at any time. (Still, don't do it too often or for the wrong reasons. You're not trying to time the market—you're supposed to be in this for the long term, and micromanaging can cost you money.)
- Employee can borrow money from the plan. (Don't do it, except for a few rare reasons, such as a down payment on a house or to pay high medical costs. Even then, only borrow if you have exhausted every other loan source, and if you know that you will be able to repay the money before you leave the company to avoid owing any taxes or tax penalties on the loan.)
- Employer pays the plan's administrative fees.
- Employer provides prompt account statements.
- Employee can make pretax and after-tax contributions.

What can you do if your plan offers only a few of these features? Complain to your benefits coordinator and your boss. Many an employee plan has been sweetened in response to the gripes of workers who complained en masse. The more complaints management hears, the more likely a paltry plan will be improved.

STEP 4 DON'T GET TAKEN FOR A RIDE BY YOUR EMPLOYER'S ESOP.

An Employee Stock Option Plan (ESOP) is another common defined-contribution retirement savings plan. Employers like these plans because they may encourage workers—who are also stockholders—to work harder for the company, but the reality is that, with an ESOP, an employer retains more control over retirement savings funds than may be possible with other retirement plans.

ESOPs can be very risky for employees. For one thing, regulations governing the plans make it very difficult for an employee to sell the stock in a timely fashion. And ESOPs are not covered by the Pension Benefits Guaranty Corporation, which is bad news for workers, because some employers go bankrupt (or squander their workers' ESOP money) and leave their workers high and dry when retirement age nears.

Q: Who determines where the money is invested—me or my employer?

A: It depends on the plan. In an "employee-directed" plan, the employee chooses between investments (typically, stocks and bonds) that are offered by the employer. But about 10 percent to 20 percent of these plans are "employer-directed"—the *employee* puts in the money, but the *employer* chooses where it gets invested.

Q: Could an employer take all that money and use it in any way it wants?

A: Yes, in an employer-directed plan. With a traditional pension, a federal law known as ARISA limits the amount of pension money that an employer can invest in its own company—in stocks and other company investments. There is no comparable law covering ESOPs. So if your employer goes bankrupt or makes bad investments, you could be out of luck at retirement time.

Q: Is opting out of my employer's ESOP plan the only way to protect my future?

A: You have to look at your whole portfolio—*all* of your investments, both outside the plan and in. If the ESOP is your only investment, you're already taking a gamble: *Your job security and financial security are both dependent on your employer.* If you have other, diversified investments, an ESOP may not be unduly risky.

Q: If I change jobs, can I take the ESOP money with me when I leave the company?

A: A former employer may choose to refund your money in dribs and drabs over several years.

STEP 5 **EXPLORE OTHER RETIREMENT SAVINGS OPTIONS IF YOU WORK FOR A NONPROFIT ORGANIZATION OR A STATE OR LOCAL GOVERNMENT.**

If you work for an educational, charitable, or religious organization, you may be eligible for a different tax-deferred plan known as a 403(b) plan. You can typically contribute the lesser of $9,500 or up to 25 percent of your salary. But if you've worked at that organization a long time, you may be able to contribute more.

Some 403(b) plans let you invest in mutual funds, but many of them limit you to annuities. Unlike with a 401(k), if you don't like the investment choices you are given with your 403(b) plan, even if you haven't left your job, you can move that money to a mutual fund custodial account. The 403(b) plan administrator probably is not going to volunteer information about this option, but the mutual fund accepting your money can give you the details. Understand that you may owe a penalty on the money you move from the unwanted 403(b) annuity to the new mutual fund, though sometimes these early-withdrawal penalties will be waived, so ask. Before you touch the money, weigh any penalty against the potential gain from moving the money to a custodial account.

If you are an employee of a state or local government, you may be eligible for a 457 plan. Currently, most eligible workers can contribute up to $7,500 per year, but if you leave your government job, you can't roll over money in this plan (in some instances, you may be able to contribute more) into an IRA. It can stay in the plan and continue to grow, tax-deferred. Or you may be able to cash it in, but you will then owe taxes on that money.

STEP 6 KNOW THE ADVANTAGES AND DISADVANTAGES OF ROTH AND TRADITIONAL IRAS (INDIVIDUAL RETIREMENT ACCOUNTS).

An IRA (Individual Retirement Account) allows most working people to shelter up to $2,000 of earned income a year. For married couples, a non-working spouse can now also open an IRA for up to $2,000 each year.

Do you qualify to deduct your IRA contribution from your federal and state taxes? If you and your spouse are not covered by a qualified pension plan at work and your income is under the yearly threshold (see the chart on page 325), you may also be able to deduct all or some of your IRA contribution on your taxes.

You can contribute to an IRA at any time during the calendar year, or in the following year up until the earlier of the date you file your income taxes or the date taxes are due (excluding extensions). But with compounding interest, every day counts, so if you have the cash, open the IRA as close to January 1 of the tax calendar year as possible (January 3, 2000, for the 2000 tax year).

	Income Limits			
	To qualify for full (partial) deductibility, your income must be under these amounts:			
Year	*Joint Filing*		*Single Filing*	
1999	$51,000	($ 61,000)	$31,000	($41,000)
2000	52,000	(62,000)	32,000	(42,000)
2001	53,000	(63,000)	33,000	(43,000)
2002	54,000	(64,000)	34,000	(44,000)
2003	60,000	(70,000)	40,000	(50,000)
2004	65,000	(75,000)	45,000	(55,000)
2005	70,000	(80,000)	50,000	(60,000)
2006	75,000	(85,000)	50,000	(60,000)
2007	80,000	(100,000)	50,000	(60,000)

Roth IRA vs. Traditional IRA

With a traditional IRA, whether you deducted the contribution or not, all earnings would be taxed at the rate for your income bracket when you withdraw that money. And if you deducted your contribution, when you withdraw that money, you will also owe taxes on all of it. But the Roth IRA, which Congress established in 1998, has some different characteristics. Specifically:

- Your contribution is not tax-deductible (regardless of your income or whether you have a retirement plan at work).
- Money you withdraw when you are over age 59½ is not taxed.
- You can withdraw, at any time, some or all of your contribution (not the earnings), tax-free. If you begin to withdraw your earnings in most cases, if you are not yet age 59½, they will be taxed, and you will also be subject to a 10 percent tax penalty. (Note: If you've held a Roth IRA for at least five years, you can withdraw up to $10,000 in earnings in order to buy a first home.)
- You don't *have* to begin withdrawing money at any time from a Roth IRA. (With a traditional IRA, you must begin withdrawals by age 70½—and a tax bill will likely follow.)
- You can continue making contributions at any age, as long as you keep working.
- When you die, your heirs can collect the balance of your Roth IRA, tax-free.

Do you qualify for a Roth IRA? Yes, if you file jointly and earn $150,000 or less (or earn $95,000 or less, and are single). Your contribution phases out beyond those income limits: up to $160,000 if you're filing jointly, and up to $110,000 if you are single.

Q: Should I open a traditional IRA or a Roth IRA?

A: For most people, the Roth is the way to go. Although you will pay taxes on the money in the year you earn it, any money you take out at age 59½ or later will be tax-free. (There are times when other distributions, or withdrawals of your original investment, are also tax-free and/or penalty-free).

Q: Should I convert a traditional IRA to a Roth IRA?

A: This is a tougher question. With traditional IRAs, most people can deduct from their income taxes the money they put in. When they withdraw it, all of the money is taxable. With the Roth, you get no deduction for the money you put in, but when you take it out at age 59½ or older, your contribution *plus earnings* is usually tax-free. Plus, unlike with a traditional IRA, no matter how old you get, you never have to start withdrawing money from a Roth IRA, so you can continue to earn on it until you need it, or leave it to your heirs tax-free. By contrast, with a traditional IRA, you must start regular withdrawals by age 70½.

A Roth IRA is also a great way to save, tax-free, for your child's college education. If you (and your spouse) put $4,000 a year ($2,000 each) into Roth IRAs from your child's birth year to age 18, you will have contributed $72,000. When it's time for college, you can withdraw that $72,000 tax-free and leave the earnings (more than $100,000) invested, to continue growing for your retirement.

Pros of a Roth IRA:

- Tax-free withdrawals if you're over age 59½ and have had a Roth IRA at least five years.
- You can continue to contribute if you're still working beyond age 70½.
- There are no mandatory withdrawals at any age.
- Money in your account can be left to your heirs without taxes if you have had your Roth IRA for at least five years.

Possible cons of converting to a Roth IRA:

- If you'll be in a lower tax bracket when you retire, it may not pay to convert your IRA and pay the tax now at that higher rate. (But if your tax bracket may *soon* drop, wait until it drops and then reconsider converting; the taxes you will owe on the conversion would be at a lower rate, but the amount you would pay when you retire would also be at a lower rate.)

- Before converting, crunch the tax numbers (your tax liability) to make sure you will have the cash to pay the tax bill before converting. Otherwise, if you must invade part of your IRA (deplete it to pay the tax bill), the amount in your IRA will be lower and you may never catch up to what your traditional IRA would have been worth after taxes. Plus, if you have to withdraw money for the conversion, you will also be subject to a tax penalty of 10 percent if you are under age 59½.

Before you make a conversion, it might be worth consulting with a fee-only financial planner. At least go to a Web site that offers software to analyze your conversion options. Possible sites to visit include: www.money.com, www.kiplinger.com, or www.troweprice.com.

Finally, if you convert your IRA but then your taxable income exceeds $100,000, you will have to undo the conversion—namely, convert out of the Roth and back into a traditional IRA. Contact the holder of your IRA for reconversion details.

STEP 7   WEIGH THE BENEFITS AND COSTS OF VARIABLE ANNUITIES.

What is an annuity? For simplicity's sake, think of it as a do-it-yourself pension. You put in a certain amount of money, and you then can draw out money for the rest of your life or for a fixed number of years.

As discussed above, with a typical pension, your employer would make contributions on your behalf over several years or decades. When you retired, you would start collecting monthly pension checks. But suppose your employer doesn't offer a traditional pension, or you've maxed out your other tax-deferred retirement savings options [such as a 401(k) plan and an IRA], but you want to make a tax-preferred investment to improve your financial picture for your later years. An annuity could do the trick.

Here's how it works: You would make one (or more) payment to the company offering the annuity. In exchange, the company would promise to pay you money for the rest of your life or for some other agreed-on time span.

With an "immediate" annuity, you hand over a lump sum of money and then start to receive annuity payments right away. By contrast, with a "deferred" annuity, which you might pay in one lump sum or over several years, you wouldn't begin to receive payments until some time in the future. A "fixed" annuity would promise to make a predetermined payment to you for a year or so, but then subsequent payments could rise or fall, based on financial conditions.

A variable annuity lets you invest your money in several mutual funds, and is offered by insurance companies, brokers, banks, and mutual fund companies. The size of your annuity payments will depend on how well these mutual fund investments did, as well as the amount of fees, commissions, and penalties you are charged.

Unlike an IRA, a variable annuity is an insurance product. Though it is often sold as a retirement savings investment, there is often a lot less here than meets the eye. It invests like many mutual funds. Contributions are NOT tax-deductible, but earnings are tax-deferred until you withdraw the money. There's no limit on the amount you can contribute. The annuity you choose may even offer a life insurance guaranty, so that if you were to die before you start collecting money, your heirs would get back at least as much as you put in as an investment.

But variable annuities are often less desirable than they first appear in the ads or in pitches from high-pressure salespeople. Here are some costs that would reduce the value of your investment:

- Sales commission.
- Yearly management fees.
- Surrender fee to withdraw money within a few years.
- Federal tax for withdrawing money before age 59½; subject to 10 percent penalty.

Should you consider a variable annuity? Maybe, but only if:

- You've maxed out your other tax-sheltered plans, such as 401(k), SEP, and Keogh. Unlike these plans, your variable annuity contributions cannot be deducted on your tax return. Variable annuities also have insurance costs.
- You've maxed out your IRA—both deductible and nondeductible. You get the same tax break with a nondeductible IRA as with a variable annuity, but you can only contribute $2,000 a year into an IRA.
- You absolutely, positively won't need the money before turning age 59½. Otherwise, you will be subject to a 10 percent penalty for early withdrawal.

- You will be able to leave the money invested for at least 10 years. Before that, the costs of a variable annuity typically exceed the benefits.
- You don't expect to need to withdraw the money in one lump sum. Although you can take a onetime-payment option, the tax hit is much worse than paying taxes each year and receiving yearly payouts.

For most people, the risks outweigh the benefits. To see if it's right for you, consult an independent financial planner (one who won't get a commission) before signing up. If you do decide to invest in an annuity, be sure to shop carefully, because fees and performance vary greatly. Banks are often the worst place to buy an annuity.

LLOYD'S LAW

Never invest IRA or Keogh money in a "tax-deferred annuity." While consumers are often sold annuities for these reasons, it's a terrible money move! IRAs and Keoghs already grow tax-deferred, so there's no reason to pay the hefty commissions and yearly fees and be saddled with the restrictions that come with annuities.

STEP 8 GET UP TO SPEED ON SPECIAL RETIREMENT SAVINGS PLANS FOR THE SELF-EMPLOYED.

If you're self-employed, as a growing number of us are, you know that you are on your own when it comes to planning for your future. There's no employer to take care of you in your old age through a pension or other retirement savings plan. The responsibility for your future is squarely on your shoulders.

Traditional and Roth IRAs cap the annual contribution at $2,000, and no one believes that that would provide enough savings for a comfortable retirement. So if you are self-employed, or have a full-time job with additional income from moonlighting, there are three good options—Keoghs, SEPs, and SIMPLE IRAs—to shelter some of this money for the future.

Keoghs

Keoghs let you stash more money and give you more investing options to choose from, but they require more paperwork than SEPs (Simplified

Employee Pensions, discussed below). High income, self-employed people, such as physicians and lawyers, often opt for a Keogh. You can open
a Keogh at mutual fund companies, banks, and brokerage houses.

There are three types of Keoghs:

1. *Money-purchase Keogh.* You can contribute up to 20 percent of
   your income, or up to $30,000. But whatever percentage of your
   income you choose, you must continue contributing that same
   percentage (not necessarily the same dollar amount) year after
   year (even if business is down that year).
2. *Profit-sharing Keogh.* You can contribute up to 15 percent of your
   income, up to $24,000. You're not required to contribute a spe-
   cific percentage of income, so you may prefer it if you have erratic
   income. It's smart to contact an accountant before trying to set
   one of these up yourself.
3. *Defined-benefit Keogh.* With this plan, you would get a fixed
   yearly income when you retire. You choose how much you want to
   get each year, then work backward to figure out how much you
   must contribute for a few years to achieve this amount. You can
   contribute up to 100 percent of your income. This plan is often
   favored by workers who have large annual incomes and are close
   to retirement.

Characteristics of all Keoghs:

- Earnings grow tax-deferred.
- You are subject to a 10 percent penalty if you withdraw money be-
  fore reaching age 59½, except for proven disability or catastrophic
  illness.
- Mandatory withdrawals must begin by age 70½.
- Payouts are tailored to your life expectancy and can be made in a
  lump sum or in installments. Taxes are due as payouts are made.
- Full-time employees must be included in the Keogh plan.

SEP (Simplified Employee Pension)

Think of a SEP as a cross between an IRA and a Keogh. It is sometimes
referred to as a "SEP IRA" or "Super IRA."

SEP characteristics:

- Your maximum annual contribution is approximately 13 percent of
  your income, up to $24,000. The contribution is tax-deductible.

- Your earnings grow, tax-deferred.
- You are subject to a 10 percent penalty if you withdraw money before reaching age 59½.
- Employees usually control how their SEP account is invested.
- Employers can contribute up to 15 percent of your pay, but you may not qualify for an employer contribution immediately, and, in hard times, an employer can skip contributions.
- Mandatory withdrawals must begin by age 70½.
- You cannot borrow from a SEP.
- SEPs require less paperwork than Keoghs do.
- SEPs are more flexible than Keoghs because contributions can vary from year to year, based on profits.

SIMPLE IRAs

Another type of retirement savings plan that is worth considering if you are self-employed is a SIMPLE (Savings Incentive Match Plan for Employees) IRA, which is designed for employers with fewer than 100 employees. A self-employed worker can use this plan to contribute up to $6,000 a year, or 100 percent of his or her salary, whichever is smaller. (The $6,000 cap will be indexed for inflation over time.)

Compared to a Keogh or SEP, this plan is especially good if you have some, but not much, self-employment earnings. Here's a comparison: To get a $6,000 contribution with a SIMPLE IRA, you need only earn $6,000. To qualify for the same $6,000 contribution with a Keogh, you would have had to earn $30,000. With a SEP IRA, you would have had to earn $46,000.

Your contribution to a SIMPLE IRA is tax-free, and the money grows, tax-deferred. The rules for opening a SIMPLE IRA are very similar to those for a traditional IRA. But the penalty for early withdrawal can be very steep. If you withdraw money from a SIMPLE IRA before turning age 59½, you are subject to a penalty of 10 percent. If you make a withdrawal within the first couple of years of starting the SIMPLE IRA plan, the penalty can skyrocket to 25 percent.

Put Your Kids Through College Even if You Can't Save Enough Money

For many parents, the measure of their success is the level of achievement reached by their children. One yardstick that many parents use is the quality (and, sometimes, the cost) of the colleges their kids attend.

The big financial squeeze for most families comes when they have to start figuring out a way to pay for their kids' college education while they're trying to save money for their own retirement and maintain their lifestyle. It's not an exaggeration to say that money choices you make here will play a part in determining where your kids can go to college, and that decision ultimately will affect them for the rest of their lives. The sooner you start, the more flexibility and choices you and your kids will have.

Chapter 31

Bankroll Your Kids'
College Years Creatively

Jeanne's Story

"Our kids are young. Stephanie's in kindergarten and Greg just started nursery school, so college is a long way off," says Jeanne J. "I quit my job when Greg was born three years ago, to stay home with my kids, so we've already done some belt-tightening.

"By staying home, I have been able to eliminate many work-related expenses. For instance, I no longer pay for child care. My commuting costs are gone, and I don't have to buy any more work clothes (although I have a pretty complete work wardrobe, which I now have no place to wear).

"We bought a house after Stephanie was born, so we have stiff monthly mortgage, tax, and insurance payments to make. My husband's company offers a 401(k) plan, and his employer matches fifty cents for every dollar, so I know we should try to max that out. We don't go on vacations. We rarely even go to the movies or out to dinner. But it's tough, maybe impossible, to save all the money we're going to need."

Tuition and other costs to attend private colleges—or even public schools—have been climbing at staggering rates. If you have school-age (or younger) children, you know that it's going to cost a lot of money—likely tens of thousands of dollars—to pay for each child's college education. You also know that you should be putting money away for your old age. (Your employer probably isn't offering you a pension, and who knows what Social Security will be paying when it's time for you to retire.)

With all those tugs on your income, you may be wondering: If you can't afford to fully fund both your retirement *and* your children's education, which should get priority? While doing television and radio news stories about paying for college, I have often asked parents which they thought should be at the head of the list.

When I first asked this question in the early '90s, most parents got it wrong—by a staggering four-to-one ratio. But the message is sinking in. Now, they only get it wrong by about three-to-two.

Here's the answer: If you can't afford to fund both your child's college education and your retirement, putting money aside for your retirement should be your first priority.

Here's why. You can borrow for your children's college education. Financial aid is available, and, in the worst case, your child can take a part-time job and go to a community college to shave costs. But *you can't borrow to fund your retirement.* Also, the way the tax laws currently are written, a dollar invested in one of the many retirement plans [such as 401(k)s and IRAs] may yield more available (after-tax) dollars when your child is ready to attend college, than if you invested that same dollar in some of the college savings plans.

When it's time for your child to attend college, you may be able to borrow against your retirement savings, or withdraw some of the money, without an undue tax burden.

Don't Believe All the Bad News You Read

Skyrocketing tuition costs make headlines, but there are still some good bargains to be had in state schools and other schools that get public funding. And most students get some financial assistance, such as loans, grants, scholarships, or a work-study job. You don't need to come up with every dollar to pay for your child's education.

Here are ten steps to financing your child's college education.

 FOLLOW THE NEW RULES OF FINANCIAL AID.

Gone are the days when parents who scrimped and saved to pay tuition got no aid, and parents who saved nothing got a free ride. Instead, financial aid is now largely determined as a percentage of a family's income (not just based on the amount saved).

If you are applying for financial aid, you will need to disclose a number of things about your personal finances, as well as your child's finances. But money in a qualified retirement savings plan is often exempted from this calculation.

Money, Money, Who's Got the Money?

When it comes to qualifying for federal financial aid, not all money is counted equally. Put simply, your child is expected to apply a much larger percentage of assets held in his or her name than you are. Thirty-five percent of your child's savings are expected to be used for his or her education. As a parent, the maximum contribution you are expected to make is no more than 5.65 percent of your assets.

Be sure to take this difference into account if you (or your child's grandparents) are considering putting money, earmarked for your child's college education, into your child's name. If your child already has some money, consider using up some of it (so your child can qualify for more financial aid). For instance, let your child pay for things that you would normally have paid for, such as a computer, school clothes, or some of his or her college tuition or other college-related expenses. (Additional ideas on qualifying for more financial aid appear later in this chapter.)

By starting to save early, investing your savings wisely, and finding aid to supplement your shortfall, you can likely send your child to a good college and still have money left for your future. The sooner you start, the faster your money will grow.

LLOYD'S LAW

Don't focus on how many dollars you will need years down the road. Parents who have successfully saved for their kids' college education typically have focused on finding ways each month to free up cash. They then find good investments that will grow but will not pose an undue risk.

STEP 2 INVEST REGULARLY.

When you've freed up cash earmarked for your child's education, where is the best place to invest it? Historically, the stock market has outperformed other types of investments, so stock mutual funds can be a good place to invest this money.

Invest on a regular basis, such as every month. Don't try to time the market based on stock tips or hunches (buying when you think prices are low, or selling when you think they are high). You'll do better by investing money on a regular schedule, regardless of stock prices. Reinvest any dividends, to increase your return.

Lower your investment risk as your child's matriculation date approaches. What goes up can also come down, and it might not rebound in time for your child's first tuition bill. Five years before your child will start college (when he or she turns 13), withdraw one year's college expenses and put the money into something safer, such as a money market account or Series EE savings bonds. The return may be lower than for stocks, but the investment won't drop in value. For each of the next three years, withdraw one year's college expenses and transfer that money to a safe investment as well.

Tip: If you've made a profit, you're going to have to pay tax on any investments you sell (the money you transfer to the safer haven). If you can afford to do it, a better move would be to keep the original investments (if you still believe they will yield a good return), and put *new* money into the safer investments.

STEP 3 — KNOW THE PROS AND CONS OF POPULAR TUITION SAVINGS PLANS.

Prepaid State Tuition Plans

Many states offer prepaid college tuition plans that promise to pay some or all of your child's tuition and other college expenses, even if college costs go through the roof. Under just the right circumstances, one of these plans may be a good deal. But unfortunately, for many parents of college-bound kids, these plans often sound better than they really are. They restrict a student's options (many will limit your child to colleges in your state). And money built up in one of these plans may keep your child from qualifying for other needed financial aid.

Only consider a prepaid plan if you have the cash to fund it completely. If you have to borrow money to pay for a prepaid plan, you'll likely spend more in loan interest than you will gain by being in the plan.

If your child doesn't go to any college, or attends a nonqualifying school (such as an out-of-state school), most plans will let parents transfer the money to another family member.

If your child doesn't go to college, or drops out, you'll likely get all of your money back, possibly with a little interest.

Education IRAs

Another college savings vehicle is the new education IRA. It lets qualifying individuals put up to $500, each year, into an IRA for a college-bound child under 18 years of age. To qualify for the full education IRA, your income must be under $150,000 if you're married (under $95,000 if you are single). You use already-taxed dollars (unlike some traditional IRAs, this one allows no tax deduction), but you will owe no tax on the earnings if you withdraw the money to pay for your child's college education.

If your child doesn't go to college or doesn't use up all the money, the remainder can be transferred to another child (or grandchild). Money left in the account when your child turns 30 will be distributed, taxed, and assessed a 10 percent penalty.

Education IRAs come with other restrictions. In any one year, you cannot contribute to an education IRA *and* a prepaid college tuition plan. You also cannot use an education IRA in the same year that you claim a Lifetime Learning credit or Hope scholarship credit. (These credits are explained below.)

Tip: If your child is older (school age), you will likely be able to invest more money in a prepaid tuition plan than in an education IRA. The prepaid plan may be a better investment if you know your child will attend a state school (or other school that is covered by your state's plan).

If you still need more money when paying for your child's education, tap a retirement IRA only as a last resort. Unlike other retirement savings plans [such as a 401(k)], you can never add the money back, so you will lose this tax-sheltered growth.

529 Plans

A new college savings plan (called a 529 plan, after the relevant section of the tax code) is being offered in a growing number of states (currently, about two dozen). Even if you don't live in one of those states, you can still take advantage of the 529 plan, but you won't get a state income tax deduction. (See the Web sites listed below for some places to open a 529-plan account.) Money invested in 529 plans grows, tax-deferred, and is taxed at your child's tax rate when it is tapped. These plans get around some of the drawbacks of prepaid state plans. For instance:

- The money is listed in a parent's name, not the student's, so it will count less against the student than would a prepaid plan when applying for financial aid.
- There's no income limit on the person contributing the money, unlike the Roth IRA and other federal savings plans.
- You can change the beneficiary if the designated child chooses not to go to college.
- The annual contribution can be up to $50,000 a year (not $500, as with an education IRA). There's a $100,000 lifetime limit per student.
- Your child has more freedom to choose his or her college. Unlike with some state plans, your child is not required to attend a school

in only one, predetermined state (or be forced to give up the earnings). This money can be used at an accredited college anywhere in the United States.

- The money grows, tax-deferred. When your child withdraws the money, that money is taxed at his or her presumably lower rate (not at the parents' tax rate).
- Contributions are deductible on a growing number of states' income tax returns.
- If your state doesn't offer a plan of its own, you can participate in an out-of-state plan, but with no state tax deduction. You should be able to transfer the money without a penalty if your state later offers a tax-deductible savings plan.
- Be aware that you cannot control how your money is allocated in these plans. Typically, 529 plans invest predominantly in stocks during the early years, but as your child ages, these plans switch to bonds and money market funds.

For more information, and to see whether your state has a 529 plan, check out these Web sites:

- www.collegesavings.org—National Association of State Treasurers.
- www.state.nh.us—A Fidelity site. Fidelity runs the New Hampshire plan (or call (800) 544-1722).
- www.nysaves.org—TIAA-CREF (Teachers Insurance and Annuity Association-College Retirement Equities Fund) runs the New York plan (or call 877-697-2837).

 STEP 4 LET HOPE AND OTHER TAX CREDITS HELP.

Trish's Story

"George and I have been saving money for our son Ed's college education almost since the day he was born," says Trish Fox. "We don't go on vacations. We rarely even go out, and are frugal with our purchases." The Foxes had accumulated almost $23,000, but then George was seriously injured in a car accident. "We had to use $5,700 of Ed's college fund to pay some of my husband's medical bills," says Trish. "Ed is now 12 and hopes to start college in five years, but I don't see how we can afford to send him to a good school."

What do you do if you haven't been able to save enough to foot the whole bill for your child's college education? Here are some loans, tax credits, and other sources of money to consider:

- Hope scholarship credit: The new Hope scholarship credit can mean a dollar-for-dollar tax credit of up to $1,500 for your child's first two years of college. You are eligible if your adjusted gross income does not exceed $100,000 ($50,000 for individual filers). It can be claimed for each college student who is a dependent in the household. If your tax liability is less than $1,500, your credit cannot exceed your tax liability.
- Lifetime Learning credit: This credit can return 20 cents on each dollar you spend, up to the first $5,000 in tuition and fees, during your third and fourth years of college and attendance at graduate school. You are eligible if your adjusted gross income does not exceed $100,000 ($50,000 for individual filers).

Tip: As your income increases, these tax credits diminish or go away altogether, so consider delaying transactions that could boost your income in the year *before* your child will apply for aid, such as selling an investment or converting a regular IRA to a Roth IRA. These transactions could lead to a big capital gain, which would boost your income and reduce the amount of aid your child might get. Do the math before beginning any transaction that could increase your income and cause you to lose these tax credits.

STEP 5 DETERMINE WHETHER AN IRA OR AN EDUCATION TAX CREDIT IS BETTER FOR YOUR NEEDS.

Which is better: an education IRA or an education tax credit? If you have several years before your child starts college, you may come out ahead by choosing an education IRA, provided you choose investments that yield high returns. When it's time to pay for your child's college costs, spend the education IRA first. Then try to qualify for one of the education tax credits.

STEP 6 LOOK HIGH AND LOW FOR LOANS.

Even if you're a student with no credit history or collateral, you still may be able to borrow some money, inexpensively. Here are some places for students and parents to start the search:

- *Stafford Loans.* Students can borrow up to $17,125 over four years, and the loans are backed by the federal government. Interest rates on these loans are relatively low, but can vary. If you are eligible for student aid, the federal government may pick up your interest while you're in college and for up to six months after you graduate. Otherwise, you will have to start paying interest while in college, or have your interest deferred until graduation. It will be tacked on to the principal you owe.

- *Perkins (federal) Loans.* Low-income ($30,000 or less) families can borrow up to $3,000 each year at low interest rates. Repayment of principal or interest is not required until nine months after graduation.
- *Plus (Parent Loans for Undergraduates) Loans.* Parents can borrow up to the full cost of college (less any financial aid) from the government, if student loans are not sufficient. A credit check is required. Repayments begin while the child is still in college. Comparison-shop—fees can run up to 4 percent of the amount borrowed, which isn't always obvious until the loan documents are prepared.
- *Personal Loan.* Students (undergraduates and graduate students) can borrow from private lenders. Repayments can be deferred until graduation. Comparison-shop: Fees, interest rates, and other terms vary.

Before you repay a student loan, explore your options. A graduated payment schedule—where your child pays back less in the early working years, when he or she is likely to be earning less, but pays more later when your child is, hopefully, earning more—may be a good option. Also, if you consistently pay on time, some education lenders may cut your interest rate by 2 percent or so. If you can't make your payments, ask your lender to let you consolidate your loans into one longer loan but ask before you've missed a scheduled loan payment.

STEP 7 UNDERSTAND THE HIDDEN COSTS AND RISKS OF EASY MONEY.

Paying for college expenses by borrowing against your home's equity looks like easy money. But think twice before you do it.

If you borrow against your home's equity to pay for your child's college costs, you may be able to write off the interest on your taxes. But you may have to start paying back the money while your child is still in college and you are still incurring additional college costs. The real drawback is that you could be forced to sell your home if you lose your job or become disabled and can't make the payments.

Borrowing against a 401(k) plan is much more expensive than it looks on the surface. Don't do it if you can avoid it. The *real* cost is how much you could have earned if you left the money in the plan. If you can't repay the full loan on time, you will owe taxes and are subject to a 10 percent penalty if you are under age 59½.

STEP 8 DON'T WASTE MONEY ON BAD COLLEGE INVESTMENTS.

Say you didn't start saving for your child's education when he or she was young. What do you do now? Unfortunately, there are plenty of anxious salespeople just waiting to help you eliminate your shortfall. But many of their financial products have serious drawbacks. Here are some popular ones that are *not* well suited for your goal.

- *Life insurance on your child or on you.* The cash value will likely grow much more slowly than you were led to believe. In fact, after sales commissions and bonuses are subtracted, the cash value on a new policy will likely be zero for the first few years. If you need life insurance, buy a good term-life policy (instead of a costlier cash-value one), and use the money you save (with lower premiums) to make separate investments that you have thoroughly checked out. *Note:* If you've already bought a cash-value life insurance policy for this purpose, don't automatically dump it. Although it might not have been a good buy, once you've paid the fees, it may make more sense to keep it. (See Chapter 13 for more information on life insurance.)
- *Tax-deferred annuities.* If you are under age 59½ when you withdraw the money, you are subject to a 10 percent tax penalty, and the issuer may charge other exit penalties, regardless of your age.
- *Zero-coupon bonds.* These can be good long-term investments, but if interest rates have gone up since you bought them, and you have to sell them before they mature, you could lose some of your principal.
- *Money market mutual funds.* Although they are good, safe places to park your money as your child gets close to college (within five years of matriculation), their after-tax return is too low for any sizable growth when your child is young and you need the money to grow quickly.
- *Gold, real estate, unit trusts, penny stocks, and lottery tickets are often sold as "good college investments."* They aren't.

Instead, stick with the other types of investments discussed earlier in this chapter, such as good, diversified mutual funds and 529 savings plans that you have thoroughly researched.

STEP 9 **POSITION YOURSELF FOR MORE FINANCIAL AID.**

Regardless of when you started saving for your child's education, or how much you've managed to save, your expected family contribution (EFC) is the amount that you would be expected to pay toward your child's college costs (tuition plus other expenses). It is a function of your annual income and savings.

The amount of financial aid your child will get is based on your prior year's assets, so good tax planning when your child is in the tenth grade could result in more financial aid. Here are some ideas for increasing your financial aid eligibility:

- Consider using up some cash, because cash counts against you when calculating financial aid.
- Pay down your mortgage. Your home's equity is excluded from the federal financial aid equation, so by paying down your mortgage you'll use up some cash. (*Note:* Check the individual school's financial aid qualifications first, because some schools *do* count home equity in *their* parents' assets equation.)
- Pay down debts, such as credit card balances, car loans, or your own student loans, to reduce your cash balance.
- Consider making major purchases (car, computer, home burglar alarm) early, before applying for aid. These purchases will reduce your cash (assets are not used in most calculations), so you may qualify for more assistance.
- Consider transferring money out of your child's name and into your own. Saving money and amassing other assets in your child's name will cost you more in lost financial aid than the same number of dollars in your name, so some financial advisers recommend transferring money out of your child's account and into your own, a "gift" from your child to you. Restrictions on gifts apply.
- Defer income or bonuses, if possible, to lower your reportable income. Your child may then qualify for more financial aid.
- This year, make charitable contributions sooner than you might have intended. Your good deed will lower the amount of cash you have.
- Go back to school yourself. The more college students in the family at any one time, the more financial aid you can qualify for. Even taking an unpaid leave of absence will lower your income and help you get more aid.

- Discourage grandparents from giving money to help pay for your child's college education. Their giving money *after* graduation, to help their grandkids pay off student loans, would be a better idea.

STEP 10 BEG FOR MORE BUCKS.

Say your child gets into a good college, but the financial aid offer isn't enough. What can you do? Ask for more. Don't accept the first offer. Many colleges will up the ante for a good reason, such as: your child received a higher financial aid offer from a competing school, or your family's financial situation has changed (a parent was laid off or became seriously ill) since your child applied to the college.

Put your request in writing. Be businesslike, but polite. A school's counteroffer is apt to be in the form of a loan, not a scholarship, so, before you accept extra loan money, weigh the pros and cons of taking on bigger debts that will have to be paid off later.

Tip: While schools often boast about how much money they will let your child have, when you're comparing offers from different schools, be sure to compare the actual number of dollars you will need to pay out of pocket.

If you are counting on financial aid, your child might want to avoid applying for "early decision." It's much harder to negotiate additional financial aid when you've already signaled to the school that your child really wants to attend there. With early decision, you won't have any other financial aid offers for that school to match.

STEP 11 SIZE UP LAST-MINUTE TUITION STRETCHERS.

Despite good planning, you may still have a shortfall, so consider these strategies:

- *Look into a work-study program.* It may take your child an extra year to earn his or her degree, but your child will earn money and get invaluable work experience that should make finding an after-college job easier.
- *Consider a community college for the first year or two.* Tuition is low at community colleges, and your child could then transfer the credits to a four-year school. If you qualify for a Hope scholarship (see above), the tax credits could cover full tuition costs.
- *Shorten your child's college stay by having him or her take Advanced Placement classes in high school.* By entering college with credits

in hand, some students can cut one or two semesters off their schedule and shave thousands off their total college bill. Also encourage taking extra credits and/or going to summer school (where you typically pay a much lower per-credit fee than as a full-time student). Your child could graduate one or two semesters early.

STEP 12 SURF FOR DOLLARS.

For more tips on qualifying for financial aid, check out the following resources:

- www.fafsa.ed.gov (You actually apply for financial aid at this site.)
- www.collegeboard.org (You can register for college board exams here.)
- www.finaid.org
- www.nelliemae.org
- www.salliemae.com
- www.ed.gov/thinkcollege/early (This Web site is run by the U.S. Department of Education.)

Chapter 32

Protect Your Teens from the College Credit Card Trap

Carly's Story

When Carly was 19 years old, and a college sophomore, she got her first credit card. "I wasn't looking to get one, but a friend said, 'My fraternity gets a dollar for each person I sign up.' I filled out an application and got a credit card. A couple months later, I got a second credit card."

Carly used her credit cards sparingly and paid her bills on time but not in full. "I was incredibly naïve," she says. "I didn't realize that by making the minimum monthly payment I was barely covering the interest and not making a dent on the balance." The "easy" money enabled Carly to make purchases (mostly books and school supplies) without asking her parents for a loan.

But before long, her balances were so high that she had trouble paying the minimum. "The bank told me to pay what I could each month, but then they increased my interest rate to 23 percent," Carly says. At that point, she was paying up to $100 a month, but the balance (including interest and fees) kept growing.

When total balances on both of Carly's cards approached $2,400, she recalls, "The sheriff tacked a warrant on my door. If I didn't pay my one bill in full, I would be in default." She broke the news to her parents. "They were mad because they paid tuition and didn't think they should have to pay this."

Her mom, Patricia, is still frustrated by the situation. "When you send your kids to college, you say, 'Don't smoke, don't drink, and don't have sex before marriage,' but you don't know to say, 'Don't get a credit card.'"

STEP 1 — UNDERSTAND THAT TEENS CHOOSE AND USE CREDIT CARDS DIFFERENTLY THAN ADULTS.

Have you had "The Talk" with your teen yet? No, not a talk about sex. Nowadays, the other talk you must have is about credit cards. Despite the fact that teens have no credit history and little or no income, consumer advocates say that credit card companies are actively pursuing (some say, targeting) them. And if your child gets a credit card and falls behind in the payments, you, like a growing number of parents, may be faced with the tough decision of whether you should pay off your child's credit card bills.

What's driving this teen credit card trend? Here are six things that credit card companies know about young consumers, and so should you.

1. *Loyalty is blind.* The adult credit card market is saturated, and studies show that consumers remain loyal to their first credit card, even if the issuer boosts interest rates and fees. Creditors realize that if they can sign up teens early, they can keep their business—and their income stream—for years. Younger teens can also be in the line of fire. Kids can unwittingly get on mailing lists when they sign up for a giveaway at a mall or return merchandise to a store. Visa and Master Card say they don't solicit kids under age 18, but, at the minimum, younger teens are getting offers for store charge cards, often without their parents' knowledge. If your high-schooler works part-time, he or she may have to sign up for a store charge card in order to take advantage of an employee shopping discount.

2. *Teens are held to easy credit standards.* Compared to working adults, teens are being held to easier credit standards. Why? Creditors understand that most parents—after paying tens of thousands of dollars in college tuition—will pay off their kids' credit card debt. Unless you cosigned your child's credit card application, you are *not* legally required to pay off your child's debt. Still, there are compelling reasons to pay it off. If you don't, your child will get negative marks on his or her credit report, which can keep him or her from getting a good job, an apartment, a car loan, and auto or health insurance after graduation. (*Note:* Many parents who have had to bail out a child knew that the child had a credit card, but assumed that *their* child would only use it prudently.)

3. *Peer pressure and free gifts are all it takes to lure teens.* Often, all it takes to snare unsuspecting teens are cheap mugs, T-shirts, or candy bars. It's almost impossible to cross a college campus without coming face-to-face with a pitch for plastic: from the ubiquitous credit card booths in student unions and bookstores, to carnival-like displays at sporting events, to student-salespeople who get paid to recruit their classmates.

4. *"Emergency" thresholds keep dropping.* Most teens initially plan to use the credit card only for "emergencies," but, over time, the threshold drops. Katrina Stevens, now 22, got a card at age 19 because of peer pressure. "All my friends had them and were living the high life—with no money," she explains. "I saw how easy it was. I didn't realize how much trouble they were in until afterward." Katrina hadn't planned to overspend, and she worked odd jobs to pay down her debt. Panic set in after she exceeded her credit limit last year. "I thought they would reject my card, but they took it, charged me a fee for exceeding the limit, and demanded I pay $500 immediately. When I got the card, I ignored the fact that I would have to pay the money back." Some teens say they got nervous the first time they used the card, but the fear passed once they made the minimum monthly payment and "nothing bad happened."

5. *Financially irresponsible behavior is rewarded.* Students who don't pay off their balance, but who pay just the minimum on their first monthly bill, typically get credit limit increases and offers for five to ten more credit cards. The interest payments can be very profitable for the banks issuing these cards.

6. *Few schools teach kids about credit.* If you haven't taught your child about credit, don't expect that your child's school has picked up the slack. Few states require any personal finance classes, and if the subject is not mandated, it's rarely taught. With budgets tight, school systems that do teach money matters often rely on free materials from the banking/credit card industry. And the omissions in these materials can have costly outcomes. For instance, industry-provided teaching aids may neglect to say that

LLOYD'S LAW

The one–two punch KOs many young cardholders. Most college students nowadays graduate not only owing tens of thousands of dollars in student loans but also owing thousands in credit card debt. This clearly puts a huge, combined drain on a new graduate's paltry income. Some recent graduates say that, to meet their debt payments, they have had to take low-paying, dead-end jobs after college, rather than pursuing higher education in professions that would be more satisfying and better paying in the long run.

if they only make the minimum monthly credit card payments, it will take them years, or decades, to pay off their balance, and they will pay several dollars in interest for every dollar they charge. Omissions like these are good for the creditor, but terrible for your teen.

So what is a parent to do? Many parents readily admit that they don't know what to tell their children about credit cards (two-thirds of adult cardholders don't pay off their credit balances each month). So, for now, few kids get any credit advice until after they are drowning in debt.

If your child racks up thousands in credit card bills, will you teach him or her more responsibility with a bailout or the advice to sink or swim? Family therapists—and many parents—say that a onetime bailout is better. But, to teach responsibility, have your child pay you back all, or at least most, of the money.

Though she's still paying off her debts, Katrina decided that cutting up her credit cards was the right option for her. "You have less freedom without credit cards, but life is better. It forces me to budget, and I've learned to spend within limits."

STEP 2 SHOW YOUR KIDS WHAT THEY NEED TO KNOW ABOUT CREDIT AND PAYING BILLS.

Despite the potential pitfalls, for your child to get one credit card while in college can be a good way to start a credit history. Here are twelve lessons for preparing your child for the responsibility before he or she leaves home.

- *Lesson 1. Show how you pay bills.* Most parents say their credit-card-carrying college kids have watched them pay bills, but many of these kids tell me they didn't pay attention. For a few months (or billing cycles), have your child sit with you while you pay bills. Have him or her fill out the check (you sign it) and put it, with the payment stub of the bill being paid, in the envelope.
- *Lesson 2. Teach how to balance a checkbook.* Most banks have simple instruction booklets or will give one-on-one lessons if you aren't comfortable explaining how to record deposits, checks, and interest and reconcile your account. Show your child how to budget, or at least how to track expenditures for one or two months. Both of you will be surprised to see where the money goes.

- *Lesson 3. Set a limit of one credit card, beginning no earlier than senior year in college.* Getting a credit card as a student may sound like a contradiction of my previous advice, but it will be easier for your child to qualify for a first card while still an undergraduate than to wait until he or she gets a job and is held to a tougher, adult credit standard.
- *Lesson 4. Keep the credit limit low: $500 to $1,000.* That's enough for emergencies.
- *Lesson 5. Specify what does/does not qualify as an "emergency."* Warn against using the card just because he or she is cash-strapped and wants a night out. An $8 pizza could end up costing over $50 when finance charges and penalty fees are added.
- *Lesson 6. Warn him not to lend the card to others.* Your child is not there to provide banking services to classmates.
- *Lesson 7. Tell him to sign the card immediately.* This cuts the chances that a thief could use it. Remind your child to keep the card in a safe (and secret) place and to report a lost card to you, and to the credit card company, immediately.
- *Lesson 8. Advise your child to hang on to receipts.* To return an item and to verify that the charge was posted accurately, your child must save the original receipt. If an error appears on the bill, your child must dispute the charge with the card issuer, in writing, within 60 days. The correct address for filing a dispute is typically different from the one for making a payment. It can be found on the back of the bill, or by calling the customer service number printed on the bill.

Tip: When a receipt is no longer needed, instruct your child to tear it up into little pieces so that no one can steal the card number from the trash can. And instruct him or her to tear up pre-approved credit offers so that someone can't steal his or her identity and send it in.

- *Lesson 9. Urge your child to pay the bill in full each month.* Many cards require that just 2 to 3 percent of the balance be paid each month—a surefire way to stay in debt for years or decades.
- *Lesson 10. Explain the penalties for paying late or sending less than the minimum.* Penalties include fees (often $29 or more per infraction) and a jacked-up interest rate. Negative marks may go on his or her credit report, making it tough to get a car loan, an apartment, or a job after college.

- *Lesson 11. Ask for notification before your child falls behind on bills.* If in doubt, have the credit card issuer send the bills to you, so you can make sure they are paid on time.
- *Lesson 12. Don't shelter younger kids from family credit problems.* Your younger children will sense something is wrong, and if you don't talk about it, they won't come to you if they need help later. Many younger siblings fall prey to the same credit card traps later, because they didn't know about their older siblings' problems.

STEP 3 **KNOW WHAT TO DO OR NOT DO IF YOUR CHILD FALLS BEHIND ON HIS OR HER BILLS.**

Glen's Story

"I got my first two credit cards when I was a freshman in college. I was a 'townie' and still lived with my parents and commuted to school each day, so I needed the cards to pay for gas and parking and miscellaneous college expenses. When my bills topped $2,000, I got a part-time job. When my bills topped $3,000, the creditor started sending notices that I was late with my payments and if they didn't get paid soon they would 'take action.'

"I didn't know what 'take action' meant and I didn't want to find out. What worried me most was that my parents would find one of these bank notices, so I asked a couple of my friends at school, 'What should I do?' My lab partner, Keifer, told me, 'Get a post office box. That's what I did. That way my parents can't see my mail and the credit card company won't know where I live.' I spent over $20—money that I needed for other stuff—to rent a P.O. box so my parents wouldn't stumble over my bills. But, of course Keifer was wrong about one thing. Even with a post office box, the credit card company still knew where to find me."

Your child could be in credit trouble if he or she is:

- Making less than the minimum monthly payments.
- Borrowing from one card to pay another card.
- Using a credit card to pay for necessities, such as groceries or gas, which will be used up before the bill ever arrives.

Delaying action when creditors are demanding payment is the worst thing any credit cardholder can do. Creditors will give the most leeway when bills are new—before they've been turned over for collection. And if you're going to pay off your child's credit card balance, you have the most negotiating clout *before* you hand over the money. Here's what to do:

- Negotiate a lower amount. Tell the creditors that you are willing to pay the debt, but ask them to remove (or at least lower) the interest charges, the penalty fees for paying late or sending less than the minimum monthly payment, and any legal fees for trying to collect from your child.
- Have the creditors set the record straight. Ask for an agreement to remove any negative marks that may have been put on your child's credit report, such as comments that he or she has defaulted or is a slow payer.
- Get all promises in writing. Before you hand over money, get a letter stating that the agreed-on amount is "Payment in full" and that no further action will be taken against your child. Write "Paid in full," on the back of the check.
- Check your child's credit report a few weeks later. If there are still negative marks listed, write to the credit bureau and send copies (you keep the originals) of the correspondence you got from the creditors. Ask the creditors to resolve it.

If your child is already behind on his or her bills, here are four costly blunders that consumers are often told will fix their problems but, in the end, could make them worse.

- *Blunder 1: Using a for-profit credit repair company.* The company can't do anything you can't do yourself, and creditors are more willing to work with consumers than with a for-profit intermediary. Besides, these companies' typical advice—to use someone else's Social Security number—can get your child into legal hot water and does nothing to improve the credit rating.

Tip: For help negotiating with creditors, call Consumer Credit Counseling Services, a nonprofit organization, at (800) 388-CCCS.

- *Blunder 2: Using a bill-paying service.* You make a monthly payment to the service and it promises to pay all your creditors. Many services abscond with consumers' money without paying creditors. You won't find out until months later, when your child's creditors notify him or her that the bills you thought were paid are long overdue.

- *Blunder 3: Taking out a costly debt consolidation loan.* Consider a debt consolidation loan *only* if it will lower the interest rate on your child's debt. But be aware that once you're late making payments, these loans are almost impossible to get. Check with your local consumer affairs office before handing money to anyone other than the original creditors.

- *Blunder 4: Filing for bankruptcy.* Don't let your child rush to file for bankruptcy. "If he's unemployed, he'll probably continue to incur debt, so bankruptcy rarely works," cautions one expert. "If he's very behind on his payments, it may make more sense to just default on the debt."

Appendix

A Time-Is-Money Calendar

What you do with your money, and when you do it, can make a big difference in your ultimate wealth. In this closing section, I will show you things you should do and the best times to do them.

January

- Open an IRA in early January, if you have the money. With compounding interest, every day counts.
- Start a folder/envelope to hold tax forms and documentation (W-2s and 1099s) as they come in.
- Check your credit card bills for ticking time bombs. Pay off what you can now, to cut your finance charges.
- Make your fourth (and final) estimated Federal income tax payment by January 15.
- Start tracking your expenses for a month to see how close you are to your savings goal of 10 percent.
- Take a home inventory of your possessions, for homeowner's insurance. Include all the holiday gifts you received in December, and the year-end business equipment that you bought. Keep this list in a safe place, and file copies at another location (but probably not in your office, where a potential thief might find it). Review the list to make sure you have adequate homeowner's coverage.
- Hire a tax preparer, if needed, between January and mid-February—before the rush.
- Challenge your real estate tax in January or February. (Check with your local government to verify dates in your community.)

February

- Buy a computer from February to June. Computer demand often peaks from the summer months (for the new school year) to December (Christmas gifts).

355

- Refinance your mortgage between February and April 1 (if you're in the market). The demand is relatively low before the spring house-hunting season begins.
- Start sprucing up your home and interviewing real estate agents if you are contemplating selling your home.
- Start tracking down missing tax documents that didn't arrive by the January 31 deadline.
- Ask the mutual fund company to compute your cost basis on sales of any mutual fund shares you may have sold last year.
- Buy a tax-prep book and/or tax-prep software if you are planning to use a computer to calculate your taxes. Keep an eye out for rebates; they start to pick up from now until April 15.

March

- Verify that you have maxed out contributions to your IRA/Keogh/SEP for last year's taxes—before you file your tax return.
- Start calculating your taxes, or double-check what the tax preparer did for you.
- Start looking for a winter vacation home to buy or rent from March through June. Since it's past "high season," there will be fewer to choose from, but sellers or landlords will be more willing to negotiate a better price.
- Reassess your portfolio, based on the taxes you see you owe this year.
- Hire a remodeling contractor and solidify your plan for any home renovations you want to accomplish this summer.
- Shop for financing for an upcoming remodeling project. Visit at least three banks and credit unions.

April

- Join a health club between April and August. Demand by new members drops as the weather warms, and attendance falls off as club members choose to exercise outdoors.
- File income taxes by April 15, or file for an extension.
- Make the first estimated income tax payment for this year by April 15, if you owe money.
- If you're entitled to an income tax refund, get it quickly by authorizing automatic deposit into your bank account. But avoid costly refund-anticipation loans.

- If you got a refund, visit the benefits coordinator at work and ask to have your withholding adjusted lower (on your W-4 form), so you can stop giving the government an interest-free loan.

May

- Shop for lower-cost long-distance service in time for Mother's Day—typically, the heaviest call day of the year.
- Shape up your credit in the spring so that you will be prepared to do popular "spring things"—shopping for a home, a car, insurance, or a new job.
- Avoid May credit card offers to "skip a payment." This popular May mailing is sent to cardholders who typically pay off their balance each month. The card issuers hope to get these customers into the costly habit of carrying a balance—and paying the finance charges that begin on the day a payment is skipped and that apply to new purchases even before you are billed.
- Use your income tax refund wisely. For instance, pay down your debt, fund your 401(k) retirement savings plans (especially if your employer is matching your contribution) and your IRA.

June

- Scrutinize credit card bills that arrive from June through September. Look for costly changes in terms (such as jacked-up fees or interest rates, or shortened grace periods) that are often slipped in during the lazy days of summer.
- Make a second estimated income tax payment (for this year) by June 15, if you owe money.
- Sell your car between June and September, when kids need cars for summer jobs or to go back to school.
- Help your children find a summer job or start a business, such as a lemonade stand.
- Talk to your spouse-to-be about money matters before you walk down the aisle together.

July

- Fund or match your child's contribution to a Roth IRA that he or she is entitled to because of a summer job.

- Help your child pay off or renegotiate college credit card bills that he or she racked up in college the previous year.
- Do some midyear tax planning.
- Rebalance your portfolio (at least twice a year).
- Pass up flight insurance. It's overpriced. If you need more life insurance, buy low-cost term life insurance that would pay no matter how you died.
- Steer clear of trip cancellation insurance. The policies typically exclude coverage for recurring illnesses and are often sold by companies that are financially weak, and unable or unwilling to pay on claims.
- Increase your savings by at least 1 percent.
- Talk to your college-bound kids about managing money and credit cards.

August

- Take advantage of "open season" on medical benefits—typically August to November (check with your employer about exact dates)—by deciding whether you want to stay with or leave your current plan.
- Get your child ready to manage money before heading off to college. Show him or her how to pay bills, write checks, and balance a checkbook.
- Get a jump on next year's remodeling projects. Start interviewing potential remodelers, and visit some construction sites while work is still in progress.
- Look for a summer vacation home to buy or rent *after* the high season, when homeowners and landlords are more willing to negotiate.
- Ask for a discount on car insurance if your child is going off to college and won't be regularly driving your car.
- File your income tax return by August 15 if you got an extension in April.

September

- Ask for a raise in September or October, when many employers draw up budgets for the next year.
- Start providing monthly highlights to your boss (if you haven't already) so that you can position yourself for a raise or promotion next year.
- Make the third estimated income tax payment by September 15 if you owe money.

- Sign up for a financial planning class during the fall semester at the local community college.

October

- Stock up on stock bargains during October, when prices often temporarily dip.
- Calculate what's left in your flexible spending account, and draw up a plan to use up any remaining money on medical or legal expenses.
- Beat the crowd by making doctor and dental appointments for you or your family, to use up flexible spending account money. Even if you don't have a flexible spending account or have already used it up, it still may pay to see doctors and dentists before year's end. If you have met your yearly deductible, and may not make it next year, make the most of it by seeing medical professionals this year.
- Play some what-ifs to cut your taxes. For instance: If you're near the 7.5 percent limit to start deducting medical expenses, should you push up elective work into this year? Or see whether you should start selling some stocks or mutual funds at a gain, in order to use up some losses you already know you have?

November

- Buy a house between Thanksgiving and New Year's. Only very motivated home sellers will show their house at this time, so they should be more realistic about the price and easier to negotiate with.
- Avoid the December mutual fund tax surprise. Don't send new money in until after the ex-dividend date.
- Make some year-end tax-saving moves, such as dumping your "dogs" (bad investments) before the end of the year so you can get the tax loss. But if you still want to own them, be sure to avoid running afoul of the "wash-sale" provision. (You can't buy back similar investments for 31 days.)
- Maximize employee benefits between now and the end of the year. Use up money in your flexible spending account, and max out your 401(k) contribution.
- Be on the lookout for so-called Christmas credit card bargains that really aren't bargains at all. They'll offer deferred billing, cash advances, and discounts for opening a store charge account.

- Use them or lose them—your frequent flyer miles and similar perks from credit cards and other rebate programs. Find out the specific rules. Some may only require you to cash in the points by year's end, but not require you to use the award certificate immediately.
- If you can't use them, donate your frequent flyer and other awards to charity. You don't get a write-off because you didn't pay for them, but the charities will appreciate your good deed.

December

- Guesstimate your taxes—based on last year's tax return and statements from mutual funds, pay stubs, and similar sources—so you will know now whether you will need to make estimated tax payments. Federal, state, and local estimated tax payments aren't due until January 15. If you pay your state or local estimated tax by December 31, and itemize your deductions, you may get to write it off this year's tax return rather than next year's.
- Make charitable contributions even if you don't have the cash. Consider charging your contributions on your credit card—you get the deduction now, but you won't have to pay your card company until next year. Donate your car (it's easier than selling it yourself). Or give appreciated stock that you've owned at least a year (you won't have to pay the capital gains tax, so the charity nets more money than if you sold the stock, paid the tax and broker's commission, and sent the charity the amount that was left).
- Speak to a customer service rep to verify that holiday gifts you are ordering online or by phone are in stock. Only then place your order, unless you don't mind giving IOUs as gifts.
- Buy a new car during the week leading up to Christmas. Few consumers buy cars as Christmas presents, but salespeople are facing month-end and year-end sales quotas, and often are more willing to haggle.
- Open, by December 31 (even if you don't have enough money to fund them), a Keogh or SEP.
- Get a Social Security number for the new baby born this year. You'll need the number for tax purposes.
- Make your January mortgage and estimated tax payments (state and local) early, so you can take the deduction on this year's tax return.
- Buy deductible purchases for your business—computers and other equipment.

- Give tax-free cash gifts to relatives, friends, and others, up to $10,000 per person. To count for this year, the checks must be deposited by December 31. (Write certified checks if year's end is near.)
- Try to postpone year-end bonuses or other income payments until next year.

Index